MW00632907

No
Higher
Honor

No Higher Honor

Saving the USS *Samuel B. Roberts*
in the Persian Gulf

BRADLEY PENISTON

Foreword by Adm. William J. Crowe Jr., USN (Ret.)

Naval Institute Press
ANNAPOLIS, MARYLAND

Naval Institute Press
291 Wood Road
Annapolis, MD 21402

Library of Congress Cataloging-in-Publication Data

Peniston, Bradley, 1968–
    No higher honor : saving the USS Samuel B. Roberts in the Persian
Gulf / Bradley Peniston.
        p. cm.
    Includes bibliographical references and index.
    ISBN 1-59114-661-5 (alk. paper)
    1. Samuel B. Roberts (Frigate : FFG-58)   2. Iran-Iraq War, 1980–
1988—Naval operations, American.   3. Submarine mines—Persian
Gulf.   I. Title.

    DS318.85.P457   2006
    955.05′42450973—dc22

                                                      2006003997

Printed in the United States of America on acid-free paper ♾

13 12 11 10 09 08 07 06   9 8 7 6 5 4 3 2
First printing

Now here is a mystery of the Service.
A man gets a boat which for two years becomes his very self—
His morning hope, his evening dream,
His joy throughout the day.

—Rudyard Kipling, *The Man and the Work*

Caught by the under-death,
In the drawing of a breath
Down went dauntless Craven,
He and his hundred!

—Henry Howard Brownell, *The Bay Fight*

"After a bit, you see, we were all pretty much on our own,
and you could really find out what your ship could do."

—Kipling, *Destroyers at Jutland*

CONTENTS

FOREWORD

Scores of volumes have been devoted to naval history, the bulk of them concerned with battles that pitted ships or aircraft against an enemy's opposing units. *No Higher Honor,* however, is the rather more unusual story of a single vessel: the USS *Samuel B. Roberts* (FFG 58). The book follows this guided missile frigate—the third U.S. warship to bear the name—from its construction in Maine to a single day of terror in the Persian Gulf, where a magnificent effort by captain and crew saved the ship from disaster.

Readers of every stripe who are captivated by maritime legends of heroism and skill will find the *Roberts*'s ultimate trial mesmerizing. The frigate was headed to a convoy assignment when it found itself in a field of naval mines laid by the Iranian military. In attempting to move clear of the mines, the ship detonated a 253-pound charge and absorbed incredible damage. Saving the ship proved a Herculean task, but the skill and unbending will of all hands eventually prevailed. The story has carved a rightful place in the annals of the U.S. Navy and stands as an inspiration to future "tin can" sailors.

This account of the struggle is riveting, but the book is a great deal more than just high adventure. It is a thoughtful endorsement of the value of preparation and training. The crew's remarkable reaction in crisis was forged in earlier months when an intelligent and determined commanding officer vowed to make his charge the best ship in the navy. There is an extensive description of the training program and priorities and the role they played in building confidence and morale. Interviews with crewmen help paint a picture of the sweat and tears that were shed in the process. This is what it takes to mold a wide array of skills into a coordinated whole. It is not easy to do.

The first ingredient is a captain who knows what he wants and who has the energy and conviction to bring the crew to his thinking. From the outset, Cdr. Paul Rinn emphasized damage control, an area that is often neglected until a unit enters its theater of operations—when it is far too late for rigorous training. Normally, commanders detail the most experienced people to operations and weaponry billets, leaving damage control to relatively junior officers. Rinn chose a different course, assigning a senior lieutenant to develop a rigorous training regimen that involved the entire crew. Officers and enlisted sailors alike were rotated through a variety of specialty schools dedicated to damage control. These steps paid rich dividends when the *Roberts* was finally tested. Of course, even the best training does not foresee all possibilities, but it can convey the knowledge necessary to meet the unexpected. The damage control preparation should be required reading for those who choose a career in the small-ship navy.

Strong and effective leadership was a hallmark of every step of the *Roberts*'s history. Rinn's strong hand and personal interest appear during the *Roberts*'s construction, preparatory training, and war-zone operations, and in the fight to save the ship. From the beginning, he took the prime responsibility for the crew's morale, its spirit, and the command's reputation, creating a sense of pride and unity that was crucial when disaster threatened. Every officer's training stresses leadership, and it is more than worthwhile to absorb a "real life" account that graphically illustrates its vital role. In essence, *No Higher Honor* is an excellent leadership textbook.

Of further interest, the book describes in some detail the difficult environment in the Persian Gulf. One moment it was placid, and the next violent—a severe test for captain and crew. Naval ships were expected to stand clear of legitimate everyday commerce, yet each skipper had to protect his command from surprise attacks. This burden required constant vigilance and a fine sense of judgment. This is bad enough in short periods of time. Over long weeks, it is exhausting and can wring a crew dry. Today, there is no alternative. Such an atmosphere is part of the new world order in which our military performs.

This story of the USS *Samuel B. Roberts* offers something to everyone who mans our warships. There is much to learn in its pages. Despite the trauma the ship faced, the reader can lay down the book with a buoyant spirit. The crew was essentially a crosscut of American society, and I suggest that their story should touch professional and laymen alike. It affirms our pride and confidence in the caliber of individuals who man our fleet and in the U.S. Navy as an institution. On a more personal level, it allows one for a few hours to be in the company of brave men.

Adm. William J. Crowe Jr., USN (Ret.)
November 2005

Admiral Crowe was Chairman of the Joint Chiefs of Staff when the *Roberts* hit the mine in April 1988, and he traveled to Dubai to inspect the damage.

ACKNOWLEDGMENTS

Among the lessons one may draw from the tale of USS *Samuel B. Roberts* (FFG 58) is that no large purpose is achieved alone. A full list of those who graciously gave their time for interviews and correspondence appears in the notes, but several deserve mention for their special generosity in sharing memories and documentary materials, including Kevin Ford, Erik Hansen, Michael Harnar, Glenn Palmer, John Preston, Paul Rinn, Eric Sorensen, Randy Tatum, and Gordan Van Hook.

The New York City office of the U.S. Navy's public affairs branch arranged a visit to the *Roberts* in Mayport, Florida, where the ship's commanding officer, Cdr. Bernard Gately Jr., went beyond the call of duty to welcome me as inspectors roamed his engineering spaces and a hurricane approached. The various holdings of the Naval Historical Center in Washington, DC, were of great use, and I thank archivist Regina Akers, historian Randy Papadopoulous, and the staff of the Ships History Branch for steering me in helpful directions. Ken Testorff of the Navy Safety Center provided access to back issues of *Fathom* magazine. Mike McLellan, a public affairs specialist at Navy Personnel Command, helped obtain *Roberts* muster rolls. Sue Pierter arranged a shipyard tour at Bath Iron Works.

Tom Cutler ushered the book through the acquisition process at Naval Institute Press, where Ron Chambers and Fred Rainbow provided early encouragement. Nathaniel Levine drew the map, cutaway, and side view of the *Roberts* with his customary competence and flair. Vago Muradian at *Defense News* provided flexibility at work at crucial moments.

Several people read parts of the manuscript and made helpful suggestions, including Christopher Cavas, Eric Greenwald, Anne Hastings Massey, Mickey Peniston, Mark Santangelo, and Phillip Thompson. Any mistakes that remain are mine alone. I owe a special debt to Portia Wu, my toughest editor and most generous supporter.

My family was endlessly encouraging during the research and writing of this book, and I dedicate it to them and to the memory of my father.

Bradley Peniston
Washington, DC
September 2005

CHRONOLOGY

12 May 1921	Samuel Booker Roberts Jr. born in San Francisco.
27 September 1942	Roberts, a U.S. Navy coxswain, mortally wounded while helping to rescue marines on Guadalcanal.
28 April 1944	First USS *Samuel B. Roberts* (DE 413) commissioned.
25 October 1944	DE 413 helps turn back the Japanese Center Force off the Philippine island of Samar, saving a U.S. invasion fleet. *Roberts* sinks after taking heavy shellfire.
20 December 1946	Second USS *Samuel B. Roberts* (DD 823) commissioned.
9 September 1970	Chief of Naval Operations Adm. Elmo R. Zumwalt Jr. launches concept study of inexpensive antisubmarine escort vessel.
11 November 1971	DD 823 sunk as training target off Puerto Rico.
April 1972	Bath Iron Works begins designing Zumwalt's new ships, which are later dubbed guided missile frigates.
25 September 1976	BIW launches USS *Oliver Hazard Perry* (FFG 7).
November 1977	Navy's Board of Inspection and Survey declares FFG 7 "the best ship in 20 years."
22 September 1980	Iraq invades Iran.
8 December 1984	BIW launches third USS *Samuel B. Roberts* (FFG 58).
1 April–20 December 1985	*Roberts*'s precommissioning crew assembles in Norfolk.

30 June–7 October 1985	4,500 BIW employees strike.
6 February 1986	Navy inspectors call *Roberts* "one of the cleanest [ships] that the Board has seen."
12 April 1986	*Roberts* commissioned, Cdr. Paul X. Rinn commanding.
8 June 1986	*Roberts* arrives in home port of Newport, Rhode Island.
27 June–24 July 1986	*Roberts* trains at Naval Station Guantánamo Bay, Cuba.
23 September 1986	*Roberts* seizes sailboat and 5.7 tons of marijuana off the Florida coast.
30 September 1986	*Roberts* receives "Mission E" awards for antisubmarine warfare, antisurface warfare, engineering, deck seamanship/navigation, damage control, and electronic warfare.
3–7 November 1986	*Roberts* passes final contract trials with fewest problems ever recorded by a *Perry*-class frigate. Called "best ship in program to date."
7 March 1987	The United States agrees to protect 11 Kuwaiti tankers in the Persian Gulf, launching Operation Earnest Will.
May 1987	In tactical readiness exam, *Roberts* notches highest damage control scores recorded to date.
17 May 1987	USS *Stark* (FFG 31) hit by two Iraqi missiles.
7 June 1987	Navy inspectors call *Roberts*'s damage control material condition the "best ever seen."

16 June–16 July 1987	At Guantánamo again, *Roberts* becomes first vessel to handle new, tougher damage scenarios while maintaining full combat watch. Called "the best REFTRA [refresher training] ship seen in two years."
25 June 1987	*Roberts*'s deployment orders change; instead of heading for the Mediterranean Sea in May, *Roberts* will leave for the Persian Gulf in January.
24 July 1987	Tanker MV *Bridgeton* hits a mine during the first Earnest Will convoy.
21 September 1987	U.S. forces catch Iranian ship *Iran Ajr* laying mines.
16 October 1987	Tanker MV *Sea Isle City* hit by Iranian missile. Three days later, American warships retaliate by shelling two oil platforms said to serve as bases for Iranian gunboats.
11 January 1988	*Roberts* departs Newport on six-month deployment.
14 February 1988	*Roberts* arrives in Persian Gulf, where schedule calls for nearly four months of patrol and convoy operations.
March 1988	*Roberts* patrols in northern Persian Gulf, guarding U.S. special operations barges.
17–21 March 1988	*Roberts* anchored in Bahrain for the deployment's first liberty call.
2 April 1988	Commander of U.S. naval forces in Gulf warns that Iranians have laid 20 mines off Kuwait in March, and more may be coming.

10 April 1988	*Roberts* sweeps its squadron's Battle E awards.
14 April 1988	*Roberts* strikes Iranian mine in central Gulf. Crew fights fire and flooding for more than four hours to save ship from sinking.
16 April 1988	*Roberts* towed into Dubai.
18 April 1988	U.S. naval forces sink or heavily damage five Iranian warships and smaller vessels in Operation Praying Mantis, the largest surface battle since World War II.
20 June 1988	Most of crew flies home to Rhode Island. Soon afterward, Rinn turns over command of *Roberts* as scheduled.
27 June 1988	*Roberts* loaded aboard heavy-lift ship *Mighty Servant 2*.
1–31 July 1988	*Mighty Servant* under way for Newport.
20 August 1988	Iran–Iraq War ends in cease-fire.
6 October 1988– 1 April 1989	*Roberts* under repair in BIW's Portland dry dock.
16 October 1989	Repairs completed for $89.5 million, $3.5 million less than estimated.
September 1990– March 1991	*Roberts* operates in Red Sea and Eastern Mediterranean during Operations Desert Shield and Desert Storm.
March 2004	*Roberts* wraps up record-breaking counterdrug deployment in Caribbean Sea.

No
Higher
Honor

CHAPTER ONE

Those Are Mines

At twenty-five knots, the sea came on quickly. Its surface, wrinkled and opaque, rushed toward the warship, split against the steel prow, and became a fleeting trail of foam pointing back toward Kuwait. Four decks above the waterline, Seaman Bobby F. Gibson leaned over the forecastle rail and twisted the focus knob on his binoculars. His metal chair, bolted to the main deck just behind the bow, afforded a panoramic view of the central Persian Gulf. The nineteen-year-old from Walkertown, North Carolina, took in the scene one small circle at a time.

Gibson ignored the horizon; the radar boys in the combat information center would spot incoming fighter jets and naval craft before any human lookout could. Instead, he lowered his gaze and surveyed the choppy surface off the port bow. He found a featureless disc of sea-water, devoid even of the trash bags and jetsam of a busy sea-lane, a dark fractal veil over the depths. The sailor rotated his head five degrees to the right, paused, repeated the motion, and then repeated it again. Each glance lasted a few seconds; each circle overlapped the next. Countless four-hour watches had honed Gibson's technique, and after three months on deployment his scan was smooth and automatic.

A lookout's duty required him to take note of ships, planes, foghorns, an unaccustomed rush of water on steel—anything seen or heard—and pass the word via the sound-powered phone that hung around his neck like a folksinger's harmonica. In busy waters, Gibson's finger rarely left the talk button. Close to shore there were dhows, the ancient sailboats that had borne the region's trade for centuries. Out here in the shipping lanes, traffic was dominated by modern merchant ships and by the super-tankers that hauled petrochemical succor to an oil-thirsty world. They went by alone or in ragged convoys, dwarfing the gray-hulled warships that herded them along. From time to time a black smudge tinted the horizon: smoke billowing from the bombed-out carcass of a tanker.

Today there wasn't much going on, and Gibson took a moment to appreciate his surroundings. The afternoon curtain of humidity and airborne dust had retreated nearly to the horizon, and yet a protective layer of cloud still shielded him from the beating April sun. A bit earlier, he had spotted a pod of dolphins off the bow, and his report to the bridge had drawn a small knot of shipmates to the forecastle. "Pretty nice," he thought.[1]

Gibson enjoyed his job; he often traded shifts with shipmates who preferred their air-conditioned refuges. The heat didn't bother the North Carolina native, and he shrugged off the desert grit that blew up from the Arabian Peninsula and down from the far-off mountains of Iran. For the Gulf was at war, and if your ship had to play shepherd in a combat zone, at least you could get the best seat in the house.

Iran and Iraq had been fighting ever since Gibson was in grade school. The land campaign had long ago devolved into a brutal, grinding stalemate, and the two countries had taken the fight to sea, where they slashed at the oil tankers that were each other's economic jugulars. Baghdad's fighter planes left smoking holes in Iranian ships, and Tehran's naval forces mounted attacks with guns and rocket-propelled grenades. Both sides were less than meticulous about identifying their prey; neutral and even friendly ships suffered the consequences. Together they had turned the inland sea into the world's most hazardous watercourse.

The United States had tried to keep out of the fray—U.S. policy makers would have preferred both sides to lose, if that were possible, but the region's oil gave it a strategic significance that could not be ignored. Reagan administration officials muddled along at arm's length, passing battlefield intelligence to Baghdad even as they secretly shipped arms to Tehran, until the Kuwaiti monarchy forced the White House's hand in late 1986 by extracting a promise to protect its tankers.

In mid-1987 the U.S. Navy launched Operation Earnest Will—its first convoy operation since World War II—and began to dispatch dozens of U.S. warships to the region. One of them was Gibson's: USS *Samuel B. Roberts* (FFG 58), a guided missile frigate on its maiden deployment. The 445-foot *Roberts* was small for a contemporary American surface combatant; it belonged to the inexpensive and oft-dismissed *Oliver Hazard Perry* class. But the ship was a stout craft, built by Maine's venerable Bath Iron Works, powered by modified aircraft engines, and better armed than it first appeared.

And its crew was second to none in the Atlantic Fleet. Cdr. Paul X. Rinn had pushed his sailors to be the best—to be the New York Yankees, as the Bronx-born combat veteran put it. Captain and crew had spent most of the previous two years at sea, mastering the myriad skills of naval warfare. Their commodore had recently named *Roberts* the best *Perry*-class frigate in his squadron, and fleet instructors declared it the best ship they'd seen in years. Two months in the Persian Gulf had put those skills to the test. Since arriving in February 1988, the crew had handled convoys, patrols, and a rescue at sea. They had chased away Iranian warships and warded off Iraqi fighters. They had guarded the secret mobile operating bases in the northern Gulf and launched black army helicopters on shadowy missions.

Danger was omnipresent. Less than a year had passed since an Iraqi jet had fired two missiles into the USS *Stark* (FFG 31), killing thirty-seven U.S. sailors. Baghdad called it a tragic accident, but the *Roberts* crew took it as a bloody warning. They had redoubled their training efforts and since arriving in the Gulf had remained constantly vigilant. On deck, the lookouts kept their eyes peeled; down in the darkened combat information center, radar operators peered at cathode-ray screens around the clock. They sorted the seething mass of green specks into tankers and warships, dhows and armed speedboats, airliners and fighter jets. Every dot concealed a different way to die—collision, accident, or deliberate attack.

But many captains—the *Roberts*'s Rinn among them—worried even more about a threat that didn't show up on radarscopes: the naval mine. Since World War II, mines had damaged more U.S. warships than missiles, guns, and bombs combined. A floating Iranian weapon had clobbered a tanker on the very first Earnest Will convoy. Its three escorting warships completed the journey in the tanker's wake, huddling behind the wounded giant. And yet the navy still afforded its surface combatants no mine-detection gear more sophisticated than a pair of binoculars and a sharp-eyed lookout.

ON THE FORECASTLE, Gibson raised his binoculars again. This time, there was something out there. A half-mile off the starboard bow, three objects bobbed some distance apart. They were black, like the ubiquitous floating trash bags. But these had protrusions and rounded carapaces—maybe they were dead sheep? Gibson had seen plenty of those bloated forms, the cast-off dead of Australian livestock carriers. These objects were different, shinier. *That's a mine!* he thought. He squeezed the round microphone under his chin, and a carbon-filled cell transformed the sound of his voice into electrical impulses. "Bridge, forecastle," he said, calling the pilothouse.

On the bridge, Lt. Robert Firehammer raised his own binoculars. A quick look told the officer of the deck what he needed to know. "All engines stop," Firehammer told the helmsman. The ship began to slow, but he decided to stamp on the brakes. "All engines back one-third," he said. The bronze blades on the *Roberts*'s seventeen-foot screw swiveled on their hubs, biting backward into the sea. The ship shuddered. Firehammer pulled a heavy black handset from a gray box beneath the windscreen. One deck down, its twin rang in the captain's L-shaped cabin.

Rinn had been going over the week's menu with Kevin Ford, the ship's head cook. It was 14 April, which meant tomorrow would be the halfway point of the deployment, and Ford had planned a steak and lobster dinner to celebrate. The captain objected to a certain item that seemed to be coming up a lot lately. "C'mon, Chief, not so much spinach, huh?" Ford just grinned; he was not above tweaking his commanding officer with a surfeit of the green leafy vegetable.

Rinn knew something was happening the moment the ship began to back down. He had commanded this ship since it was an inanimate pile of steel on a Maine riverbank, and he felt every vibration as if it were his own body. He answered the phone, and in almost the same movement was out the door and up the ladder to the bridge. Through the door to the bridge wing, the floating black forms were clearly visible less than half a mile away—three of them, lined up. *Those are mines,* Rinn thought.

In a minefield the only clear path to safety was the wake. The captain was an excellent shiphandler, by instinct and by years at sea, but backing a frigate wasn't easy. It was hydrodynamically akin to throwing a paper airplane backward. Rinn gripped the rail and gazed aft to the pale white stripe that stretched back to clear water. The ship began to creep backward, powered by a pair of electric outboard motors customarily used for docking in safe harbor. Moments went by. *We're going to get out,* he told himself. There were those, later, who imagined they heard a scrape of metal on metal.

The explosion grabbed the frigate and shook it from stem to stern. The ship flexed, flipping Gibson backward out of his chair. Superhot gases rushed through a hole in the hull, setting fires at the ship's very core. A wall of seawater followed within seconds, ripping open fuel tanks and flooding the engine room. Far above, a ball of flame erupted from the ship's stack, and fiery chunks of debris rained down on the deck. With reflexes imbued by thousands of hours of drills, sailors rushed to pull hoses from bulkhead racks. But when they pulled the levers on the heavy brass nozzles, mere trickles came out. Somewhere under their feet, something was very wrong.

It would take Rinn and his crew hours to add up all the clues, but the news they gathered early on wasn't good. The main engine room and another capacious engineering space were inundated with oil-slicked water, and a third compartment was filling rapidly. Lose that one, and the frigate would likely plunge to the bottom of the Gulf. The *Samuel B. Roberts* was flooding, on fire, surrounded by sharks and sea snakes, alone in a minefield in a sea at war. Its crew was fighting for their lives. But they faced the battle well prepared, well led, and with a sturdy ship beneath their feet. The outcome of the next few hours would, in no small part, be determined by events that began many years before.

CHAPTER TWO

Paul Rinn and the *Roberts*

Paul Rinn, as he liked to say, was not a tough guy, but he could play the part. Born in 1946 and raised in the Bronx, Rinn grew up on the top floor of a five-story walkup near East 200th Street and Webster Avenue. Located about four miles north of Yankee Stadium, it could be a rough neighborhood. He bore the scars of a street youth in New York, including a .22-caliber bullet hole in his leg from an impromptu altercation. One summer, he got a union card and worked the New York docks, taking the 5:30 AM train to the longshoremen's hall downtown. There was plenty of work for a six-foot-tall rookie. Many nights he came home weary, dreading the five-flight climb to bed.

But the Rinn family valued education—his mother was a grade school teacher, his father a law school graduate who helped manage the city's real estate—so Paul traveled several miles uptown each morning to Mount St. Michael Academy, a Catholic high school for boys. Founded by the Marist Brothers teaching order, the high school had a grassy twenty-two-acre campus that offered a bit of respite from the city's pressures. More important, it offered a fine education. When Rinn graduated in 1964, he enrolled at the order's Marist College, about sixty miles up the Hudson River in Poughkeepsie.[1]

He found an academic mentor in Thomas Casey, a philosophy professor who pushed his students to set lofty and humanitarian goals. Casey drew Rinn into scholarship and pushed him to grapple with ideas. The professor counted on the Bronx kid to enliven the classroom discussion, and the student esteemed his teacher's insights—at least until his senior year, when he took Casey's course on early American pragmatism. It was a difficult class. A uniquely American strain of philosophy that emerged in the late 1800s, pragmatism encouraged its adherents to seek moral and ethical truths scientifically, by advancing hypotheses through action and testing them through experience. What could not be tested, what could not be controlled, should be ignored.

Rinn found this ridiculously abstruse. It just didn't seem to apply to the concrete things in life, like his varsity rowing team, which was making a serious run for the small-school national championship. Rinn and his teammates spent hours on the Hudson River each day, endlessly honing the simple techniques of the sweep oar.

Nor did he see how pragmatism applied to the U.S. Navy officer's commission he expected to take upon graduation. Rinn had fallen in love with the sea service through his older brother, a naval officer. Paul had visited Greg's ship in New York Harbor and became entranced with his brother's shipmates and their tales. World travelers, sworn to defend the country, they were different from anyone he'd known in high school or college. "The SWOs [surface warfare officers] were the coolest guys I ever met," Rinn said. "They were fearless and had a hell of a good time."

And pragmatism certainly didn't seem to apply to the deepening conflict in Southeast Asia, which would one day introduce him to combat.

One late spring day, Rinn launched into a classroom tirade against pragmatism and the hypocritical classmates who pretended to see some relevance to their own lives. After class the student apologized to his professor but refused to concede his point: "None of this stuff you're teaching is ever going to matter." He would eat those words.

Rinn's naval career began well. He took his commission in 1968 through the Reserve Officer Candidate program and spent seventeen months running the combat information center of the aging destroyer USS *Sarsfield* (DD 837). His performance earned him a spot promotion to lieutenant and the assignment of ship's operations officer.[2] Suitably impressed, the navy's personnel office picked Rinn for a far tougher job. The assignment would change the young officer and the way he looked at leadership.

In 1972 the U.S. withdrawal from Vietnam was well under way; within a year all conventional combat units would be gone. But war still raged across Indochina, and thousands of Americans remained behind as advisers. The navy taught Lieutenant Rinn to speak Thai and Cambodian and then sent him far up the Mekong River, past Vietnam's delta and into the thousand-mile valley that divided Laos and Thailand. As a military trainer and counterinsurgency adviser, Rinn found himself working and fighting beside a grab bag of American and local forces: U.S. Marines and brown-water sailors, SEAL commandos, Cambodian troops, Laotian irregulars, and Royal Thai Navy sailors. He helped build bases along a four-hundred-mile stretch of the Mekong—one near the Thai city of Nong Khai, another by the ancient Lao capital of Vientiane—and used them to launch river patrols and assaults against Cambodia's Khmer Rouge and other groups.[3]

One day Rinn led a small group of Americans and Thais up the river to the base at Bon Pisai. The reconnaissance mission soon turned difficult; fighting on the river erupted swiftly and at close quarters as Rinn and his men pressed on toward their objective. That night, they lit a fire and brooded on the long trip back to home base. *Everyone in Cambodia probably knows where we are,* Rinn thought. *Our chances of getting out of here alive are slim to none.*

His men were shaken as well, so Rinn said what he could to buck them up. He started along the lines of *You can't worry about what you can't control,* and as his men began to perk up, he realized his words had a familiar ring. Elements of pragmatist philosophy, long dissolved into some nether region of his brain, began to crystallize. To Rinn's utter surprise, the ideas he had dismissed in a Hudson Valley classroom were surfacing along the Mekong River. *If you worry about what you can't control, you lose focus. You make bad decisions.*

"I found myself talking to my men, explaining to them a pragmatic viewpoint of what had happened to us and why we needed to pick ourselves up and go on and do what we needed to do," he said later. "Why we had to go on and make things better if we could."

When his group finally made it back to their base, Rinn penned a note to his former professor. *I'm writing this letter 5,000 miles from nowhere,* he began. *A couple years ago, I told you that nothing you had told me in that class applied. I'm writing to tell you that I was wrong . . . What you taught will help us keep our sanity in the future and go on with our lives.*[4]

This was the lesson Paul Rinn took from Southeast Asia: you had to let go of the things you could do nothing about and focus with all your intensity on the things you could change. Combat stretched you beyond anything you ever thought possible; if you weren't already prepared, it was too late. He asked himself, then and later, *What prevented the enemy from killing me? How can I keep them from killing my guys?* For Rinn, these became the central questions of military command.

He continued to get the kind of assignments that marked a rising young officer. As weapons officer aboard the frigate USS *Blakely* (FF 1072), Rinn shot half a dozen practice missiles; as an exchange officer in Halifax, Nova Scotia, he ran operations for the 1st Canadian Destroyer Squadron. He earned admission as a lieutenant commander to the Naval War College in Newport, Rhode Island, and graduated with distinction in 1981. He completed a pair of tours as second in command: first as executive officer of the frigate USS *Bowen* (FF 1079), then as chief staff officer of Destroyer Squadron 36.

In 1983 the navy certified Rinn for command at sea, the most singular authority granted by the U.S. military. He was thirty-six years old, junior for a warship captain—possibly the first skipper from the class of 1968. But Rinn had watched his own superiors carefully for fifteen years, learning from their strengths and weaknesses, building his own leadership style. Now he would get to exercise it in the fullest way the navy offered.

Service officials soon picked a ship for him: a *Perry*-class guided missile frigate, designated FFG 58 and named Samuel B. Roberts after a heroic Navy coxswain. Rinn could scarcely believe his good fortune. He believed in the power of heritage to guide a crew, and a captain could scarcely ask for better exemplars than the World War II hero and the two previous ships that bore his name. But as yet the frigate existed only on the paper of the navy's master shipbuilding plan, though the construction order had already been dealt to a Maine shipyard. Instead of merely taking command of a ship and its crew, Rinn would help assemble them both.

IN APRIL 1985 the sailors who would man the *Roberts* began to gather in barracks at Norfolk Naval Station in Virginia, the sprawling home of the Atlantic Fleet. The group—formally, the *Samuel B. Roberts* Precommissioning Detachment—included about 150 crew members, three-quarters of the frigate's full complement. Fewer than half had ever been to sea, but all had survived boot camp, and some had received training in their shipboard job specialties. Still, this was just a start. All told, they would spend tens of thousands of hours in classrooms and simulators before they even boarded their ship.

The job of U.S. Navy sailor had long required more than a doughty attitude and a roll in the walk. A modern warship is among the world's most complex artifacts. It carries weapons, radars, generators, and a thousand other components, all interdependent and packed into a slim hull built for battle. Its crew must maintain, fix, and wield their gear in peace and war. The *Roberts* sailors had come to Norfolk, nearly a thousand miles south of their nascent ship, to learn how to operate it as a team.

They began with courses on damage control (DC). This was the craft of minimizing the effect of injury on a ship's ability to fight. A fervent approach to damage control is the necessary corollary to the independent and martial nature of a warship. At sea there is no one to help when enemy shells rain down and oily seawater rises in the engine room. And there is no time to hesitate or fumble; the first few minutes after taking a hit can determine the fate of a ship. To survive naval combat, the skills of damage control must become as familiar, as ingrained as drawing breath. So the *Roberts* sailors absorbed lectures on flooding and how to stop it and then drove across the base to practice in simulators that drove them batty with leaky pipes, punctured bulkheads, and split seams. Firefighting came next: lessons in the morning were followed by afternoons of hell in the two-story fire trainer called USS Buttercup.

After DC school, it was time for more technical training. The members of the *Roberts* detachment scattered across the United States. Gas turbine systems technicians learned about their frigate's propulsion plant in Great Lakes, Illinois, and then traveled to Philadelphia to stand watches in a mock engine room. Sonar technicians boned up on the care and feeding of the SQS-56, whose hull-mounted microphones would help them find enemy submarines. Fire controlmen learned to wield the Mk 92 system, which used the frigate's radar to guide its missiles and naval gun. The ship's officers had their own study programs. Engineers, for example, spent fourteen weeks at Great Lakes, flew to Newport for three weeks' study of gas turbines, and then headed to Philadelphia for a month of drills.[5]

Rinn himself spent much of 1985 in classrooms and ersatz ships. The navy had a lengthy curriculum for first-time frigate skippers. It started with numbing amounts of *Perry*-related mechanical detail delivered in a fourteen-week course at an Idaho training facility, moved on to Newport with courses on frigate propulsion, and then to Virginia and California for combat systems and tactics. The course wrapped up with six weeks back in Rhode Island, where prospective commanding officers discussed everything from corrosion control to the etiquette of visiting a foreign port.[6]

During a break, Rinn flew to Norfolk. The first meeting he called was with his chief petty officers. He intended to set the tone for his command, and he wanted to start with the chiefs. On the organizational chart, a chief works for a junior officer and transmits orders to more junior petty officers and seamen. But U.S. Navy chiefs have a stature that paper does not convey: they are the seen-it-all experts, the iron-fisted overlords of their sailors, the self-appointed repositories of naval heritage. The officers may give the orders, but the chiefs run the ship.

So Rinn called his chiefs to him and began to talk.

Number one, I am not just some guy who came out of the woods in Washington, DC. I served in Southeast Asia. I served off Lebanon. I've been in the Gulf of Sidra. I know what it is like to go into combat. I know what it is like to face the enemy. I know what it's like to think you're going to die, and I know what it's like to kill other people.

I know what it takes to make a ship the best, and quite frankly, there aren't any second-place awards in combat. I don't intend this ship to be a second-place ship. I want this ship to be the best ship there ever was. I want this ship to be a ship that everybody talks about, and more importantly, that everybody's proud to serve on.

But the key is that I want every sailor who ever served on the ship to think this is the best thing he could ever possibly have done with his life for those three years. And if they don't feel that way, then I will feel that I have failed. Not you—*I* will have failed.

I want this to be a professional platform where nothing but professionalism is accepted. I expect that the chain of command will work, and I expect all of you to be in the chain of command.

So you'll be empowered to lead, to teach. I expect you to lead
your men and to teach the officers. And if I find that you are not
doing that, I will be in your face immediately.[7]

Chief Gunner's Mate Tom Reinert ate this up like warrior's manna.
Few aboard the *Roberts* had more years at sea than Reinert, the senior
enlisted man in the ship's ordnance division. None was more determined
to make the brand-new frigate a standout in the fleet.

Like most Americans who graduated from high school in 1970, Reinert had faced a choice: go to college, or join the military. For the ship-
infatuated teenager from St. Petersburg, Florida, it was an easy decision;
he'd never much cared for school. But once in the navy, Reinert was
surprised to discover that he liked to study when the subject interested
him. So he graduated with honors from five-inch gun school and then
displayed such mastery of the Mark 13 missile launcher that the instructors asked him to stick around to teach the class. In 1984 Reinert
requested duty aboard the *Roberts,* savoring the challenge of turning a
new crew into one of the fleet's best.

In particular, the gunner had his eye on the "Battle E" awards. Every
eighteen months, ships were tested for their "battle efficiency" in gunnery, communications, engineering, and six other areas. "Mission 'E's"
were awarded for outstanding ability in a specific category; a winning
crew hastened to break out its paintbrushes and daub the record of its
achievement under the bridge. A white capital "E" denoted excellence
in communications, a red "DC" for damage control, and so forth. But
the most coveted and prestigious award was the Battle E itself, which
went to the best ship of its class in its squadron. The winning ship
marked its achievement on the bridge with a big black-shadowed "E,"
just like the hull number on the bow and not much smaller. Moreover,
the award came with a personal decoration for each crew member: a
dark-blue ribbon bearing a little silvery "E." The *Roberts's* squadron,
Naval Surface Group Four, contained nine *Perry*-class frigates. Only one
could win.

On Reinert's previous sea tour, the gunners couldn't even remember
the last time they won a mission E. He had refused to leave the destroyer
without one, and his team eventually painted their capital letter on the

bridge. But the exhausting effort convinced him that it was much easier to start good than to get good. He intended the *Roberts* to earn an "E" the first chance they got.

Reinert found the other chiefs of similar mind, and they bonded over barbeque and beers at the Virginia Beach motel they designated their precommissioning headquarters. They dubbed themselves the "Sammy B Fun Bunch" and launched forays to the beachfront bars in custom T-shirts. "It was tight right from the get-go," said Chuck Dumas, a signalman first class who joined the *Roberts* in May 1985 and was eventually advanced to chief. "With a lot of ships, you have these pockets of people who have their own little world. With the *Roberts* it was different; it seemed like everybody worked together on everything. If there was something to be done, there were plenty of people to take care of it . . . That chiefs' mess was ninety-five percent top-notch, and they led by example. Totally. If there was a working party, they would get involved with it. They wouldn't just stand there and direct."

Dumas credited the crew's success to Rinn's early messages, and to the chiefs for running with them. "Right from the start, we said, 'This is the *Sammy B. Roberts,* and this is the way we're going to do it,'" Dumas said. "Every sailor that came, it was instilled in his brain basically that, look, this is the third *Sammy B,* and we want to uphold every tradition to the utmost."[8]

That was just the spirit Rinn had sought. A good crew is a proud crew, and the captain believed that pride could start with a connection to the name painted in black letters on the ship's stern. He said: "From the beginning, every sailor who came aboard that ship, we taught them the tradition. Who was Samuel B. Roberts? I've been on ships where the sailors don't have a clue who the ship is named after. Not on *Samuel B. Roberts*. They knew who Samuel B. Roberts was."[9]

THE SHIP'S NAMESAKE was born in 1921 to a pair of navy veterans in San Francisco. His father was a former machinist's mate; his mother had answered a World War I call for clerical "yeomanettes." Samuel Booker Roberts Jr. enlisted in the naval reserve in 1939, flashing a cockeyed smile at a boot camp photographer. The navy taught him the skills of a coxswain—a master of small boats—and early duty took him from

California to Iceland and back. Then Roberts was assigned to the USS *Bellatrix* (AK 20), an eight-thousand-ton amphibious cargo ship, and sent into battle in the South Pacific.[10]

In August 1942 the *Bellatrix* and eighty-two other ships launched the assault on Guadalcanal, America's first counterpunch at Japanese territory. For two days Roberts and other coxswains ferried troops and gear to shore. Then four allied cruisers were sunk off nearby Savo Island, and the navy called a hasty retreat. The move stranded nineteen thousand marines in enemy territory with four days of supplies. Roberts and two dozen other navy and coast guard sailors volunteered to run a hastily constructed supply post farther down the coast. For seven miserably hot weeks they piloted their Higgins boats from a former coconut plantation at Lunga Point, hauling food and ammunition to the troops.

On 27 September several hundred marines piled into a dozen of the wooden boats and headed up to a beach near the Matanikau River, where Lt. Col. Chesty Puller, the legendary combat leader, hoped to outflank a Japanese strongpoint.[11] Roberts and the other coxswains dropped the troops off and headed back to base. But half a mile inland, the marines stumbled upon dug-in enemy soldiers. A passing U.S. dive-bomber picked up their distress call and flashed a message to Lunga Point. The sailors clambered back into their boats and sailed to the beach. The marines burst from the trees at a dead run, with Japanese machine gunners tracking them across the sand with deadly bursts. The sailors returned fire, but their light .30-caliber slugs offered little deterrence. Roberts had volunteered to create a diversion in just this situation, and so the coxswain pulled his boat off the beach and back into the surf. Running wide open at ten knots, he cruised up and down the shoreline, drawing the deadly attention of the Japanese troops. The distraction eased the pressure on the marines, and the other boats gathered them up, pulled off the beach, and turned to go. Roberts held his own boat in range a fatal moment too long, and machine-gun bullets caught him in the neck. He died aboard a medical evacuation flight.[12] The coxswain received a posthumous Navy Cross, the service's second-highest decoration.[13]

Within months, the navy bestowed upon Coxswain Roberts an even rarer honor: it gave his name to a warship. In April 1944 the fleet commissioned USS *Samuel B. Roberts* (DE 413), an eighteen-hundred-ton destroyer escort—essentially, a pocket-sized destroyer lightly armed with a pair of five-inch guns and a triple rack of torpedo tubes.[14] Like Paul Rinn's guided missile frigate, the first *Roberts* was built to shepherd troopships and merchant craft, and to do it at a bargain price. Yet the deeds of this diminutive warship would deepen the luster of its name. Before the year was out, the *Roberts* would help seal the fate of the Japanese empire amid the largest naval battle ever fought.[15]

Responsibility for preparing the *Roberts* and its crew belonged to its first and only commanding officer, Lt. Cdr. Robert Copeland. Perhaps thirty of the ship's roughly two hundred sailors had ever been to sea; the rest were farm boys and city kids who had been hastily introduced to naval warfare in Norfolk. A naval reservist and lawyer from Tacoma, Washington, Copeland worked hard to ready his sailors for battle. "A good ship is actually no good without a good crew," the captain told an interviewer long after the war. "A good crew can do pretty well with even a passable ship; but when you have a good ship and then get an A-1 crew, you've got something that can't be beaten."[16] Its training complete, the *Roberts* sailed west to join the greatest armada ever assembled.

In October 1944 the U.S. Seventh Fleet, a collection of more than seven hundred troop transports, battleships, cruisers, and supply ships, disgorged thousands of army troops onto the beaches of the Philippine island of Leyte. The invasion threatened Japan's entire war effort; the loss of the Philippines would sever access to Indochinese oil and immobilize what remained of the imperial fleet. Desperate, the imperial high command threw its last strength into an attempt to repel the landing fleet.

The Battle of Leyte Gulf began badly for the Japanese. American warships annihilated a flotilla that crept in from the south.[17] But hope glimmered in Tokyo when a northern stratagem stripped the Seventh Fleet of its northern guard: the U.S. Third Fleet was lured from its station by a toothless group of empty-decked Japanese aircraft carriers. On October 25 a Japanese battleship squadron plunged through the defensive gap. Built around the super-battleship *Yamato,* this center force mustered three other battleships, eight cruisers, and eleven destroyers. With the Third Fleet gone, only a baker's dozen of Seventh Fleet warships stood between the *Yamato* group and the wallowing U.S. troopships in Leyte Gulf.

This was Task Unit 77.4.3, which went by the radio call sign Taffy 3. It consisted of six escort aircraft carriers, four destroyers, and three destroyer escorts, including the *Roberts*. Copeland had been up all night, ear pressed to the radio, anxiously following the action to the south. By dawn, he was breathing a bit more easily. The southern battle had become a rout, while the Third Fleet—he believed—still covered the northern flank. The impression was shattered around 6:30 AM when the *Yamato* sent salvoes of 18.1-inch naval shells, each the size of a tree trunk, whistling in from eighteen miles away. Hundred-foot geysers bloomed green and purple, dyed to help gunners track their shots. Taffy 3 lacked even a single gun to reach the distant battleships, and the commanding admiral ordered his force to run.[18]

On the bridge of the *Roberts,* the helmsman wrenched his ship toward nearby splashes, hoping to outguess the Japanese gunners as they corrected their aim. Near misses doused the bridge. The incoming fire grew heavier. At 7:42 the admiral concluded that Taffy 3 would not survive five more minutes of pounding. He ordered his destroyers and destroyer escorts—the seven "small boys"—to turn and attack. It was a suicide mission, and Copeland knew it; his fifty-four-pound shells could not penetrate Japanese armor. Yet he told his crew that they would do what damage they could. Belching a thick screen of covering smoke, the *Roberts* charged the enemy.[19]

In the melee that followed, the small boys of Taffy 3 wreaked havoc upon their lumbering foes. Dodging and weaving at twenty knots, Copeland pressed his torpedo attack on a cruiser. Two miles from his target, he loosed a two-fish spread. A flash appeared below the mast. "We got her!" someone yelled. Copeland hauled his ship around and set upon another cruiser that was stalking the U.S. carriers.[20] His gunners poured a jumble of five-inch gunfire onto its superstructure: standard rounds, armor-piercing shells, antiaircraft munitions, even illumination flares. But eventually, luck ran out for the *Roberts.* A trio of eight-inch shells ripped through the port side, disdaining to explode against something as flimsy as a destroyer escort but crippling the ship with brute momentum. After coming almost unscathed through nearly two hours of combat, the limping craft became easy prey. Fourteen-inch shells soon finished her off. At 9:10 AM Copeland ordered his crew to abandon ship.

The battle raged on, and it took several days for the navy to rescue the survivors of Taffy 3. By the time a group of U.S. landing craft found them two days after the battle, only 133 living *Roberts* crew members, dehydrated and delirious, could be pulled from the oily sea. But their effort had been enough. The furious counterattack of the small boys, along with heroic efforts by army and navy planes, had convinced the Japanese commander that he faced a much more powerful force of heavy cruisers and carriers. As DE 413 slipped to the bottom, the center force retired to the north. World War II dragged on for nearly a year, but Japan had lost its last chance to salvage a different ending.[21]

In his battle report, Robert Copeland delivered the ultimate encomium to his sailors: "The crew were informed over the loudspeaker system at the beginning of the action of the Commanding Officer's estimate of the situation; that is, a fight against overwhelming odds from which survival could not be expected, during which time we would do what damage we could. In the face of this knowledge, the men zealously manned their stations wherever they might be, and fought and worked with such calmness, courage, and efficiency that no higher honor could be conceived than to command such a group of men."

The U.S. Navy commemorates valiant ships as well as valiant sailors, so in late 1946 the service commissioned a second *Samuel B. Roberts*. No half-pint destroyer escort, the twenty-four-hundred-ton DD 823 belonged to the formidable *Gearing* class, the final word in World War II destroyers. Operating out of Newport, the "Steamin' *Sammy B*" established a reputation for nabbing bit parts in big events—a sort of naval Forrest Gump. DD 823 sailed with the first naval squadron to transit the St. Lawrence Seaway and was the last warship through the Suez Canal before war shut the waterway in the 1950s.[22] In October 1962 the destroyer sped south to help turn back Soviet ships bearing missile parts to Cuba; the next year, the ship gathered up the rubber gloves and oil that rose over the grave of the nuclear attack submarine USS *Thresher* (SSN 593).[23]

The *Roberts* earned its two battle stars in 1965: one for bombarding enemy positions on Hainan Island; another for action off Vietnam, where it stood plane guard as the USS *Enterprise* (CVN 65) delivered history's first air strikes from a nuclear-powered aircraft carrier.[24] (More than three decades hence, the "Big E" would return the favor, exacting revenge for the mining of the third *Samuel B. Roberts*.) By 1970 the second *Sammy B* was worn out. The crew stripped the destroyer for decommissioning, and gunners aboard newer warships sank it for practice off Puerto Rico.[25]

RINN BELIEVED GOOD sailors carried a sense of heritage in their sea bags. The heroes of the past offered a standard to meet, a path to follow, a spur to excellence. "Joining the navy made you aware that you were part of history, doing things people had done before you," he said. "You thought, 'Maybe if I do what they did, it will help me.'" The connection was as much emotional as intellectual for Rinn, who could get quite worked up while discussing the tardy rescue of the survivors of DE 413.

So the captain-to-be set out to embed his ship's heritage into the fiber of its crew. He eagerly tore into a packet of information from the Naval Historical Center in Washington.[26] He borrowed Coxswain Roberts's Navy Cross from his family and had it framed in a shadowbox for the officers' wardroom. He commissioned a bronze plaque listing the DE 413 sailors who fought in the battle off Samar. He plucked the ship's official motto— "No Higher Honor"—from Copeland's battle report; it described a good skipper's attitude toward good sailors. And he stocked the ship's small store with a slim navy-blue hardcover book: Robert Copeland's memoir.

> We sold 400 copies of that book in the store—*The Legend of the Sammy B.*—so they knew who Samuel Booker Roberts was and how he got the Navy Cross, and they knew about DE 413 and how it made an impossible attack. They met the survivors. They knew there was something before them and something that was awful good, it was awful courageous, and was awful brave.
>
> More importantly, it was a small ship [about which] everybody said, "What can you do?" Turn back a bunch of Japanese cruisers, that's what. And go in harm's way. And look at hell in the face and say, "Fuck you."

Rinn intended to mold his own ship in that image.

He had a head start of sorts. His *Perry*-class frigate was another kind of ship about which many said: "What can you do?" The answer to that began in a New England shipyard.

CHAPTER THREE

A Bath-Built Ship

A small Maine city seemed hardly the place to find a naval shipyard late in the twentieth century. Its location, tucked amid the forests that were so vital to an earlier era's craft, was far from the steel plants that fed modern shipyards. Autumn came early and spring late to the banks of the Kennebec River. In between there were months of biting cold and snow, when outdoor labor became a grueling feat of endurance. But Bath had good reason to call itself the City of Ships. A tiny band of British settlers had pioneered New World shipbuilding on the Kennebec more than a dozen years before the *Mayflower* landed at Plymouth, and a thriving industry had grown up in the first decades of American independence. Shipwrights found a natural home in the river town, which was sheltered from Atlantic storms, supplied by local timber, and blessed with a three-mile stretch of ruler-straight riverbank—the Long Reach—whose gentle slope fell at once to deep water.[1]

In 1884 a local Civil War hero by the name of Thomas Worcester Hyde issued stock for his machinery firm, a thriving concern built around a fifty-year-old foundry, and incorporated it as Bath Iron Works Ltd. (BIW).[2] Hyde's company soon ushered Maine into steel-ship manufacture with a U.S. Navy order for two 205-foot gunboats; over the next half century, BIW built everything from the battleship USS *Georgia* (BB 15) to J. P. Morgan's $3.5 million yacht.[3] But the Maine yard became best known for its destroyers. During World War II Bath turned out eighty-two of the fast, slender-hulled warships—more than the entire German Reich or the Japanese empire.[4] Its vessels were delivered faster, cheaper, and with fewer defects than other yards', and they earned a near-mythic reputation for endurance under fire. The destroyer USS *Laffey* (DD 724)— "the ship that would not die"—shrugged off German shells at Normandy,

steamed halfway around the world, and survived hits from five kami-
kazes and four bombs at Okinawa.[5] The coming of the Cold War seemed
to cement Bath's primacy among U.S. destroyer builders; between 1950
and 1965, BIW designed more than half of the navy's smaller surface
combatants: destroyers, destroyer escorts, frigates.[6] "Bath-built is best-
built," the saying went.[7]

But by the late 1960s the Maine firm struggled to compete with larger
shipyards that were bankrolled by deep-pocketed defense conglomer-
ates. Bath took a tough blow in June 1970, when it lost a bid for the mammoth thirty-ship contract to build the state-of-the-art DX destroyer. The
job, awarded in a selection process noted for political influence and shift-
ing rules, went to Litton-Ingalls in Pascagoula, Mississippi. The loss of the
DX, which was the last destroyer-type ship the navy planned to build for
some years, left Bath's future as a military shipbuilder uncertain.

Several weeks later, two BIW executives flew to Washington for a
meeting with the head of U.S. Navy shipbuilding. William Haggett, the
yard's marketing manager, was one of these; company president James
Goodrich was the other. Both men had spent much time in the capital
city, pitching their services to admirals and members of Congress. This
time, however, they sought an augury on their yard's future. They had
requested an appointment with Rear Adm. Nathan Sonenshein, the
powerful chief of the Bureau of Ships, and they were not encouraged
by the time slot: 7:00 AM. This was early for a business meeting, even by
military standards, and it seemed to portend no good.

An aide ushered the men from Bath into Sonenshein's Pentagon office,
and Haggett got right to the point. "How would you suggest we move
ahead in a way that allows us to maintain our hundred-year history of
doing work with the navy?" he asked the admiral. "Is there repair work
we might do?"[8]

Sonenshein was blunt. "Now that we have awarded the DX contract
to Litton, I can see no further need for the Bath Iron Works in any of the
Navy's future programs," the admiral said.[9] Sonenshein likely held no particular animus against Bath; he was a champion of efficiency who believed
the United States was already carrying excess industrial capacity.[10]

But Haggett was furious. BIW was smaller than its rivals, but its design
and production proposal had outlasted all but one in the contest for the

DX. The Maine yard had been building destroyers since the sleek warships were invented, and Haggett, who had been raised in Bath by a father who ran the yard's tin shop, did not intend to stop.

The problem was that BIW wasn't building much of anything at that point. For the first time in thirty-seven years, there were no new ships on the building ways, and the yard was limping along on upgrade jobs. In a dismal mood, Goodrich and Haggett boarded a plane at nearby Washington National Airport and headed back to BIW, grimly determined to keep their yard alive. They realized that Bath would have to adapt to survive. Over the next few years, the yard scratched up enough work to stay afloat, taking in subcontracts for other naval yards, building commercial tankers and container ships. And against all odds, Goodrich and Haggett persuaded their board of directors to fund a $14 million overhaul of the yard. The renovation would introduce a process called modular construction and put BIW back on its industry's cutting edge.

Modular construction reflected a fundamental change in the nature of warships. In the age of wooden ships the assembly of a vessel's structure had generally consumed more time and effort than installing its fittings. Shipwrights laid down a timber backbone and then labored under the sun to attach ribs, decks, and masts. But warships had evolved. Steam replaced sail, electricity replaced candles, plumbing replaced slop buckets. Along came radar, electronics, and computers, with miles of wiring to knot them together. A ship's innards began to demand far more labor than its skeleton and skin.

But working inside the hull was unwieldy and tiresome, and therefore slow and expensive. The solution: build the ship in pieces, and stack the massive chunks as if building a toy boat from blocks. The advantages were nearly endless. Work proceeded in a workshop, not a cramped, half-built hull. Fittings and other components flowed easily into position. Even bathroom breaks were more convenient. Bath had long crafted small chunks of ships indoors, but the Japanese and Scandinavians had rebuilt entire shipyards based on the concept. Now BIW followed their lead. The Maine workers raised a 480-foot assembly hall that became the state's largest building. They erected a forty-story monster crane. Built to hoist modules the size of diesel locomotives, its candy-striped tower loomed above the river town, blurring local television reception.[11]

The timing of the renovation was excellent. Bath would soon return to the ranks of naval shipbuilders, thanks to its revamped yard—and the innovative leader who had recently taken command of the navy.

AT FORTY-NINE, Adm. Elmo R. Zumwalt Jr. was the youngest chief of naval operations (CNO) in U.S. history, and he swept into the navy's top office like a man in a hurry. In a flurry of mid-1970 edicts called Z-grams, Zumwalt cancelled burdensome "chicken regulations" such as the prohibition of beards and took steps to reduce sexism and racism. The new CNO also introduced a bold shipbuilding strategy called High-Low, which envisioned a fleet comprised of a few top-of-the-line ships—*Nimitz*-class aircraft carriers, nuclear submarines, and guided missile cruisers—and a large number of relatively inexpensive ones.[12] The plan drew fire from admirals accustomed to the navy's usual price-is-no-object approach, who argued that lesser warships would hinder, not help the fleet. But simple math showed that the navy, with too many World War II–era ships overdue for retirement, could not afford costly replacements.[13]

In September, Zumwalt asked his ship designers to sketch out a "patrol frigate": a lightly armed, twenty-knot escort craft to shepherd cargo ships.[14] They reported that a thirty-seven-hundred-ton frigate might be built for $50 million. The CNO cut the weight limit by three hundred tons and the price by $5 million. Then he told his ship designers to sharpen their pencils and get to work.[15]

They roughed out a fairly typical construction for the patrol frigate— a steel hull with riblike frames every eight feet—but the compromises began immediately. Instead of half-inch plates of high-tensile alloy, the hull would be covered with medium steel just three-quarters as strong. The superstructure would be built of aluminum, a light metal that resists saltwater corrosion but burns at temperatures that only singe steel.[16] Tougher materials would buttress the structure at key points: the main deck and keel would be built of HY-80 steel, and strips of the double-strength alloy would run along the top of the hull.[17]

Compromise followed compromise. Instead of a two-rail missile launcher, the frigate would carry the Mk 13, a "one-armed bandit" that reloaded after every shot.[18] Rather than state-of-the-art sonar, the frigate would get the smaller, less expensive, and less capable SQS-56; sonar technicians called it the "Helen Keller" system. And the patrol frigate would receive the SPS-49 air-search radar in lieu of a "three-dimensional" model that could determine an aircraft's range, heading, *and* altitude— making it the navy's only missile ship whose long-range sensor could not tell the height of its targets. None of these sacrifices was easy. Zumwalt's designers soothed themselves with assurances that their patrol frigate would never be a frontline unit, and that there would always be other, more capable ships nearby.[19]

How to arm this austere new ship? If planners fitted the slender hull with antiship Harpoon missiles and antiair Standard missiles, they would have to jettison the bulky pepperbox launcher that fired antisubmarine ASROC missiles—and then how would the frigate fight subs?[20] After a bit of thought, the planners proposed a bold move: ditch the ASROCs and rely on the ship's helicopter. This required a leap of faith; no anti-submarine warship had ever depended so heavily on its aircraft. But the LAMPS helicopter (Light Airborne Multi-Purpose System) was no ordinary rotorcraft. The LAMPS stalked its quarry with floating sonobuoy microphones and a chin-mounted radar. Stubby antenna swapped radar and sonar data with its mother frigate, allowing the ship's company and aircrew to draw a lethal net around their prey. By the time the *Roberts* came along, a LAMPS-equipped warship would be the surface navy's most lethal sub-killing machine.

The patrol frigate may have been built to economy-car standards, but it would move on Corvette engines: twin 20,000-horsepower General Electric LM-2500 gas turbines. These were marinized versions of GE's aircraft jet engines. Like their airborne cousins, marine gas turbines burn atomized fuel to spin a core at thousands of revolutions per minute. In an aircraft, thrust comes from the combustion's exhaust; in a ship, the whirling core is yoked through a reduction gear to the ship's screw. Compared to the hellish boiler rooms that powered steamships, gas tur-bines offered all sorts of benefits: they took up less space, required fewer engineers, could be started up with the press of a button. Gas turbine ships were the sports cars of the naval world, able to accelerate far faster then their steam-powered brethren. The engineers even added a bit of insurance: electrically powered, retractable outboard motors mounted beneath the forward superstructure. Dubbed auxiliary propulsion units

(APUs), the 325-horsepower units swung out in pods to help the ship maneuver in tight harbors—or in the event of catastrophic damage, pull it to safety at four or five knots, a feature the *Roberts* crew would one day find quite useful.[21]

In May 1971 the planners presented their work to Zumwalt, who approved it with delight, named it the PF 109 class, and launched a competition among shipyards to finish the design.[22]

GOODRICH AND HAGGETT leaped to bid on the job, and it didn't take long for coastal Maine's newspapers to pick up the near-forgotten scent of victory. In February 1972 Bath Iron Works won the contract to lay out preliminary blueprints for the PF 109; the following year, the yard received a $92.4 million contract to build the lead ship.[23] Bath Iron Works, once dismissed by the chief of navy shipbuilding, was back.

The yard's architects and engineers began to lay out the innumerable details of a modern warship. They strove to keep things simple for the sake of cost and structural strength. They drew and redrew blueprints until the ironworkers could shape most of the ship's thousands of steel plates with no more than two cuts, and the welders could put them in place with no more than two welds. BIW officials persuaded the navy to allow stock L-shaped metal braces instead of the customary T-beams produced by cutting I-beams in half—an astonishingly labor-intensive process.[24] Defying convention, Bath's designers placed the engine room aft of the ship's center. This allowed the berthing and dining spaces to be clumped together, pushed noisy machinery away from the bow sonar, and vented corrosive exhaust leeward of radar antennae. For all of this, the future crew of the *Roberts* would one day be grateful.

Construction began in March 1975 on the first ship, which was redesignated FFG 7 and named *Oliver Hazard Perry* after the hero of the 1813 Battle of Lake Erie. One by one, the ship's thirty-six modules were assembled, lifted onto the ways, and welded into place. *Perry* was launched in September 1976 and put to sea a year later for formal acceptance trials. These proceeded under the exacting eye of Vice Adm. Joseph D. Bulkeley, president of the navy's Board of Inspection and Survey. As a young man, Bulkeley had received the Medal of Honor for spiriting Gen. Douglas MacArthur from Japanese clutches in his plywood

PT boat. Forty-five years later he was a living legend and a crusty, demanding inspector.

Haggett permitted himself a moment of pride as he watched the *Perry* pull away from the pier and head down the Kennebec to the Gulf of Maine. The ship's graceful hull began at the raked shark's-nose bow and sloped in a long curve to the flight deck aft. The superstructure was a long and boxy dog bone: beam-wide at the bridge, narrow amidships, and flared aft to accommodate twin helicopter hangars. But would the ship pass inspection?

A few days later, Haggett held his breath as the frigate hove into view around a bend of the Kennebec. The ship was two days early. Through the crisp fall air, the onlookers spied a broom tied to the mast, the traditional symbol of a clean sweep of its tests—and then a second broom appeared as well. The trials had gone all but flawlessly, and Bulkeley had cut the trials short. "A magnificent ship,"[25] the old sea dog declared. "The best ship in 20 years."[26]

Over the next decade, the Maine yard built twenty-one more *Perry* frigates, and the program blossomed into a model for naval shipbuilders. "Destroyer Built On Time, Under Budget," the *Washington Post* marveled in late 1978: "Here on the banks of the Kennebec River, a strange thing is happening in this era of Navy ships being delivered years late and way over the original price tag. The venerable Bath Iron Works, which started building ships for the Navy in 1890, is building a new breed of destroyer on time and under the agreed-upon price."[27] The yard was rigorous about applying lessons from one ship to the next, and almost every vessel was delivered earlier and cheaper than its predecessors. It took 2.5 million man-hours to build the *Perry*, but just 1.4 million to deliver Bath's twelfth frigate, the USS *Aubrey Fitch* (FFG 34).[28]

By the time work began on the third *Samuel B. Roberts* in October 1983, the yard's workers could practically build one of the ships in their sleep. Like its predecessor *Perrys*, FFG 58 began life in a fabrication plant in the nearby town of Hardings. Trains bore raw steel onto the sidings of a blue prefab building, where metalworkers cut the beams, trimmed the plates, and stacked them on flatcars for the seven-mile trip up to Bath. There, welders and shipfitters began to assemble the plates into modules. The following spring, a candy-striped crane removed the first gray chunk of ship from the long assembly building and lifted it into place on the ways. A month later, the gas turbines were lowered into the main engine room. Work continued through the summer, and as autumn tinted the nearby forests, the frigate's slender hull began to take form.[29]

PAUL RINN ARRIVED in Maine a few chilly weeks after Labor Day of 1984. He had left his family behind in Charleston, South Carolina; he and his wife, Pamela, had decided not to uproot their three children, and after surviving three of Paul's deployments in four years, Pamela was more than capable of running the household. Rinn took up residence in a small cliff-top house on Bailey Island, one of the bits of piney land that crowd Casco Bay. The summer folk had long gone, and most of the remaining inhabitants were watermen, taciturn old salts who stacked their lobster traps like cordwood along the roads.

On most mornings, Rinn went to grab coffee and a doughnut at the local general store, where regulars in woolly sweaters warmed themselves around a potbellied stove. But the naval officer's early attempts to scratch up some conversation were met with silence. After three weeks of this, he began to wonder whether he would eat breakfast alone for the next two years. Driving home one night, Rinn stopped his Volvo to give a shivering teenager a lift. The next evening, he found a lobster and a six-pack of beer in a shopping bag on his doorstep—a thank-you from the kid's mother. The day after that, he stopped to pick up his coffee. "Mornin', Cap'n," someone said.

In Bath, Rinn found a half-built ship surrounded by scaffolding like an eight-story stand of bamboo. He buried himself in thick books of specifications, studying his nascent frigate's structure and equipment. He spent hours among half-built hull forms, picking his way among the power cables, chatting and joking with welders and electricians. He showed up early and left late.

The navy had brought Rinn to town a full year before the ship's scheduled delivery, to help oversee its construction. The job officially belonged to the local deputies of the Supervisor of Ships (SupShip), who worked out of a white building across the street from the yard. The SupShip officers measured BIW's progress against a contract the size of a phone book. But a ship's prospective commanding officer brought a gimlet eye to the process. The captain would one day take the ship to sea, trusting his life and his sailors to the builders' workmanship.

The skipper's job required a certain diplomatic touch. He had no formal power and could not order so much as the repainting of a passageway. Almost every request was supposed to come from the SupShip's office and every alteration cleared through Washington. But a captain learned to do deck plate business over coffee with BIW supervisors. An amicable relationship with the managers and shipyard leaders could help solve problems without an inch of red tape.

William Haggett, who had been recently appointed the shipyard's top executive, found Rinn exacting but easy to work with, professional but warm—in fact, one of the savviest skippers to come down the pike. "He was doing all the things that a wise commanding officer does to get the very best ship: working closely and cooperatively with the shipyard, and the workers in the shipyard on the deck plates," Haggett said. "And the first-line supervisors, getting to know them by first name. And getting to know the CEO of the shipyard."

When Rinn started asking for changes, he sought ways to make things turn out well for everyone. "Let's turn this vacant space forward into an extra potable-water tank," he might say, "and I'll let you skip the decorative tiling somewhere else."

Haggett soon told his employees to work with the commander on anything that didn't cost extra or bend the rules too far. "Rinn was—I was going to say demanding, but he wasn't demanding," the shipyard executive said. "He was a politician more than a guy who would stand up there and yell and scream. He wouldn't do any of that. He just worked with our people, and he was smart enough to come in [on] weekends."[30]

FOR ALL OF Admiral Bulkeley's praise, the *Perry* frigates had not enjoyed a universally warm welcome in the fleet. The FFGs' small fuel tanks, limited communications suite, and twenty-eight-knot top speed had not endeared them to U.S. commodores. Critics evinced little hope that the ships' slender hulls could accommodate much-needed improvements. The disdain had increased with the introduction of the USS *Ticonderoga* guided missile cruisers and their Aegis combat system, a high-tech marvel of advanced radar and weapons that could make a frigate sailor feel like a second-class citizen. One lieutenant commander wrote that the guided missile frigate was in peril of becoming "the Navy's square peg of the 1980s."[31]

But others, mostly veterans of *Perry* ships, leaped to their defense. One former skipper noted that his FFG had beaten most rivals at spotting and shooting aerial targets, and predicted that the arrival of the improved LAMPS-3 helicopter and the towed sonar array would transform the frigate into a perfectly competent sub hunter.[32] An Australian exchange officer aboard USS *Flatley* (FFG 21) cited all manner of missions accomplished: patrolling the Persian Gulf, shadowing Soviet ships in the Caribbean, protecting an aircraft carrier in the Mediterranean. "FFG 7s are fast becoming the utility ship of the Navy," he wrote.

And in May 1984 the debate drew a letter from the future commanding officer of the *Roberts*. "When operated aggressively, the FFG 7 is a superb antisubmarine warfare pouncer inside the outer screen," Paul Rinn wrote to the editors of *Proceedings,* the naval professionals' journal. He argued that the ship was well suited to hunt down subs that managed to get past the first ring of escorts that surrounded a carrier. But he warned, "The ability of an individual platform to integrate into the carrier battle group and perform in different mission areas simultaneously depends largely on the proficiency of her crew and the aggressiveness of the ship's on-board leadership."[33]

Here was a thought that had yet to be advanced in thousands of printed words, and it was pure Rinn: give me a frigate and a good crew, and, come game time, we're gonna knock it out of the park.

THREE U.S. WARSHIPS slid from their concrete wombs on 8 December 1984. One was USS *Pittsburgh* (SSN 720), a nuclear-powered attack submarine in Groton, Connecticut. Another was the salvage ship USS *Grapple* (ARS 53) in Sturgeon Bay, Wisconsin. The third was the *Samuel B. Roberts*. Although no one could have known it at the time—the 600-Ship Navy was still a dream alive—the service would never again launch three ships in a single day.[34]

In Maine the BIW launch crew rose before dawn to complete the preparations. The checklist was long but familiar, burnished over a century that had sent 393 ships into the Kennebec River. Workers swaddled the prow of the *Roberts* in bunting and replaced the concrete keel blocks with a sliding wooden cradle. Signal flags flapped merrily on long catenaries. The newly complete hull, with its smooth coats of gray and ochre paint, belied the work that remained. Bits of scaffolding surrounded the unpainted superstructure, and a wooden plug occupied the missile launcher's place on the forecastle. But the tall web of steel and wood that had surrounded the ship was gone, and the slender hull perched naked and precarious atop its launch cradle. Towering over the snow-dappled building ways, the *Roberts* looked ill at ease, as if itching to move on.

By noon, thousands of workers and other well-wishers had folded themselves into metal chairs on the concrete. On the forecastle high above, sailors peeped over the lifelines. Paul Rinn escorted his wife onto a whitewashed lumber dais under the looming prow, where they joined a cluster of dignitaries, including two congressmen. There was even a survivor of DE 413: Jack Roberts, brother of the ship's namesake.[35]

Bath's city band played the national anthem, the politicians spoke, a chaplain delivered an invocation. Jack's wife, Ivonette, broke a beribboned champagne bottle against a small plate welded to the bow and jumped back as the wine foamed over.[36] Bath's launchers pulled the trigger, and the *Roberts* moved smartly down the ways. One BIW engineer pulled a pencil from a battered notebook wrapped with a rubber band. In precise letters, Erik Hansen noted the time, date, and speed as the ship moved down the ways. His book held the same data for each of the yard's twenty previous frigates.

The *Roberts* plunged into the river, and tugboats shepherded it to a nearby pier. But more than a year of work still lay ahead for the workers of Bath—and for the frigate's crew, whose members were starting to trickle into town.

CHAPTER FOUR

Damage Control for Breakfast

The man who built the *Roberts*'s damage control team hadn't wanted the job. At thirty-one, Lt. Eric Sorensen was a bit older than his peers, thanks to his enlisted service in the U.S. Coast Guard and a couple of years as a charter boat captain. But he was no less determined to make a career of the navy, and had worked hard to get his commissioned service off to a fast start.

Sorensen had paid his dues aboard the destroyer USS *Briscoe* (DD 977), starting out in charge of the line handlers and working his way into the combat information center. He had accepted orders to the yet-to-be-commissioned *Roberts* in hopes of earning the engineering qualification that would round out his resume. It would mean back-to-back tours at sea, but it would be worth it—if he could talk his way into an engine room job. So he was displeased to learn that his new skipper intended to make him the damage control assistant (DCA). Adding insult to injury, contemporary naval culture held that the job generally belonged to a very junior officer, not a lieutenant on his second sea tour.[1] But Rinn was looking for a take-charge officer to make sure damage control drills were no afterthought. In Sorensen, whom *Briscoe*'s skipper had called "bold and supremely self-confident," he had his man.

Sorensen's deck plate confidence dated from his youth. Young Eric spent his childhood weekends working on the charter boats that plied the waters near his Cape Cod home. At seventeen, bored with home and high school, he dropped out to join the coast guard. The service designated him a boatswain's mate—a job for those saltiest of sailors who handle lines, helm boats, chip paint, and keep the decks shipshape—and sent him to serve on a long-endurance cutter in the North Atlantic. Sorensen, a very junior sailor, was given charge of a five-person whaleboat crew on the cutter. Putting his small wooden craft into winter seas off Labrador, he learned what it meant to hold others' lives in his hands.

Sorensen made petty officer second class in a lightning-quick thirty months and then left the service. For a time, he ran a charter-boat service out of Cape Cod. But the waterfront life wore him down, and he eventually followed the advice of an older waterman and headed off to college.

A chance visit by a frigate to Boston Harbor stirred memories of his service, and as the semesters passed, the idea of returning to the coast guard—as an officer—took hold. A year before graduation, Sorensen applied to the officer candidate program and sent a copy of the application to the navy as well. Months passed without news, and Sorensen grew frustrated, then angry at his former service's indifference. When acceptance letters to both programs finally arrived, the former Coastie packed his bags for the navy's Officer Candidate School (OCS) in Newport.

OCS was the sixteen-week training program for officers-to-be who had neither matriculated at the U.S. Naval Academy nor taken ROTC (Reserve Officers' Training Corps) courses at a civilian college. Sorensen did well at the school, where his enlisted service gave him a head start on the coursework. Then he pulled a back muscle during one of the school's occasional field days ("mandatory fun," the students called them), and by nightfall could barely move. After ten days in bed he learned that administrators were planning to drop him back to the next class of candidates. Sorensen dragged himself to the classrooms and attended lectures lying down on the buildings' heaters. He had missed seven exams, but they were in basic seamanship and navigation, so he took them without studying, and passed. Three weeks later he was appointed regimental commander of his graduation group, the Newport equivalent of class president. "The highlight of my fifteen-year navy career: OCS," he said, dryly.[2]

In July 1981 Sorensen reported to the *Briscoe* in Norfolk. He was given the job of assistant first lieutenant, the deputy to the officer in charge of keeping up the ship's decks. Sorensen passed the next six months much as he had his coast guard days: teaching knots, boat handling, maintenance, and other elements of traditional watercraft to the *Briscoe*'s junior sailors. He qualified to drive the ship after about eight weeks at sea, a process that generally takes new officers more than half a year.

By the time Sorensen finished his *Briscoe* tour in November 1984, he reckoned he had the makings of a well-launched career. He had added stints as first lieutenant and combat information center officer to his service jacket, and he had a plan for his time aboard the *Roberts*. He intended to wangle the job of main propulsion assistant, second only to the chief engineer in responsibility for the warship's power plant. He would earn his certification as engineering officer of the watch and would emerge from the job with qualifications to conn warships, run their engineering plants, and fight their combat systems. In short, he would have punched all the tickets, as the saying went, and set himself squarely on the road to lieutenant commander.[3]

Paul Rinn had other plans. The prospective commanding officer believed that damage control, like mine warfare, often received more lip service than priority. The navy spent billions of dollars on antiaircraft missiles and millions of hours learning to fire them—yet the U.S. surface fleet had not shot down a single plane since the Vietnam War. But a warship risked collision and grounding every time it left a pier, and a shipboard fire could break out any day of the week. "You drive for show, and putt for dough," Rinn said.[4]

A crew had to know how to fight their ship, but they also needed to know how to save it—and quickly. Trauma doctors and nurses speak of the "golden hour" that follows a life-threatening injury; the chances of survival sharply diminish if not treated within sixty minutes. The margin was even slimmer for a ship, where fires and floods could rage out of control in a mere quarter hour. Rinn intended to train his crew to fight fires and patch holes skillfully, without hesitation and in the direst of circumstances.

On a frigate, responsibility for DC training belonged, at least nominally, to the executive officer and chief engineer. In practice, the burden rested on the damage control assistant. It was the DCA's job to draw up training regimens and to lead senior enlisted sailors in drilling the crew.[5] But the junior officer who customarily held the office found it tough to compete for the crew's attention. And he often found himself woefully underprepared—reading the instructor's manuals one moment and teaching crews the next.

Rinn thought this a dangerous custom. He wanted someone experienced, someone with the rank and temperament to cut through the welter of daily activities. He'd met Eric Sorensen aboard the *Briscoe;* as chief of staff of the destroyer's squadron, he'd read the fitness report that declared the lieutenant "bold and supremely self-confident." Rinn was delighted when Sorensen received orders to the *Roberts*. He turned down the lieutenant's request for an engineer's post. "No," Rinn told him, "I want you to be DCA."

Sorensen squawked. "Captain, I don't want the job," the lieutenant said.

"Well, Eric, I want you to be the DCA, and it's not your choice," Rinn said.

> I need a smart guy who's been around the navy and someone who is very pigheaded, and Eric, you fit the bill. You're the perfect DCA. You know the navy, you know the ship, and you're not going to stand for anything until you get your way. That's what I want. I want a DCA who will make this ship capable of fighting.
>
> I don't need an ensign who comes in and hasn't a clue about anything, who's going to get pushed around by every department head on the ship, who's going to be told to jump in the lake, who isn't willing to go up to some chief petty officer and say, "We're going to drill today." So you're going to do that job, Eric, and you're going to do it well.[6]

Six months later, after absorbing the contents of various engineering and damage control schools, the new DCA reported in at Bath.

IT WAS EARLY 1985 and most of the crew was still in Norfolk. The *Roberts* was moored to a BIW pier but far from habitable, so Sorensen rented a small house on the river for $125 a week. For the next few months, his job consisted of learning every space and piece of equipment on his new ship—a task he shared with his boss, chief engineer Lt. Gordan Van Hook. Neither had any experience with *Perry*-class frigates, yet both were charged with knowing the ship better than their own bodies. Together, they made a game of it. "If I put my foot through this bulkhead, what's going to come through?" Van Hook would ask. "Is it air, fuel oil, water?"

As Sorensen worked to learn the ship, he roughed out a plan for teaching damage control to the crew. The first problem, as he saw it, was the official textbook, which was overlong, boring, and repetitive. If something could be said in ten thousand words, he concluded, the navy would say it in twenty thousand. Sorensen decided to write his own handbook. Personal computers had begun to populate homes and offices, but the navy was having none of that. So Sorensen booted up the ship's SNAP II, a refrigerator-sized administrative computer with rudimentary text-handling tools, and began pecking away.

Thou shalt keep our ship watertight, he began. It was easy enough for his students to understand why a hole in the bottom of a rowboat was bad news. When any hull and its contents outweigh the water they displace, the craft sinks. But things are a bit more complicated aboard a warship. For one thing, it is generally tougher for a single hole to cause trouble. The smooth gray hull of the *Roberts* hid a bewildering warren of more than a hundred compartments, but Sorensen taught his sailors to look for the bulkheads that ran from bilge to main deck. These vertical walls divided the ship into eleven watertight sections, reducing the amount of seawater that might accumulate through a single breach in the hull. This made it unlikely—though far from impossible—that a single hole might admit enough weight to sink the ship.

There were two caveats. First, the effectiveness of this compartmentalization depended on the crew's absolute dedication to shutting the appropriate doors, hatches, and valves. One mistake could flood twice the space. Green sailors learned to dog the hatches behind them, often assisted by profanity-laced reminders from their senior shipmates.[7]

Second, a flooded compartment is more dangerous than it may appear. Liquid flowing inside a hull reduces stability much more than the equivalent weight of a solid material. The phenomenon is called the free surface effect, and it is easily demonstrated. Fill a five-gallon bucket to the halfway mark. Pick it up with both hands, and tilt it back and forth to get the water moving. Now walk forward, and feel how the liquid's movement pulls you to and fro. A flooded compartment tugs a ship in much the same way. Picture a ship at sea in a storm, taking on seawater as it batters its way through the waves. With each roll, water rushes to the lower side of a compartment, weighing the ship down, slowing its return to vertical. Such a ship loses stability at a rate roughly proportional to the square of its flooded area. Things get much worse if the hull is breached below the waterline. Laid open to the sea, a ship loses stability in proportion to the cube of the flooded area.

Thou shalt believe in our ship and her ability to withstand severe damage, Sorensen wrote. A ship holed by a naval shell is not usually in immediate danger of sinking by flood, thanks to compartmentalization. While it is certainly necessary to begin plugging the leak immediately, water is not a ship's most fearsome enemy—it's fire. At sea, a small blaze can swiftly become a conflagration.

Many factors complicate the task of the naval firefighter. A warship contains a witches' brew of volatile materials: fuel, lubricants, coolants, paint, bedding—not to mention weaponry. What extinguishes one blaze may feed another; water douses a wastebasket fire but sloshes burning grease across the countertop. Cramped conditions prevail; firefighters to assemble in passageways too narrow for two to walk abreast and to wrestle pressurized hoses through steel warrens. High voltages, magnetic fields, and radar beams threaten invisible harm. Smoke builds to opacity when vents are shut to prevent its spread. Yet where sailors in flame-retardant gear find it difficult to move, fire does not. Heat passes easily through metal decks and bulkheads. Superhot gases scream down air ducts. Thick bundles of electrical cables become conduits for flame. And unlike municipal firefighters, sailors have nowhere to retreat. So the *Roberts,* like all warships, was stuffed with gear to help its crew extinguish blazes.

Thou shalt know the use of thy damage control equipment and keep it holy, Sorensen wrote. For starters, there were six dozen portable extinguishers charged with carbon dioxide gas or potassium bicarbonate powder. But for serious blazes, the frigate carried enough firefighting gear to outfit a town's fire department. The list started with 160 fire hoses: fifty-foot lengths of tough cotton fabric, double-jacketed against punctures and rubber-lined against leaks. Each had a coupling that accepted a heavy brass nozzle, which could deliver a cannonlike stream or a dense cooling fog. As with any power tool, a fire hose under pressure required careful use. A dropped nozzle could lash out like a spitting cobra.

The hoses could screw together to make longer hoses, a simple concept that became complex in practice. For one thing, they came in different widths—mostly 1 1/2 inches, some 2 1/2—and there were fittings that allowed, say, one hose to feed two more. Brass couplings helped everything fit together, but rigging for a fire could feel like doing a jig-saw puzzle.[8]

The water for firefighting came from the sea. It was drawn into the ship by five pumps, pressurized to 150 pounds per square inch, and piped around the ship in eight-inch copper-nickel fire mains. It could be tapped at five dozen fireplugs, or, in certain compartments, rained down from overhead sprinklers.[9]

There were options for fires that resisted ordinary water. Several of the ship's spaces could be flooded with inflammable gases. The missile magazines were guarded by six fifty-pound canisters of carbon dioxide. The engine room and machinery spaces could be pumped full of Halon, a colorless, odorless gas with a density nearly five times that of air. When these spaces were in danger, flashing lights and sirens warned their human occupants to get out or be suffocated along with the flames.

For fuel fires, the seawater could be mixed with a detergent-like chem-ical called aqueous film-forming foam (AFFF). A solution of one part AFFF and nineteen parts water would spread over a burning surface, trapping the flammable vapors from diesel oil, jet fuel, or paint thinner. The ship had eight stations that dispensed premixed "A-triple-F"; it could also be drawn from five-gallon drums and mixed in fire hoses on the fly.

It was vital to keep track of the water drawn aboard. "One of the hazards of fighting a fire aboard a ship is that it is possible to sink the ship while putting out the fire," Sorensen wrote. During World War II, New York City fireboats doused a blaze aboard the French luxury liner SS *Normandie,* which proceeded to capsize under the extra weight.[10] A 2 1/2-inch hose could put a ton of seawater inside the hull every minute, and what you poured onto the flames, you had to get rid of, preferably sooner rather than later.[11]

To avoid the *Normandie*'s fate, the *Roberts* was built with six-inch drainage pipes in the bilges and stocked with eight gas-powered portable pumps. There were also four eductors, simple and ingenious devices that harnessed water pressure to create suction. An eductor resembled a two-foot pipe with an extra intake near one end. You attached a pres-surized fire hose to one end and a drainage hose to the other and then turned on the water. The high-pressure stream created a low-pressure zone inside the eductor, sucking water through the intake and sending it down the drainage tube.

Thou shalt protect thyself so that thou can protect our ship. This started with clothing. When the alarm sent sailors to general quarters, they tucked pants into socks, rolled down sleeves, and buttoned up collars to the neck. Hats were replaced with flash hoods that resembled thin brown cotton ski masks. On deck, sailors donned helmets and lifejackets; firefighters inside the ship added fire-resistant outfits and Nomex gloves.

A sailor trapped by flame or smoke could grab an emergency-egress breathing device, EEBD for short. When its transparent bag was fitted over the head, a soda-can-sized canister of chemicals generated enough oxygen for fifteen minutes of escape time. Firefighters used a sturdier contraption called the OBA, for oxygen breathing apparatus. A sailor donned a scuba-type mask and a chest harness, screwed on a canister—they looked like oversized green whiskey flasks—and pulled a lanyard. That set off a chemical reaction inside the flask that produced enough oxygen to keep a person going for an hour, or so the manufacturer claimed. The wise sailor, however, worked for no more than a half hour before swapping for another green flask. Sorensen suspected that he had not yet seen just how fast a truly scared sailor could burn through an OBA canister. "Figure twelve to fourteen minutes in a really tough situation," the lieutenant told his crew.[12]

Thou shalt report any damage to the nearest damage control station. A ship's DC effort began at its repair lockers, the cramped storehouses that held the tools of the damage controlman's trade: helmets, flashlights, crowbars, and so forth. A *Perry*-class frigate had three of them. Repair Locker 2 handled emergencies forward, Repair 3 took care of the ship's after spaces, and Repair 5 dealt with the main engine room. The lockers served as muster points, as conference rooms, and as emergency workshops. When a locker team attacked a fire, it generally did so in five-person groups. A scene leader directed the effort, while an investigator looked for hot spots amid the smoke and steam. Two hosemen hugged the pressurized tube, keeping it in place, while the nozzleman directed water at the blaze. And hose skills were just the beginning. There were thirty-five distinct damage control roles, each with its own set of tasks: leak plugger, stretcher bearer, and so on. A repair locker needed at least one sailor who was qualified to handle each role.[13]

In a major crisis, the frigate's DC effort would be directed from Damage Control Central, an eight-by-ten-foot nook in the engineering control room. One wall contained a panel whose lights indicated temperature and fireplug status around the ship. DC Central was dominated by a plotting table, where the DCA and several enlisted assistants scribbled grease-pencil hieroglyphics on laminated deck charts. In the ship's steel honeycomb, losing track of fire or flooding could be fatal.

Thou shalt take every possible step to save our ship (and thyself) as long as a bit of hope remains. This meant, among other things, stanching the rush of seawater from a pipe or through a ragged hole in the hull. The modern U.S. Navy taught several ways to attack a leak; some of the techniques would have been familiar to Admiral Lord Nelson's English tars. A mallet could be used to pound wedges of yellow pine or Douglas fir into the gap. Smaller holes might be plugged with natural fibers that would swell when wet: rags, cloth, the oily hemp strands called oakum. To be sure, technology had updated some equipment. There was fiberglass cloth to wrap around split pipes, and steel plates to be welded over bulkhead punctures.

Structural damage called for shoring, the craft of using wood or metal beams to brace weakened hull plates and bulkheads. Telescoping steel supports were quick to set up; the blue-painted beams were easily wedged into position. But serious problems often required complicated patterns of wooden beams: T-bracing, I-bracing, K-bracing, all named for the letters they resembled. The ship carried about fifty yards of four-by-four-foot beams and handsaws to cut them to size.

Thou shalt keep cool; thou shalt not give up our ship. Every sailor was expected to know the basics of damage control. But repair teams needed a firm grasp on all firefighting and shoring methods—and a degree of innovation and improvisation as well; combat damage, after all, rarely occurred the same way twice.

Sorensen condensed all this, and more, into an eighty-six-page reference guide that would fit in a hip pocket. Rinn wrote a foreword for the pale-blue volume. "War-damage reports have shown that if a damaged vessel survives the first 10 minutes, it will probably live to fight again," the captain wrote. "This indicates that initial corrective action is vitally important. What YOU do when a casualty occurs may determine our survival. This booklet will provide you with the basics. Read it, reread it, and know it. Learn damage control procedures as if your life depended on them—it very well may."[14]

Armed with his new textbook, Sorensen became relentless in drilling the crew. Old hands agreed that no one else taught the subject with Eric Sorensen's quiet intensity. "Damage control on the *Sammy B* was different than anywhere else I had been," recalled chief gunner and damage control training team member Reinert, who had served on aircraft carriers and destroyers. "At most commands, you had to be damage-control qualified and know how to fight fires. On the *Sammy B,* everyone probably felt like they were part of a hose team because of the way we did training."[15]

As new sailors arrived in Bath, Sorensen would spread out a deck diagram and hit them with an introductory lecture he called "the micro-to-macro-to-micro approach for the farm boys from Iowa." A *Perry*-class frigate was a "three-space ship," he began. "It's divided into 11 watertight compartments. Any three of these compartments can flood completely, and the ship will settle into the water a certain amount, but it'll still float.

"But if that fourth compartment begins to flood, the ship is going to capsize, and it's going to sink. That's why it's so important that you know how to plug that hole in the bulkhead, or use that pipe-patching kit, because you don't want that fourth compartment to flood, do you? No, you don't."

Once a sailor realized that his life depended on knowing this stuff, his education had begun. Studying the handbook was just a starting point. The crew of the *Roberts* learned to patch and shore, and to handle each position on a hose team. They memorized the layout of vital equipment in the engine room and machinery spaces.

When someone needed help, Sorensen would stay with him for a quarter hour, two hours, whatever it took. "The guy eats damage control for breakfast," the crew said. Nor was Sorensen alone in his efforts. As the enlisted crew began to show up at Bath, Sorensen had wheedled

and arm-twisted Reinert and about twenty senior sailors into joining the
ship's DC training team. Most were first-class and chief petty officers, but
Sorensen chose a few second-classes who showed enthusiasm for the
extra duty. Together, they pushed the ship into a routine: every four
hours, a new watch, a new team on duty, and a new damage control
drill.

PRIVATELY, SORENSEN HAD reached a disturbing conclusion about the
frigate. Damage control school had taught him to do back-of-the-envelope
calculations concerning the hydrodynamic stability of a floating hull,
and he wasn't convinced *Roberts* actually was a three-space ship. Each
new class of warship was generally designed with extra space and buoyancy to accommodate the new guns and gear that might be invented
and installed during its two-decade lifespan. Many classes began with
hundreds of tons of reserve buoyancy, but the *Perry* frigates, whose
design had been squeezed for every penny, had been built with only a
fifty-ton margin. Yet in the nine years that separated the launch of *Oliver
Hazard Perry* from that of *Roberts,* the navy had added four feet of
length and several hundred tons to the basic FFG design.

The additional weight reduced the ability of *Roberts* to right itself
when rolling in heavy weather; it recovered more slowly than its predecessor *Perrys,* and, in extremis, would capsize sooner. More ominously,
the extra tons also eliminated some of the stability that allowed the frigate
to absorb combat damage and keep fighting. Sorensen wasn't convinced
Roberts could lose three spaces and survive.

CHAPTER FIVE

Putting to Sea

As spring 1985 turned to summer in Norfolk, the members of the *Roberts's* precommissioning detachment wrapped up their individual studies and began to depart for the collective training that would meld them into a fighting crew. The combat systems team headed out to learn the art of modern naval warfare at a ridge-top facility overlooking San Diego Harbor. Among them was John Preston, a fire controlman third class. Sailors came from all over, but Preston's story was fairly typical of the *Roberts's* junior personnel; he had been drawn to the navy, somewhat reluctantly, as an escape from a humdrum existence.

Preston had grown up in Craig, Colorado, population eight thousand, and developed a nineteen-year-old's dread of growing old there. Finished with high school, and with no money for college, Preston was working a dead-end job at the local auto dealership. *Right now, I'm just a nice Christian boy who works for four bucks an hour and has no life,* he told himself. *But I am not going to allow myself to dry up and blow away in this little hick town in the middle of nowhere.*

A church acquaintance steered him toward the navy, but it wasn't a quick sell. Still fresh in Preston's mind was a recent *Saturday Night Live* spoof of the service's recruiting commercials. Over footage of sailors cleaning toilets, a voice intoned, "It's not just an adventure, it's a job." There was also the recruiter himself, a cigarette-stained chief petty officer who quarreled loudly with his wife while Preston took a military aptitude test in their kitchen. And there was Shelley, a young friend from church who pleaded with him to stay.

Despite it all, Preston signed up. In November 1983 he forced back tears, boarded a Trailways bus, and headed off to San Diego. At boot camp he was morbidly cheered by the presence of some older fellows.

These guys must be real losers, he thought. *At least I only wasted one year of my post–high school life doing nothing. Some of these guys are almost thirty!*

In less than two years—having endured recruit training, a lonely graduation, plenty of midnight watches, and lots of toilet-cleaning duty—Fire Controlman 3rd Class Preston graduated near the top of his class in Mk 92 missile launcher school. His skill earned him a choice of assignments, and he picked a brand-new frigate that was under construction in Maine.

Preston joined the *Roberts* in August 1985, driving across the country in his Toyota pickup to meet up with the rest of the frigate's combat systems team in San Diego. The day before he checked in at the Point Loma training center, he chose the wrong second to glance at a map. His truck veered from the road and plowed into a parked car. Another sailor happened along and took the bruised and bloodied Preston to a naval hospital, where a corpsman diagnosed a separated right shoulder and put a dozen stitches in his head.

"I got some extra here," the corpsman said.

"Extra what?" Preston asked.

"Extra skin," the corpsman replied. "Do you want it?"

Preston gritted his teeth and went to class.[1]

The Point Loma ridge offered spectacular views of the harbor, the Coronado Peninsula, and the Pacific Ocean—provided, that is, you were not inside a classroom or one of the shipboard simulators. That, of course, was where Preston joined Lt. Cmdr. Glenn Palmer and thirty-nine other sailors.

The combat information center (CIC) had long replaced the bridge as the fighting heart of a modern warship. In the darkened space just below and behind the pilothouse, the *Roberts* sailors would huddle over green screens, reaching out with electronic eyes to find their enemies. In battle, the captain would be in the CIC, making the decisions to fire. The center's enlisted personnel included radar operators, who used the frigate's three kinds of radar to find objects afloat or aloft; sonar operators, who used computers and headphones to track the invisible craft below the waves; operations specialists, who identified ships, aircraft, and missiles by their electronic emissions; and fire controlmen, who used the data from their shipmates to guide their own ship's guns and missiles. Together, they ran the *Roberts*'s electronic and mechanical eyes, ears, and fists.

The Point Loma course required hours of classroom study, but the lectures alternated with exciting mock battles in the simulated combat information center. Palmer's team sank fleets of computer-generated Soviet ships, downed imaginary air wings, and shredded swarms of pretend missiles. They learned fast, and finished the six-week course with more honor graduates than any previous frigate. A chief operations specialist by the name of Monigle notched the highest personal grade point average to date. Overall, the *Roberts* team had earned the highest grades ever received by a frigate crew.[2]

ON THE LAST day of June 1985, some forty-five hundred BIW shipyard workers walked off the job. Negotiations for a three-year contract had stalled, bringing most work on the *Roberts* to a halt. Builder's trials in August, acceptance trials in September, and commissioning in November—all were postponed. The delays discomfited yard executives and dismayed the SupShip officials.[3] But Rinn and the *Roberts* crew saw the delay as a gift of precious time. While workers picketed outside the BIW gates, the sailors of FFG 58 finished up the required precommissioning curriculum and then signed up for more. Gunner Reinert added certifications in small arms and ship's defense to his qualifications and spent the next several months passing his newfound knowledge to his shipmates. Soon more than half the crew was qualified to fire .45-caliber pistols, M-14 rifles, and 12-gauge shotguns.[4]

As the strike dragged into autumn, the *Roberts* sailors exhausted the navy's voluminous course book; they turned to various light construction projects around the base, repairing barracks and repainting buildings. Winter was creeping toward the Maine coast when the BIW employees' patience, and their strike fund, finally dwindled and disappeared. Union members approved a new contract on 7 October, and work on the *Roberts* resumed the following day.[5]

Not long afterward, FFG 58's sailors broke camp in Norfolk and headed north, leaving a dazzled set of instructors in their wake. "*Samuel B. Roberts* was without a doubt the most impressive of the many FFG 7 class precommissioning detachments to conduct training here at Fleet Training Center, Norfolk," the center's commander wrote. He ticked off the crew's accomplishments: *Roberts* sailors completed eighty-two different courses, for a sky-high total of three thousand classroom days. No disciplinary infractions. No drug busts. Forty-five promotions and fourteen personal awards had been granted. The local Jaycees even forwarded a note of appreciation for the *Roberts*'s community service efforts. "It is obvious," the training commander wrote, "that their ship will quickly be established as a 'front runner' in the fleet, one that does it right, on time, every time."[6]

BLIZZARDS SOON ENFOLDED coastal Maine, producing a season so cold and snowy that even the local lobstermen took notice. In Bath, the *Roberts* sailors spent long dark days on the ship, watching and learning. Gunner Reinert made sure his sailors were in attendance whenever one of the frigate's weapons went into place. When nothing much interesting was going on, the sailors crawled all over their ship, going hand over hand along pipes and cable runs, committing the systems to memory.

Like Reinert and Rinn, Lt. Gordan Van Hook was intent on training his junior sailors. The ship's chief engineer was responsible for the ship's propulsion system, electrical plant, pumps, filters, distillers, air conditioners, and myriad other gear. It was one of the navy's most demanding posts, and like any good officer, Van Hook knew he was only as good at his job as his sailors were at theirs.

So the chief engineer played Sorensen's kick-a-hole game with them and sent them on scavenger hunts around the ship. They took field trips to a half-built *Perry* frigate a few hundred yards away. "We'd take them over to the *Kauffman* [FFG 69] to let them see a bare-bones, not-in-the-water ship, walk around the spaces, see what was above you, below you."[7]

But the lieutenant knew enough to let his senior enlisted personnel do most of the teaching. "Van Hook was kind of hands off," said Robert Bent, a chief electrician's mate. "He let [Chief Dave] Walker and experienced guys handle it. A lot of engineers would have had us painting the barracks; he wanted us down learning the stuff. He was no-nonsense for that kind of thing."[8]

Over the months, Van Hook developed a strong working relationship with two right-hand men: Chief Alex Perez, who knew the electrical systems of turbines like the back of his meaty hand, and Chief Walker, a mechanical specialist and a master problem-solver. The two chiefs paired up well. Perez was a firm but fair leader with a knack for paperwork and daily management, while Walker was a roguish sort who wore his hair long and affected aircrew-style flight suits for himself and his engineers. Van Hook considered Walker something of an administrative disaster, but when things went violently wrong, he was the guy you wanted around.

The chief engineer himself was rather young for his job; the Newport, Rhode Island, native had just five years' commissioned service as an officer. But more than a bit of saltwater flowed in his veins. One grandfather had graduated from the U.S. Naval Academy in 1909, the other one in 1924, and a great-uncle in 1926. Gordon's own father, from the class of '51, had commanded several ships and retired as a captain after twenty-seven years in uniform. The family's list of alumni went into double digits once you started counting cousins.

Yet Van Hook's entry into naval service was far from preordained. Under the sway of a "hippie older sister," he said, he matriculated at Texas A&M, where he earned a degree in wildlife and fisheries management. It was only when he began musing about joining the coast guard that his father put in a gentle word for the navy's Officer Candidate School. Perhaps obeying some buried genetic compulsion, Van Hook gave it a try—and loved the navy immediately. The junior officer had proven his mechanical ability on his first sea tour when he mastered the steam-puffing monstrosity that was the propulsion plant of an *Adams*-class destroyer. Sterling performance reviews propelled him to a prestigious two-year stint as an admiral's aide in San Diego and then a posting to the precommissioning *Roberts*.

Compared to the old destroyer, his *Perry*-class ship was a lot more pleasant to operate, if not exactly simpler. He had gas turbines tucked into soundproof boxes, not steam boilers roaring away in hellish engine rooms. Getting under way meant a ten-minute checklist, not a four-hour wait for warming pipes. And much of the plant could be operated by remote control, from the engineering nerve center called Central Control Station.

The BIW strike gave Van Hook five extra months to prepare for the ship's commissioning, now rescheduled for April 1986, and the chief engineer was nothing but happy about it. "It got us off to a great start, made the crew much closer, more together, much better trained," he said.[9]

The time in Bath wasn't all work. The chiefs' Fun Bunch established a comfortable end-of-day routine at the Muddy Rudder restaurant down the road in Yarmouth.[10] The sailors formed recreational sports teams that took on squads from other ships and from the P-3 Orion squadrons at nearby Brunswick Naval Air Station. The basketball and volleyball squads notched notable successes.

Rick Raymond signed up for the hockey squad. An operations specialist (OS) second class, he was part of Palmer's combat systems team. But Raymond wasn't a typical "twidget"—navy slang for sailors who worked with computers. Born in Brooklyn, raised in New Jersey, he had been a sheet metalworker until overfamiliarity with the unemployment line propelled him to the local recruiter's office. He asked to be a hull technician, which would have put his metalworking skills to use, but the navy made him an OS instead. Nevertheless, when Raymond arrived aboard the *Roberts* for his second sea tour, he fell in with the engineers and was eventually assigned to a fire party in Repair Locker 3—an unusual general quarters post for an OS. "Didn't bother me," he said. "That was my personality: 'Doesn't mind getting greasy and dirty.'"

Raymond's hockey team competed, or tried to, on the ice rink at nearby Bowdoin College. "We made the Bad News Bears look like the New York Yankees," he said. "There were guys on the team who had to hold on to the boards to skate up and down the ice. We would get beat so bad they would turn the scoreboard off. But the camaraderie we had as a team was special, and we always had the largest crowd of fans cheering for us."[11]

A WARSHIP IS never so fussed over as during the rituals that place it in commissioned service. On 12 April the sky above the shipyard was thick with gray clouds, just a few shades lighter than the ship's spotless paint job. A damp wind stirred signal flags, strung in long catenaries from stem to mast to stern. Tricolor stripes of bunting iced the deckhouse. A pale canvas amidships protected a wooden dais from the intermittent drizzle.

The cold air held the smells of wet pavement and industrial grit and the far-off tang of the sea.

The *Roberts* had made its maiden voyages in January and February, excursions of a few days' duration meant to prove its worthiness as a navy warship. The ship had done far more than meet the standard; crusty old Vice Adm. John D. Bulkeley, still the navy's chief inspector, declared the frigate "excellent" in most areas and one of the cleanest ships he'd ever seen.[12] On 1 April the local SupShip deputy had signed an ordinary-looking government form, and *Roberts* became the property of the United States government.[13] But more than the sales transaction, more even than a first taste of saltwater, the commissioning rites marked the start of a ship's active life.

The crew of the *Roberts,* 182 sailors strong, stood in ranks on the pier. Coats had been banned so that the crew members might present a sharper appearance, and the junior sailors shivered in their dark blue jumpers and white Dixie-cup hats.[14] The officers wore dress blues and the accoutrements of rank: gloves, medals, and swords. "Commissioning was a lot of spit-and-polish stuff. For the most part very few of us appreciated the preparation," recalled Mike Roberts, a signalman from Rochester, New York. "The actual ceremony was cool, in retrospect. Most of us didn't realize at the time how rare it was."[15]

A conversational hum rose from the crowd, punctuated by the scrape of folding chairs on concrete and service standards from the navy band. The gathering audience was mostly Bath Iron Works employees and local dignitaries, but plenty more were Rinn's personal guests. The gregarious commanding officer had invited scores of people to share one of the big days of his life.[16] Among them were nearly three dozen survivors of the first *Samuel B. Roberts*. Rinn had tracked them down with the help of the DE 413 shipmates' association. They wore ball caps emblazoned with the hull numbers of all three *Roberts* ships, and they had placed a sign by the ship: "Congratulations Bath Iron Works From The Survivors Of The 'Sammy B.'"[17] Rinn and his sailors had unveiled a sign of their own: a heavy bronze plaque listing the crew members of DE 413. They had spent months hunting down the muster list from the day the destroyer escort went down. The plaque would be mounted near the quarterdeck and would serve as a reminder of strength in the ship's trials to come.[18]

At half past eleven, the band stilled their instruments, and a chaplain offered a blessing. Capt. Paul Aquilino, the commodore of the *Roberts*'s squadron, stepped to the podium and read the order placing the ship in commission.[19] In so doing, the commander of the Newport-based Surface Group Four accepted the task of supervising the new ship as it prepared for deployment nearly two years hence. But Aquilino's new burden paled next to the one that had just settled onto Paul Rinn. Even in the modern age of radio and data networks, there was no job that carried as much autonomy and responsibility as a warship captain at sea.

Rinn stepped to the podium and faced his crew. The sailors came to attention, awaiting the traditional first order of a commissioned ship, and their captain gave it: "Man our ship and bring her to life!"

At most commissionings these words triggered a pell-mell sprint for the gangways. The *Roberts* sailors remained stock-still. An aging gentleman in a dark suit rose from his seat. He was Lloyd A. Gurnett, the damage control officer of DE 413, and the last man to leave his mortally wounded ship at Leyte Gulf. Gurnett climbed the gangway, strode to the coaming, and saluted the officer of the deck. Then he made his way back down the ramp. The crowd cheered and the crew broke for the brows, adding their own hollering to the joyful noise. The ship itself came mechanically alive; gun and missile launcher dipped and swung; radar antennae rotated—"a little dance," said Glenn Palmer, who had choreographed it with his sailors. Rinn ordered the first watch to be set, and the *Roberts* became a functioning warship.

At the podium, 2nd Fleet commander Vice Adm. Henry C. Mustin rose to speak. Mustin was the son of an admiral, grandson of the first pilot to fly from a ship's catapult, and, like Rinn, a decorated veteran of the Southeast Asian river campaigns. The admiral invoked the valor of Coxswain Roberts. "In the navy's hall of heroes, no name shines more brightly than that one," said Mustin. The admiral saluted the survivors of DE 413. "They steamed those little ships into the valley of death," he told the crowd. "I feel pretty humble about talking about it in their presence." It would not be the last time Mustin would praise a ship named *Samuel B. Roberts*.

Rinn started his own speech—"Great things come from great traditions," he said—but it had started to rain again, so he cut it short. He told the former *Roberts* crew members in the audience, "You are our inspiration. You are our spirit." And he asked his crew for three cheers "for those who have built our ship, and those who sailed before us."[20]

FOR ALL ITS Currier-and-Ives charm, the twelve-mile passage from the Long Reach to the Gulf of Maine was no sleigh ride. Here and there the channel narrowed until a sailor could toss a bolt onto either of the rocky banks. The Kennebec River wound past fields and forests, churches and clapboard farmhouses, menacing rocks and pebbled beaches. In winter the landscape was painted in fresh snow, and warships nosed gently between ice sheets that covered the river like a giant's flagstones. But the *Roberts* was making the journey in May, and spring was starting to color the riverbanks in shades of pale green.

The frigate passed beneath the granite walls of abandoned Fort Popham, picked its way past the bobbing buoys of lobster traps, and headed south to the open sea. In the coming year the crew would sail *Roberts* from the city of its birth, put into its home port, and head south to Cuba for a shakedown cruise—the first tough test of the young ship's capabilities and their own acumen. The ship would also earn their first decoration for operational valor.

Clear of the islands of Casco Bay, the bridge crew opened *Roberts* up and let it run. The frigate leaned like a young racehorse, the modern analogue of the square-rigged man-o'-war, a true and proper heir to the frigates of old. The bow sliced the water at twenty-five knots; the stern threw up a low, rumbling rooster tail. The ship was fast, no doubt about it. During a full-power run off Cuba later in the year, *Roberts* would set a *Perry*-class record by hitting thirty-one knots.[21]

Within hours of the ship's departure from Maine, the frigate entered rough water. The chiefs laughed at the young pups who turned green as the ship bulled its way through the swells. Still, most stayed gamely at their stations, gripping plastic bags, for adrenaline was flowing as well. "It's the first time you're working as a team together to get this huge ship where it's supposed to go," said signalman Chuck Dumas.[22]

Paul Rinn took the opportunity to introduce some of his junior officers to the art of conning the ship, or "driving" it, as surface warfare officers were wont to say. Like most warships, a *Perry* frigate was guided by any of several qualified crew members. The designated conning officer directed verbal orders to an enlisted helmsman, who steered the forty-one-hundred-ton warship with a three-inch replica of a sailing ship's wheel.

Like every class of watercraft on the sea, the *Perrys* had their quirks, many related to their single-screw, single-rudder design. For one thing, they turned a bit faster to port than to starboard. For another, their boxy silhouettes caught the wind evenly and would happily lie broadside to it, while most destroyer-type ships tended to swing away from the wind bow-first. And at very low speeds the stern tended to "walk" to starboard. This made it somewhat easier to moor portside to a pier, and somewhat more difficult to depart from such a mooring. In difficult situations, the conning officer had the option of lowering the auxiliary propulsion units, clamping the propeller shaft into motionlessness, and sidling up to the pier. A good frigate driver learned to use these quirks to his advantage.[23]

For all of this, driving a *Perry* was a dream compared to handling steam-powered ships. *Roberts*'s twin gas turbines provided plenty of power on demand, and its variable-pitch propeller could all but make the ship dance. The seventeen-foot propeller had five blades mounted on individual spindles. As the helmsman took the ship up to fifteen knots, the computer-controlled blades swiveled to take bigger bites of the water. To go faster, the gas turbines sped up. For an emergency stop, the blades would reverse their angle, dragging the ship from flank speed to dead stop in two lengths of its hull. A frigate plowing backward at twelve knots could stop, reverse course, and hit its twenty-nine-knot flank speed within a hundred seconds.

Rinn, a fine shiphandler himself, loved teaching other people to drive. He had learned the craft from his skippers on *Sarsfield* and *Blakely*.[24] But Rinn learned something else from these men, who rarely took the helm when they could let junior officers do it: good captains are as much teachers as warfighters. "They gave you the football and let you play the game. And they said, 'If you made a mistake, you learn,'" Rinn said.

He adopted the practice as a tenet of leadership. "Your job as a CO was to fight the ship, no doubt about it," he said. "But it was also to train your people. If you died in the first five minutes of the battle, they'd fight on without you. They'd just say, 'Okay, he's gone, but we can do this.'"

One basic skill was the Anderson turn, a full-power circle used to rescue a sailor fallen overboard. To practice, someone would toss a buoy over the side, and the officer of the deck would practice zooming around in a turn that would bring the ship up behind the hapless sailor.

Rinn described the man-overboard lesson like this:

> I took everybody out into the bridge wing and said, "I don't know whether you've ever been trained on how to do a man-overboard drill, but I doubt it.
>
> "Let me just tell you this: man-overboard drills are not a test of your manhood. It's not a test to see how fast you can drive the ship, and charge out there and run the guy over in the water. If you go too fast, you're going to scare him to death, or miss him."
>
> Recovering a man at sea or driving the ship is like hitting a guy throwing a curveball or fastball. I hate to use these analogies, but it really is. Always try to stand in the same place and use a physical marker somewhere on the bridge wing that doesn't move. That way, you have reference points. In baseball, when guys look at the pitcher on the mound, they size him up so that when his hand hits a certain point, he's flinging. That's how you hit a fastball. A curveball, same thing. You watch to see the environment.
>
> I took everybody out on the starboard bridge wing, and I said, "Okay, everybody close your eyes."

The officers crowded onto the oblong open-air platform. Rinn pointed to the bobbing buoy and raised his voice to give the order to the enlisted helmsman in the pilothouse.

> "Engines ahead flank, right full rudder." I count to ninety seconds. And then I pointed and said, "Open your eyes and look out there. What do you see? It's the man in the water."
>
> So I did it about three times. Every time you hear "man overboard," and you say, "Engines ahead flank, right or left full rudder," you can be sure that in two minutes he will be there. Even if you can't see him, you can know that's where he is, okay?
>
> Now that you know that, you have to bring the ship around to get in that position, so just trust that that's where he is. Now bring

him around to this cone over here at forty-five degrees. This is a highly maneuverable gas-turbine ship.

I said, "Whenever you drive the ship, you always stand here next to the pelorus [a navigation tool]. Always. Always, always.

"If you're not standing here, you're like a tennis player who gets out of position on the court. And if a guy hits a shot at his ankle, it doesn't matter how good he is, he can't return it. If you're out of position, you can't do the job."

Good athletes always go to the place where they know they can execute the game. If you play badminton against an eighty-year-old man and he knows badminton, he runs you all over the court, and he kills you. And he hasn't moved. Why? Because he knows how to play the game. He knows the alleys.

"It's physics, man. So stand right here."

And every time a guy didn't do it, I'd go out and give him hell, and say, "What the fuck are you doing? I told you where to stand. Stand there!"

Because they would immediately screw it up. They'd stand in the wrong place, and they'd get all botched up. And I'd say, "Why are you so thick? I told you, stand here." And I'd ask, "What doesn't move here? The ocean moves, the sun moves, the water moves. The ship doesn't move. The ship's always going to be the same.

"If you're standing here, guess what is always going to be here? The corner of the bridge wing, this pelorus over here, these voice tubes down here, and you use them just like you use a sight on a gun."

It's called seamanship. You teach them how to use their ship. As if it's part of your body.

I eventually got them all indoctrinated on how to do it. And to a man, they could all get a man to the side of the ship in under three minutes. And they could teach anybody else to do it. I'd bring the enlisted men up there and teach them to do it.[25]

Rinn could use shiphandling lessons to teach other ideas as well. One day, the captain walked into the wardroom around lunchtime.

I said, "Remember what I told you: that a man-overboard drill isn't a test of your manhood. You remember that? Well, I'm a pretty straight guy. You can believe what I say, right?"

And they all said, "Oh yes, sir."

I said, "Well, I lied. Today, it's a test of your manhood."

And they all went, "What?"

There was a lesson. I always believed that lessons are a very good way of teaching people how to do things right. Just like officers are your men's best protection, and your men's best friend, the CO sometimes can be the biggest prick in the world, and he's doing it for a reason, and they don't have to know it. And you're not there to explain it to them. You're not trying to win a popularity contest.

The reason I did this was that the combat systems officer, a guy by the name of Glenn Palmer, was kind of different by the wardroom's standards. But Glenn was a good guy. I liked him a lot. He worked incredibly hard, and I trusted him.

I said, "Today, we are going to have a competition."

And there was a prize. I said, "Whoever wins this, I'm going to take out to dinner in the most expensive restaurant in Newport, you and your wife, or you and your girlfriend."

So everybody says, all right. So we go up on the bridge, and everybody's making a good run of it. Racing around. About fourteen people. I got up there and it was really super. I had a stopwatch. It was the way you want your wardroom to be. These guys were great. They were all aggressive.

The first five or six guys are all at two minutes, fifty-six seconds; two minutes, thirty-six seconds. It's great. They're all hauling around, driving the ship at thirty-one knots. The ship's heeling over, and I'm loving it. I'm thinking this is what being a cruiser-destroyer guy is all about. I'm telling them stories about black smoke and white water.

Palmer steps up. He's like the sixth or seventh guy and he says, "Man overboard, starboard side. Engines ahead flank. Engines stop. Engines back full."

He stopped the ship on a dime—gas turbine ship—and backs up: one minute and ten seconds. Glenn's going to win.

And everyone's pissed off: "You cheated." Some of the remarks to Palmer were in jest. But a lot of them weren't.

And I thought, "We're all a team here, and these guys talk about Glenn being a nerd. Well, that means we're not a team. We're a bunch of bullies, and we like to pick on a guy in our wardroom."

Glenn used to drive me nuts, because he was a little different. But that didn't mean he wasn't a good officer. And he worked his ass off. That's the one thing I was so impressed with the guy. He just really worked hard. He did his job very, very well.

So we get down to the wardroom, and I told Glenn I'd take him out to dinner. So Glenn left the wardroom, and I told everyone else to stick around.

I said, "I do have a comment for you guys. You know, this was a lot of fun, wasn't it?"

They said, "Yes, Palmer won. He cheated."

I said, "He didn't cheat; he was better than you. Smarter than you. You're pissed off because the geek beat you, aren't you?"

And everyone looked at me, and I said, "Yes, that's right: the geek. That's what you guys call him. That sucks. Because you know what? What's worse than anything is, the geek kicked your ass, didn't he?

"So let me teach a lesson about combat. My friends, you may think that guy out there doesn't look like an all-American. You may think he doesn't look like much of anything. He'll kick your ass and kill you, okay?

"Learn this lesson today. You went up against a guy who out-thought you and smoked your asses. And you call him a name—pretty bad—and he blew you away. So my question to you is, 'What day are we going to meet somebody on the high seas that you don't think much of, and he blows us away?' So don't ever forget the lesson you learned today, and don't ever call him a geek again."

Total silence. I got up and said, "I hope you enjoyed your lunch. See you later." And you could have heard a pin drop.

It was a very good lesson, and they viewed Glenn Palmer very differently after that day.[26]

THE SHIP PAID a short visit to Annapolis, Maryland, serving as window dressing for the U.S. Naval Academy's graduation week. Then there were two weeks of sweet liberty in Newport, the ship's new home. The colonial-era city, long a center of naval training, had recently been returned to duty as a home port for a quartet of frigates and destroyers. Many of the married sailors had already installed their families in navy housing along Narragansett Bay. But the reunion was soon over.

In mid-June the ship weighed anchor for U.S. Naval Station Guantánamo Bay, Cuba. "Gitmo," as sailors and marines called it, was one of the U.S. military's odder installations. For starters, it sat on communist land, an accident of history whose roots lay in the Spanish-American War. After U.S. troops seized the island's eastern tip in 1898, a permanent lease was drawn up with the Cuban government, and marines had occupied the area ever since. Fidel Castro's 1959 revolution prompted better defenses—barbed wire, gun emplacements, the western hemisphere's largest minefield—but could not stop Cuban troops from taking the occasional potshot with a rifle.

The navy eventually established a training facility at Gitmo, and a predeployment visit became a rite of passage for Atlantic Fleet crews. From before sunrise to long after midnight, the instructors worked a ship and its crew to exhaustion, pushing them through lesson after lesson, drill after drill, honing their skills in damage control, engineering procedures, and naval combat. For many crews, Gitmo was the toughest action they ever saw.

The *Roberts* arrived on 27 June 1986 and spent the next five weeks almost constantly on the go. A typical day went like this:

3:00 AM: Reveille
3:15:   Sweepers: clean the ship
3:30:   Breakfast
4:15:   Morning muster
4:30:   Convene the sea-and-anchor team
5:30:   Anchor in Guantánamo Bay
6:15:   Weigh anchor and get under way
8:30:   General quarters exercise
11:30:   Lunch

Noon: Next exercise
12:30 PM: Convene the sea-and-anchor team
  1:30:   Moor at training center pier
  2:15:   Damage control drills
  4:45:   Dinner
  5:45:   Convene sea-and-anchor team
  6:15:   Get under way
  7:00:   Electronic warfare exercises
  7:30:   Eight o'clock reports
  8:00:   Movies on the mess deck
 10:00:   Taps
 10:30:   More antiship exercises
 11:59:   Sailing off Cuban coast
  3:45 AM: Reveille

Even the occasional afternoon off wasn't much to write home about. Temperatures hovered in the nineties, and there wasn't anywhere to go anyway.[27] Besides the barracks, training centers, and gun emplacements, Gitmo consisted largely of a Navy Exchange store, an outdoor movie theater, an un-air-conditioned self-serve laundry, and a McDonalds. You couldn't really stroll the landscape on the forty-five-square-mile base because of the lizards and land crabs. Even sliding into second base on the softball diamond might draw a nasty infection from the bacteria that lived in the local dirt—though the *Roberts* team ignored the peril and won the Independence Day tournament.[28] Social life was all but nonexistent; the place was dubbed "Gitno" by those who most acutely felt the absence of women.

So crews threw themselves into damage control drills. Sorensen had taught the sailors well, but the Gitmo team made them better. The instructors' exercises were tougher and more complicated than those that the ship's DC training team could set up. "It was always kind of the worst-nightmare kind of thing," Signalman Roberts said. "Sometimes there literally was a reveille after a night with no taps."[29]

Van Hook's engineers faced an operational propulsion plant examination (OPPE), an exacting review that could turn engineering heads prematurely gray. Many ships survived Gitmo and the OPPE by packing the watch bill with experienced chief petty officers instead of green ensigns and junior lieutenants, but Van Hook had pushed to do it right. Most of the senior watch stations were filled by officers, as they would be in combat, and their preparation paid off in "superb" grades, the highest compliment an official navy report can bestow.[30]

When the ship departed in late July, it left very impressed trainers in its wake. The instructors graded the *Roberts* "outstanding" in navigation, anchoring, transferring items at sea, and gathering intelligence. The ship's overall report grade, through more than thirty-five exercises, was 87.1 percent, or "good"—unusual for a crew with so few weeks at sea.

As the *Roberts* prepared to leave Cuba behind, another *Perry*-class frigate flashed a message over the water. "PAUL THANKS FOR YOUR SUPPORT AND GOOD WISHES HAVE A SAFE TRIP TO CHARLESTON HOPE TO SEE YOU IN MAYPORT SOON REGARDS GLENN." It was Cmdr. Glenn Brindel, skipper of the *Stark* (FFG 31), who was readying his own guided missile frigate for deployment.[31] The next time Rinn heard from the *Stark,* the news would not be good.

THE *ROBERTS* SPENT much of rest of the summer in Caribbean waters. In the exercise ranges off Puerto Rico, the ship sent half a dozen Standard missiles skyward after orange jet-powered drones. Time and again, the bulky launcher on the forecastle whirled into loading position, tilting its arm to accept the missile that popped up from the magazine below. With frightening speed, the arm came down and the launcher swiveled to starboard. Under the launch rail, guidance fins unfolded and snapped into place, and the weapon departed in a puff of white smoke. In an eyeblink it was miles away, leaving radar operators to track its kill or its ignominious descent to the waves.

In September a coast guard drug-enforcement team came aboard and helped the crew track down and seize a smuggler's sailboat. The bust netted nearly six tons of marijuana and earned the ship the coast guard's Meritorious Unit Commendation.

The *Roberts* closed out its first calendar year of commissioned service amid a flurry of praise. After a four-day search for construction flaws, a navy evaluator declared the *Roberts* the best *Perry*-class ship to date.[32] The Atlantic Fleet commander took note of "a highly professional crew

getting their ship off to the right start . . . Well done and keep charg-
ing."[33] And when the Battle E results were announced, the crew had
earned Mission Es in seven of the nine categories, including air defense,
engineering, and damage control.

But they were also left with goals to strive for. Commodore Aquilino
denied the *Roberts* the squadron's overall Battle E, ruling that FFG 58
had been in service too short a time. And Gunner Reinert had met half
of his objectives: his crew had received the antisubmarine warfare prize,
but the gunnery prize had eluded them.

As wintry storms drew a curtain on a busy and successful season, the
Roberts returned to the state of its birth for a few months of light repairs
and equipment installation at Bath Iron Works' dry dock in Portland,
Maine.[34] Since its April commissioning, frigate and crew had spent seven
weeks in BIW yards and more than four months at sea or elsewhere—
and less than two months in its new Rhode Island home.[35]

The holidays provided the sailors of FFG 58 a few weeks' respite from
the demands of the naval life, a chance to think about friends and family
and life outside a steel hull. But in a faraway land untouched by snow,
war and politics were shaping their destiny.

CHAPTER SIX

Drawing Swords

As the *Roberts* began its yard repairs in late 1986, the crew could be forgiven if they generally skipped the *Portland Press-Herald*'s wire stories about the Iran-Iraq war. There seemed little reason to suspect the frigate might somehow become caught in the bloody conflict, which had already ground on longer than World War II with little U.S. involvement.

Iraqi president Saddam Hussein had lit the flame in 1980, pouring troops across his eastern frontier to seize land and oil in the chaotic aftermath of Tehran's Islamic revolution.[1] But the incursion galvanized a divided country, and Iranian troops soon bludgeoned the invaders back to the border. Unfortunately for the region, Ayatollah Ruhollah Khomeini proceeded to duplicate his enemy's blunder by mounting his own push into Iraq. The Baghdad strongman rallied his war-weary citizenry, and the conflict soon devolved into a brutal stalemate, pocked with fruitless offensives and punctuated with missile explosions in crowded neighborhoods. In the first three years of war, some three hundred thousand Iranian troops and civilians died, along with nearly sixty-five thousand Iraqis.[2]

By 1984 Saddam wanted peace, but he could neither eject the Iranian forces nor swallow Khomeini's heavy reparation demands. So he sought instead the aid of more powerful nations who might enforce a cease-fire. The Iraqi leader knew that long years of slaughter had not moved the West to intervene, but he thought he knew what would. The maritime traffic of the Persian Gulf included a steady procession of deep-draft oil tankers, whose capacious holds slaked one-tenth of the world's daily demand. Saddam's plan was simple: sink tankers, hurt oil-thirsty countries, and let *them* stop the war.

The strategy turned a sprinkling of maritime attacks into a new battlefront. In March 1984 a pair of shiny new Dassault Super-Etendards lifted off an Iraqi runway and headed southeast down the Gulf. Their wings bore Exocet missiles, the ship killers that had sunk a British destroyer in the 1982 Falklands War. South of Kharg Island, the pilots locked their radars onto a sea-level blip, let fly two missiles, and set a Greek tanker ablaze.[3] Four attacks followed in as many weeks, all on ships bound for or bearing away from Iran. Tehran soon struck back in kind.[4]

The "tanker war" littered the shipping channels with burning vessels. Seventy-one ships were hit in 1984, 47 the following year, and 111 the year after that. Few of the big tankers actually sank, thanks to their spill-proofed double hulls, but dozens were declared total losses.[5] Both sides preferred to sink enemy cargo, but one merchant ship looked much like another. Adding to the confusion, Iraq shipped its oil from ports in Kuwait and Saudi Arabia. The pillars of black smoke that rose above the hazy horizon frequently pointed back to neutral or even friendly craft.

Western action in the Gulf was long in coming, and it did not take the form Saddam had envisioned. In late 1986 the oil kingdom of Kuwait, tired of the attacks on its merchant fleet, asked Washington to provide naval escorts for its tankers through the war zone. American foreign policy toward the Persian Gulf might charitably have been described as muddled. Publicly, U.S. officials professed neutrality in the conflict. But Khomeini's coup had transformed Iran, a staunch and well-armed U.S. ally under the shah, into a bitter enemy. The Reagan administration had tried to rally an international arms embargo—while secretly shipping U.S. weapons and gear to Tehran in attempts to free hostages elsewhere in the Middle East and to fund the Nicaraguan contras. Meanwhile, Washington had restored diplomatic relations with Baghdad in 1983 and had begun the covert supply of battlefield intelligence to Iraq.[6]

But the Kuwaitis proved better geopoliticians than Saddam. Even as Washington began to declare the request for a naval escort, the monarchy's diplomats were inviting Moscow to do the job. The idea of Soviet warships protecting the world's energy jugular was too much for the White House to bear. In March 1987, U.S. officials announced an upcoming series of convoys, to be dubbed Operation Earnest Will. The U.S. Navy had patrolled the Gulf since World War II. But this new effort would require a far heavier presence—as many as three dozen ships in and around the region.

The buildup had barely begun when disaster struck. One of the first new ships to arrive was the *Stark*, Cdr. Glenn Brindel commanding. Ten months earlier, Brindel had flashed a friendly message to Rinn across the tropical waters of Guantánamo Harbor. Now his frigate was on patrol in the middle of a war zone—and fairly relaxed about it. Neither the chaff launchers nor the Phalanx CIWS (close-in weapons system), an anti-missile weapon, was turned on. The .50-caliber machine guns were unloaded, their gunners lying down near the mounts. In the combat information center, just one of the weapons control consoles was manned.

Just before sundown on 17 May, an Iraqi pilot in an F-1 Mirage jet headed down the Gulf, scanning his instruments, looking for tankers. In the *Stark*'s darkened CIC, an operations specialist picked up the Mirage on his screen: track number 2202, range two hundred miles, headed inbound. The jet was pointed past the ship, four miles off the port beam. The sailor passed the word to his skipper.

At two minutes after 9:00 PM, the Mirage locked its Cyrano-IV fire-control radar onto the *Stark*. The frigate's instruments lit up in warning. A sailor asked permission to send a standard "back off" message to the Iraqi pilot. "No, wait," came the reply.

At 9:05, the Mirage banked left, toward the warship. At just over twenty-two miles' distance, the pilot launched his first Exocet. The missile leveled out a dozen feet above the waves, accelerated to nearly the speed of sound, and turned on its radar-homing seeker. Twenty seconds later, another Exocet dropped from a wing and lit off toward the *Stark*.

The ship's tactical action officer later recalled no warning of the launches, though the ship's radar and electronic countermeasures system were both built to sound such an alarm. The ship popped neither chaff nor flares. The Phalanx weapon—conceived, developed, and purchased for a moment such as this—remained in standby mode.

The first Exocet punched through the *Stark*'s hull near the port bridge wing, eight feet above the waterline. It bored a flaming hole through berthing spaces, the post office, and the ship's store, spewing rocket propellant along its path. Burning at thirty-five hundred degrees, the weapon ground to a halt in a corner of the chiefs' quarters and failed to explode. The second missile, which hit five feet farther forward, deto-nated as designed.

The fires burned for almost a day, incinerating the crew's quarters, the radar room, and finally, the combat information center. Nearly one-fifth of the crew was incapacitated in the attack. Twenty-nine men were killed immediately; eight more died later.[7]

By the time the *Stark* was towed into Bahrain, a shaken U.S. Navy was already trying to figure out what had gone wrong. Why had the ship failed to defend itself? The service's formal investigation blamed Brindel for failing to "provide combat-oriented leadership." But the investigators also noted that the navy leadership had failed to sound the warning about accidental attacks from Iraqi jets. Instead, Gulf skippers had been told to keep a sharp eye for Iranian mines and admonished not to embarrass the United States by acting precipitously.[8] One contributor to *Proceedings* wondered whether America's naval service was breeding leaders who could handle a split-second switch from diplomacy to combat, saying: "The Navy's natural selection during peacetime mirrors American society. We have always imagined a gulf between war and peace. We have attempted to separate cleanly our values and our behavior accordingly, and this has limited our effectiveness in a world of shadow conflict, or 'violent peace.' Even when we bridge that gulf and formally go to war, the mental transformation from gentility to the warrior's ethic that demands unconditional surrender takes time. How long does it take the warrior to emerge?"[9]

The news of the *Stark* reached the *Roberts* at sea as it headed south for some exercises off the Virginia capes.[10] The report shocked the crew. Many had a buddy aboard the *Stark;* some had acquaintances among the dead. Everyone knew the two frigates shared the same weapons, the same systems, the same vulnerabilities. Lester Chaffin, an electrician's mate first class, studied the missiles' paths and the damage done, and counted the shipmates who would have perished if the missiles had struck his own ship.

Rinn had known Brindel since their Naval War College days, and the classmates had renewed their ties at Gitmo the previous summer. "When I got that message, I sat on the bridge of the ship," he recalled.

And the XO [executive officer], Bill Clark, came back about thirty minutes later. I hadn't said a word to anybody, and he said, "Are you okay?" And I said, "No, I'm not. I'm sitting here thinking, 'What twenty-nine guys would I would give up on this ship that I'd ever be able to sleep again?" Couldn't do it; wouldn't ever want to do it. So if there was anything that put a stamp on [my intensity], it was that I was never going to let that happen. How do you do it? How do you ever prevent it? You work as hard as you can.[11]

Rinn saw the *Stark* as the mistake of a guy who hadn't been mentally ready. He vowed never to let an enemy take the first shot. Training aboard the *Roberts,* always intense, ratcheted up a notch.

IN JUNE 1987 the *Roberts* headed once again for Guantánamo Bay. A year earlier the crew had merely been confident. This time, they set sail with a gleam in their eye and a knife in their teeth. The frigate had aced its recent readiness exam, and its helicopter detachment had notched a flawless flight certification. The commander of the Atlantic Surface Fleet sent kudos: "Your DC material condition was the best ever seen by the inspectors, and your crew's average score of 94 on the General DC Test has set the standard for others to follow."[12] At Gitmo, the *Roberts* crew intended to break every record in the book.

But the instructors were waiting for them. The curriculum that the *Roberts* had faced a year ago was among the casualties of the hellish chemical fires aboard the *Stark*. In the month since the attack, the damage control testers had devised more complex scenarios intended to put a warship's crew in the *Stark's* shoes. *Roberts* would be the first ship to face the new test.[13]

For three weeks, the crew moved through one exam after another with aplomb. The bridge watch notched the best seamanship and navigation grades in two years. Van Hook's engineers ran through the comprehensive set of equipment-failure scenarios—then did it twice more just for practice. The frigate's sonar operators locked onto the nuclear attack submarine USS *Scamp* (SSN 558) with helicopter and towed array, pounding away on the hapless sub for three extra days. Gitmo trainers deemed it the "the most impressive operation of its type held to date."[14]

The big test, a "mass conflagration" drill, arrived on 14 July. The instructors arrayed themselves around the ship, ready to dock points for any missteps. At a whisper from an instructor in CIC, one of the operations specialists called out a warning: "Missile inbound, starboard side!" The Gitmo instructors clicked their stopwatches, and the game was on.

Rinn sent the crew to general quarters, but the "missiles" struck while hatches were still being dogged. The ship's repair teams sprang into action as instructors around the ship narrated the scenario to grim-faced *Roberts* sailors. The first missile plunged into the ship's exhaust stack, knocking out electrical power. The ship's interior grew dim as fluorescent lamps went out and battery-powered battle lanterns came on. The roof of the starboard helicopter hangar collapsed. Class Alpha and Bravo fires erupted in the hangar bay and the midships passageway.

A second missile slammed into the ship moments later, exploding in the central office complex under the flight deck. The blast punctured decks and bulkheads, and thick black smoke spread inside the ship. A fire main ruptured. Main propulsion and communications followed electrical power into oblivion. The explosions "killed" or "wounded" just about everyone in the superstructure aft of the signal bridge; fantail, flight deck, hangars, central office, supply office—all gone.

Repair Lockers 3 and 5 leaped to work, with Rinn, Van Hook, and Sorensen in charge. The sailors diagnosed the damaged fire main and closed valves to stop the leak. They opened crossover connections to draw water from the undamaged pipes. They connected fire hoses and began to attack the blazes. They shored up failing bulkheads with wood and steel.

The instructors ratcheted up the pressure. Twenty minutes into the fight, the CIWS magazine atop the hangar deck blew up from the heat, further weakening the ship's beleaguered superstructure. Moments later, the welding gases in an aft storage room exploded, blowing another six-foot hole in the side of the ship. That "killed" Rinn, and the instructor snarled at him with a look that said, "You're an idiot for standing next to a flammable locker without moving its contents to a safe location." It was a lesson he would not forget.

The instructors were merciless. They walked among the hose teams, sending scene leaders and nozzle operators to the sidelines with a tap on the shoulder and a terse "you're dead." Others they squirted with blood-red liquid, leaving them "wounded" for the corpsmen to save if they could.

The imaginary toll was worse than the *Stark's*; nearly one-third of the *Roberts's* 165-member crew were pronounced dead. But the crew, cross-trained to a fare-thee-well, was unflappable. As chiefs and first-class petty officers fell, junior petty officers and seamen slid smoothly into their places.[15] Through it all, Rinn kept the bridge and CIC teams in their seats, monitoring their surroundings for more attacks.

When it was over, the crew was winded but victorious. The instructors were a bit stunned. Their unanimous verdict: the *Roberts* sailors had saved their ship—and could have fought off more enemies as well. The senior tester praised the crew's "originality and initiative," "excellent crew participation," and "superb leadership." It was, he declared, the best mass conflagration drill he had ever witnessed.[16]

The Gitmo training commander tacked up a framed photo of FFG 58 outside his office and gushed about the ship to the three-star head of the Atlantic Surface Fleet. "The entire crew presented an eager, aggressive attitude and refused to let any problem set them back. Superior leadership and a keen sense of pride in their ship enabled them to function as a complete team," he wrote. "USS *Samuel B. Roberts* departed GTMO as one of the best REFTRA [refresher training] combatants trained in years."[17]

The *Roberts* would need all that expertise soon. Half a world away, the first Operation Earnest Will convoy was assembling on the far side of the Arabian Peninsula.

THE MV *BRIDGETON,* anchored off the eastern coast of Oman, defied the eye's attempt to take its measure. The supertanker's weather deck stretched a quarter mile from stem to stern and 230 feet across the beam. From time to time a Filipino sailor appeared on the rim of that vast steel plain, pedaling a bicycle on some errand. The ship's double-bottomed hull could hold nearly 120 million gallons of crude oil, enough to keep Japan, the vessel's birth nation, running for eight hours. For a decade the 413,000-ton tanker had gone by the name *al-Rekkah* and had reigned as the largest ship in Kuwait's fleet—indeed, the biggest under any Middle Eastern flag.

The giant ship had recently surrendered that title, not because any larger contender had appeared, but because it no longer sailed under the

Kuwaiti flag. Under the deal negotiated between Washington and Kuwait City, *al-Rekkah* and ten other Kuwaiti ships had shifted their country of registration to garner U.S. naval protection.

The crew of what was now the *Bridgeton* had marked the change in a ceremony in the Gulf of Oman, hauling the kingdom's banner down the stern mast and running up the Stars and Stripes. The funnel, which had advertised the Kuwait Oil Tanker Company, already bore the red "C" of the Chesapeake Shipping Company. The new name had been painted over the old one on the stern, and the new home port lettered in white: Philadelphia. The ship would never visit its purported home; the river city's piers were too shallow to accommodate its seven-story draft.[18]

The *Bridgeton* weighed anchor along with a reflagged liquid propane carrier, and four U.S. Navy warships fanned out around them. The nine-thousand-ton cruiser USS *Fox* (CG 33), the largest of the escorts, was a gnat beside the behemoth.

On 22 July 1987 the first Earnest Will convoy moved into the Strait of Hormuz and headed toward Kuwait, beginning a journey of nearly five hundred miles through a war zone. The seven-year toll on commercial shipping stood at 333 watercraft damaged or sunk, according to famed insurer Lloyd's of London. The total for the year to date was 65.[19]

The *Bridgeton* was within a day of its destination when it became a naval statistic. Around 6:30 AM, the ship's American skipper and his bridge team heard a distant metal-on-metal clank. Then the deck began to undulate. The sailors grabbed for the railings and hung on. "It felt like a five-hundred-ton hammer hit us up forward," the ship's skipper recalled.[20] There was only one likely explanation: the tanker had hit a naval mine. But the leviathan was unable to stop—even emergency reverse thrust could not halt a supertanker in less than three miles—and the *Bridgeton* barreled on, making sixteen knots through a minefield. When the ship finally came to rest, the crew discovered a jagged hole the size of a squash court in the port bow. But the double hull kept the ship afloat. Soon the convoy was steaming onward to Kuwait, with one change in formation: the warships trailed *Bridgeton* in a meek line.[21] None of the thin-skinned escorts dared break trail.

This was not the first live mine U.S. forces had found in Gulf waters. Mines had damaged at least one other commercial ship in the Gulf in

1987, and possibly two or three. About a dozen of the stealthy floating bombs had been detected and destroyed, but how many more were out there was anyone's guess.

Stealth and simplicity made mines cheaper and often more cost-effective than just about any other naval weapon. During World War II, for example, U.S. submarines sank roughly five million tons of Japanese shipping, at an approximate cost of one hundred dollars per ton. By contrast, mines dropped by B-29 bombers in 1945 sent about 1.25 million tons of shipping to the bottom—and at one-sixth the cost per ton.[22] Another statistic: in the half century after World War II, eighteen U.S. warships were damaged by hostile action. Fourteen of them hit mines.

Nevertheless, until the attack on the *Bridgeton,* naval leaders had remained largely complacent about the threat of mines in the Persian Gulf. It was a chronic oversight. U.S. Navy culture had long treated countermine operations as the ugly duckling of naval warfare. It was slow, painstaking, unglamorous work. And few admirals argued for spending money on bottom-search sonars instead of cruise missiles, fighter jets, and nuclear submarines.[23]

In the wake of the attack on the supertanker, the navy airlifted eight minesweeping RH-53D Sea Dragon helicopters to the Gulf. Four small wooden-hulled boats arrived a bit later on the back of an amphibious assault ship. But it took until late October for the navy to get its most capable mine hunters into action: six oceangoing minesweepers, none less than thirty-five years old, most relegated to the naval reserve, and so rickety that most of them were towed across the ocean to spare them wear and tear.[24]

Iranian officials, who had originally attributed the hole in *Bridgeton's* hull to "the hand of Allah," confessed to laying mines after another merchant ship mysteriously sank near the Strait of Hormuz. But Tehran insisted that its weapons were meant only for "coastal defense." By autumn, shadowy U.S. forces would expose that as a lie.[25]

By September 1987 Operation Earnest Will was in full swing. Almost every day a U.S.–led convoy would depart from the Fujairah anchorage and head into the strait, while another group of tankers, bellies heavy with oil and gas, left Kuwait for the open sea. Many of the reflagged ships carried a U.S. liaison officer—generally a reservist called up from a civilian job, for the navy had not performed convoys since World War II and had no active-duty officers trained for the task. All told, the United States had nearly thirty warships in or near the Gulf, including the battleship USS *Missouri* (BB 63).[26]

But that was just the public face of the U.S. military operations in the region. The Pentagon also secretly dispatched an ecumenical group of elite forces: army special-operations helicopters, navy patrol-boat operators and SEAL commandos, marine security details. Operating under the classified code name Prime Chance, they set up shop aboard a pair of leased oil barges anchored in the northern Gulf. Mostly, they hunted armed speedboats operated by the Pasdaran, or Revolutionary Guards, a paramilitary organization whose naval role was attacking merchants with machine guns and rocket-propelled grenades.[27]

Operation Prime Chance was also meant to catch Iranian minelayers, and on 21 September, it succeeded. After nightfall, a pair of army helicopters lifted off from the frigate USS *Jarrett* (FFG 33), their pilots flying with night vision goggles. They zeroed in on a small amphibious ship, the *Iran Ajr,* that was creeping along about fifty miles off the coast of Bahrain. As the pilots watched, Iranian sailors dropped heavy objects the size of fifty-five-gallon drums into the water. The army pilots radioed their findings to the navy commander in the Gulf, who responded: "Stop the mining." The pilots sprayed the ship with rockets and machine guns, and a team of navy SEALs stormed the deck. They gathered up an intelligence bonanza—minefield charts and nine M-08 mines—then scuttled the ship in deep water.[28]

The sinking of the *Iran Ajr* hardly slowed attacks on merchant ships. Three dozen were hit in September alone. On 16 October an antiship missile flashed from its launch container on Iran's Fao Peninsula and struck the tanker *Sea Isle City* at anchor off Kuwait, blinding its American captain. It was the first attack on a reflagged ship since the *Bridgeton,* and it drew retaliation three days later. U.S. destroyers shelled a pair of defunct oil platforms that served as forward bases for Pasdaran speedboats. The chaos in the Gulf was getting worse.[29]

THE RUMORS STARTED on a rainy Veterans Day in Newport. A late-autumn drizzle forced an American Legion memorial ceremony off a trim park lawn and into the century-old city hall. As several dozen people rearranged themselves in the city council's chambers, a navy commander in dress blues stepped to the lectern. The event's organizers had invited Paul Rinn to make a speech, and characteristically, he had equipped himself with a relevant bit of history. The captain regaled his audience with tales of the 1st Rhode Island Artillery company at Gettysburg, and he asked listeners to remember the sacrifices of U.S. servicemen and women and the families they leave behind.

It was a moving speech—at least the editorial writers at the *Providence Journal* found it so. But an almost offhand remark by one of the speakers set tongues wagging across the waterfront: he wished Rinn and his crew smooth sailing in the Middle East. The next day's newspaper carried a denial by *Roberts*'s executive officer that the ship had received any such orders. "The way it's set up, you have to join the Sixth Fleet in the Mediterranean first, then we get our assignments," Lt. Cdr. William Clark said. "If we're ordered to the Middle East, we won't know until thirty days prior to deployment." But he added that the navy considered the guided-missile frigate "the best kind of ship for that environment."

As for the crew, Clark said, "I think the overall attitude of the ship would be like if you were driving down the highway and saw a bad accident that just happened. You can feel the adrenaline pumping a little stronger, and you're curious."[30]

The XO was being cagey. He and Rinn had known differently for months. In late June the commodore of Surface Group Four had passed along a tip: the navy, in the wake of the *Stark* attack, had decided that every frigate once slated for a Mediterranean deployment would go to the Gulf instead. This required the *Roberts* to deploy in January, six months earlier than planned. "Know this news not the best you've heard today," Aquilino wrote.

But now, despite Clark's official denials, the cat was out of the bag. Everyone took the news a bit differently. Gunner Tom Reinert was phlegmatic. For one thing, he'd been predicting this for months. Moreover, he'd been to the Gulf twice already. His only disappointment was that his antisubmarine warfare team, which had worked so hard and received such praise, would be largely idle in the shallow Gulf, where no subs sailed.[31]

Others were not so sanguine. "In the late 1980s, the biggest fear for a young man just out of high school joining the navy was the possibility of finding himself on a ship in the dreaded Persian Gulf," recalled Joe Baker, a fireman from New Mexico. "In civilian land, it's like a rumor. But in the navy, people were talking about it all the time."[32]

John Preston recalled one gunner's mate who freaked out at the news: "I can't go there, man!" The tension showed in frayed nerves and squabbles. Preston recalled the argument that broke out between two junior petty officers in a forward passageway. As he watched, the ship's serviceman broke open a tin of red paint and dumped it over the engineman's head, spattering the missile magazine, the passageway, and both sailors. Preston just kept walking. That looked like a fun cleanup, he thought.[33]

The crew took comfort in the knowledge that no ship on the East Coast was readier for battle. In recent exams, gas turbine inspectors had declared Van Hook's team the best frigate engineering department they'd seen in two years. The aviation department earned the first flawless score the testers had ever issued. And in a no-notice damage control inspection, all three repair lockers received the highest possible grades—the best performance in the Atlantic Fleet.[34] Palmer's combat systems team was ready to go as well. Over the course of the year, the frigate had shot off an unusual amount of ordnance: five thousand rounds of small-caliber ammo, three thousand rounds of CWIS shells, three hundred 76-mm shells, a pair of Standard missiles, and two Mk 46 exercise torpedoes.[35]

Off the Massachusetts coast, the CIC crew had dueled with air force fighters until they could bring them down in their sleep. When the F-15s came out to play, Rinn had his radar operators dim their displays until the pilots radioed in from twenty miles out. The fighters would kick in the afterburners, drop to 250 feet, and go supersonic. When they flashed overhead, dragging a roar that could dissolve teeth, the sonic boom hit the ship like a hammer. Books plummeted from shelves; the hangar door fell off its hinges. But down in CIC, the fire controlmen had locked up the jet in plenty of time to greet it with a missile. To Rinn, that skill was worth any incidental damage by shockwave.[36]

DEPLOYMENT WAS SET for 11 January. The crew scattered across the country for the Christmas holidays and then returned for two hectic weeks of "packing the ship." The engineers checked off a long list of spare parts and supplies: synthetic lubricating oil for the gas turbines, mineral oil for the reduction gear, acetylene tanks for welding, refrigerants for the air conditioners, nitrogen for the flight deck. They loaded rags, logbooks, and paper forms; citric acid to clean the ship's freshwater distillers; canisters of bromine to make the water potable; and bales of cheesecloth to protect their machinery from the dusty Gulf air.[37]

Chief Cook Kevin Ford and his team of mess management specialists hustled to load their own refrigerated storerooms. In the rush, an order form typo brought the delivery of not one hundred, but one thousand five-pound bags of sugar—fully two and a half tons. An expert in the art of *cumshaw,* or barter, Ford had the extra sugar loaded aboard. He reckoned it might come in handy on deployment.[38]

A lot of new DC items arrived in the weeks before deployment. The *Stark* had revealed a need to keep smoke from spreading through passageways without obstructing firefighters. The navy had responded with smoke curtains—seven-pound, two-paneled drapes to be hung over hatchways. The service also sent a dozen portable radios.

Meanwhile, the crew stocked up on shoring beams. They obtained ten extra ten-foot four-by-four planks to add to their authorized issue of ten twelve-footers, and swapped six of their five-foot extendable steel supports for eleven-footers, giving them eighteen of the longer blue ones.[39]

The crew scoured the Newport waterfront for OBAs, the full-face masks that allowed firefighters to work amid the toxic fumes of a shipboard fire. The frigate was allocated 120 oxygen canisters—far too few.[40] In Sorensen's ten-page post-Gitmo memo, he had noted that the *Roberts* had expended their entire store during the mass conflagration exercise. When the exam ended, half of the sailors were wearing strips of masking tape labeled "OBA" in place of the real thing.

The *Stark* proved his point. Before it left for the Gulf, the crew had rounded up nearly four hundred canisters—and this had not been nearly enough. In the twenty-four hours that followed the missile strike, the crew used them all up—plus hundreds more flown onto the burning frigate from nearby U.S. warships.[41] Sorensen recommended each frigate should deploy with no fewer than eight hundred canisters. The DC teams scrounged up as many OBAs as they could lay their hands on. Even parts and carcasses were stripped and rebuilt to add to the total.

Sorensen would have been proud to see the effort, but he was no longer aboard the ship. He had been rotated off as scheduled, and turned the job over to a replacement, Ens. Ken Rassler. The crew of the *Roberts* would face its deployment without their first DC leader. They also had a new executive officer; Clark rotated off and was replaced by Lt. Cdr. John Eckelberry, a veteran of several Gulf deployments.

Eventually, even the last-minute tasks were done. All the extra gear made for a very crowded ship—particularly since FFGs weren't large to begin with, nor designed for extended patrols. The *Samuel B. Roberts*, mustering 215 souls and displacing 4,712.25 gross tons, was ready to go to war.[42]

ON 11 JANUARY 1988 Glenn Palmer awoke well before dawn. He switched on a light in his family's Newport house, rolled out of bed, and headed downstairs to collect a last batch of laundry. Rachel, a three-year-old in pink flannel pajamas, was waiting at the top of the stairs. "Hold me, Daddy," she said, and stretched out her arms.

For Palmer, preparing to sail meant preparing his family to stay behind. This would be his fourth deployment—he'd been to the western Pacific, the Mediterranean, even around South America. His wife, Kathy, and their three children had developed rituals to help bear the separation. A construction-paper chain hung in the kitchen of their Newport house, 184 links long. Each morning one of the kids would tear off a colored loop, marking the slow but steady passage of Daddy's deployment.[43]

Putting to sea was always a risky business, and there had been plenty of tension during Palmer's Cold War missions. But for the first time in their nine-year marriage, the couple had talked about what the family might do if Glenn failed to return. Things felt more dangerous this time—his ship was headed for a combat zone that had already taken the lives of thirty-seven U.S. sailors. There was another reason as well: Kathy was pregnant with the Palmers' fourth child. The baby was due in March, which meant that Glenn would miss the birth—along with the couple's wedding anniversary and the birthdays of their three other kids.

The couple had decided that if Glenn died, Kathy and the kids would move in with his mother. And with that, Kathy laid the matter in God's hands. "I know there'll be times when I'm depressed," she told a newspaper reporter who was writing about the imminent departure of the *Roberts*. "The first time it'll hit me will be when I have the baby, and I expect Glenn to bring me flowers and see the baby, and he won't be there." Palmer, the son of a minister and a graduate of a Christian college in Michigan, shared his wife's faith and her sadness. "You can't say you love people and say you want to be away from them for six months," he said.

But there was another feeling, too: eagerness, an adrenaline trickle. It was a natural feeling of a naval officer in his twelfth year of service, especially one who had spent two solid years preparing himself, his ship, and his crew for a fight. The time had come to ride his warship into harm's way. "This is basically what I'm getting paid for," he said. "I'm putting my money where my mouth is. I'm not going to say I'm not afraid. But it's a healthy fear, a respect."[44]

The family gathered in the early morning darkness, and Palmer asked God to see them through their six-month separation. Then they climbed into the Caprice station wagon—little Rachel squeezed between her brother and sister in the backseat, her parents holding hands in front—and drove the five minutes to the naval station.

At the pier, Palmer embraced his wife and hugged his children. Then, as dawn broke, he turned and strode toward the gray form of his ship, dark against the cloudless sky.

Around him, shipmates were saying their own farewells. Most of the crew was already aboard ship; they were young and single, most from towns and cities far from Rhode Island, and had no one to see them off. Such was the final addition to the crew, Christopher Pond, a hull technician third class. Pond had slipped aboard just hours earlier—2:00 AM, as a matter of fact—and had received surprising news from the petty officer on duty at the quarterdeck. "You still have four more days of leave left," the petty officer said, fingering a date on Pond's transfer documents. "I would take it if I were you."[45]

Pond had listened in disbelief. His orders had said nothing about his new ship's imminent departure or its destination. A native of Lebanon,

Pennsylvania, the nineteen-year-old was just back from a two-year tour aboard a support ship moored near the Italian island of Sardinia. The hull technician was still readjusting to life on American soil, and the idea of setting off on a six-month deployment before lunch arrived as something of a shock. For a moment, he was tempted to take his hard-earned leave and let the navy worry about getting him to the *Roberts* after it departed. Then he shrugged. *Better to stay aboard than be shuffled around the world trying to catch up to my ship,* he thought.

At 9:00 AM a navy band played "God Bless America," and the frigate moved away from the pier. A small clot of family and friends waved as the ship headed out into the blue-gray Narragansett Bay. Moments later, another frigate pushed away from an adjacent pier: *Roberts*'s squadron-mate USS *Simpson* (FFG 56). One after the other, the warships passed beneath the long suspended span of the Jamestown Bridge, south past the rocky Dumplings, and out toward the Atlantic Ocean.

Left behind on the Newport pier was Aquilino. For eighteen months the commodore of Surface Group Four had guided and supported the *Roberts* as it proceeded from a newly commissioned watercraft to a deploying warship. Now he could only watch the frigate go with a mixture of pride, concern, and envy. Later that afternoon, he sent a message out to the departing ship, wishing them Godspeed as they headed for the closest thing the navy had to a front line.[46]

Three years of training had forged the *Roberts*'s two hundred and fifteen sailors into a fighting team. Thousands upon thousands of hours of preparation had honed their skills. But drills couldn't compare to duty in the Gulf, where the action lasted not hours but days and weeks. And thoughts of *Bridgeton, Sea Isle City,* and *Stark* hung like specters in the salt air.

USS *Samuel B. Roberts* (FFG 58) being outfitted in the dry dock at Bath Iron Works in Maine, ca. summer 1985. *Courtesy General Dynamics Bath Iron Works*

Lt. Gordan Van Hook, chief engineer (left), and Lt. Eric Sorensen, damage control assistant, in officers' country aboard the *Roberts,* ca. 1986. *Courtesy Eric Sorensen*

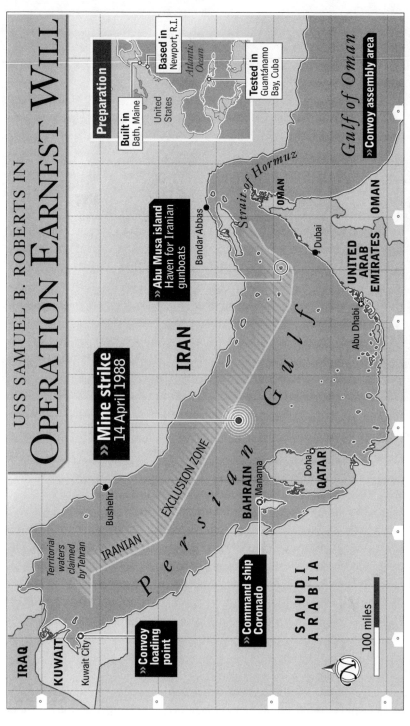

USS SAMUEL B. ROBERTS IN
OPERATION EARNEST WILL

Preparation

Built in
Bath, Maine

Based in
Newport, R.I.

Tested in
Guantánamo Bay, Cuba

United States

Atlantic Ocean

IRAQ

KUWAIT

Kuwait City

>> Convoy loading point

Territorial waters claimed by Tehran

IRANIAN

EXCLUSION ZONE

Bushehr

Persian Gulf

>> Mine strike
14 April 1988

IRAN

>> Abu Musa island
Haven for Iranian gunboats

Bandar Abbas

Strait of Hormuz

OMAN

Gulf of Oman

>> Convoy assembly area

BAHRAIN

Manama

>> Command ship
Coronado

QATAR

Doha

SAUDI
ARABIA

UNITED
ARAB
EMIRATES

Dubai

Abu Dhabi

OMAN

100 miles

Map of the Persian Gulf; (inset) the Atlantic Seaboard of the United States. *Courtesy Natban Levine*

An artist's conception of the mine blast, which occurred in the central Persian Gulf about 4:50 PM local time, 14 April 1988.
Chris Stopa

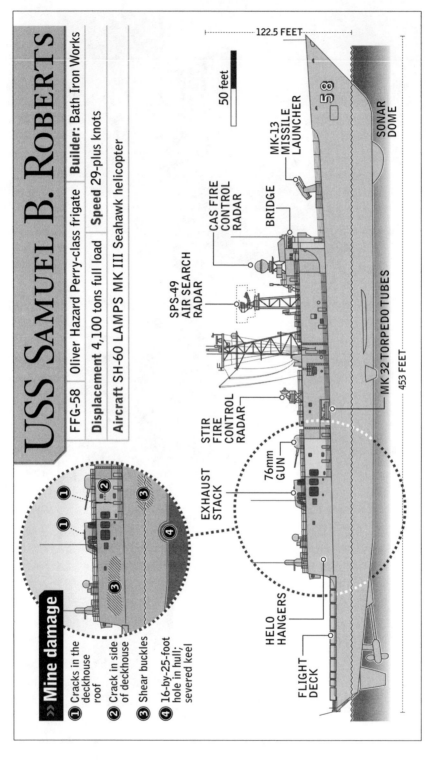

USS Samuel B. Roberts

FFG-58	Oliver Hazard Perry-class frigate	**Builder:** Bath Iron Works
	Displacement 4,100 tons full load	**Speed** 29-plus knots
	Aircraft SH-60 LAMPS MK III Seahawk helicopter	

» Mine damage

1. Cracks in the deckhouse roof
2. Crack in side of deckhouse
3. Shear buckles
4. 16-by-25-foot hole in hull; severed keel

122.5 FEET

50 feet

453 FEET

SPS-49 AIR SEARCH RADAR

CAS FIRE CONTROL RADAR

BRIDGE

MK-13 MISSILE LAUNCHER

SONAR DOME

STIR FIRE CONTROL RADAR

EXHAUST STACK

76mm GUN

MK 32 TORPEDO TUBES

HELO HANGERS

FLIGHT DECK

58

Side view of the USS *Samuel B. Roberts* shows mine damage. *Courtesy Nathan Levine*

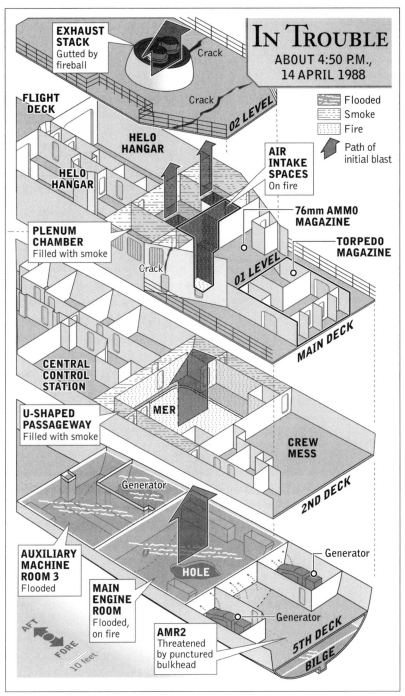

Cutaway of the *Roberts* shows fire, flood, and smoke damage. *Courtesy Nathan Levine*

The mine blast punctured the aft bulkhead of Auxiliary Machine Room 2, allowing seawater to pour in from the inundated main engine room. This photo shows one of the extendable steel shoring members the crew used to brace unorthodox soft patches on the bulkhead, and illustrates the cramped conditions in which the AMR2 damage control effort took place. *Courtesy Eric Sorensen*

An unidentified sailor stands amid a tangle of fire hoses used to extinguish the blaze and to drain the ship. *Courtesy Eric Sorensen*

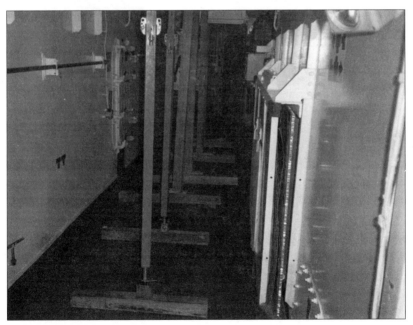

This I-type shoring was installed in the center passageway aft of the quarterdeck on 15 April 1988. The shoring, which used the final bits of wood available after the damage control effort, was an attempt to stabilize the ship amid fears that it might break up during the tow to Dubai, UAE. *Courtesy Eric Sorensen*

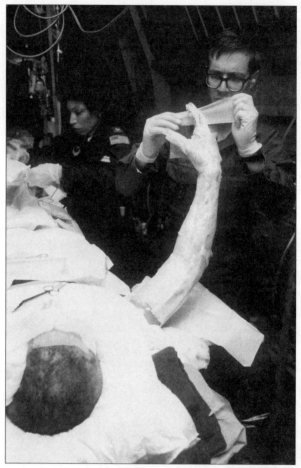

Gas Turbine Systems Technician (Electrical) 3rd Class David J. Burbine receives fresh dressings en route to Germany aboard a U.S. Air Force C-141B Starlifter. *Sgt. Douglas K. Lingefelt, U.S. Air Force*

Cracked in three places, the aluminum superstructure was braced with 3/4-inch phosphor-bronze cables on 15 April 1988. Here, Signalman 1st Class (SW) Serge E. Kingery stands roving security patrol atop the port gas turbine access plate as the *Roberts* sits at Dubai Drydocks in late April 1988. One of the cracks is visible to either side of the plate. *Courtesy Eric Sorensen*

Roberts in dry dock in Dubai, ca. May 1988. *Photographer's Mate 1st Class Chuck Mussi, U.S. Navy*

View of the *Roberts's* hull breach from dry dock floor, 3 May 1988. *Photographer's Mate 2nd Class Rudy D. Pahoyo, U.S. Navy*

A look into the *Roberts's* mangled main engine room from dry dock floor, 3 May 1988. *Photographer's Mate 2nd Class Rudy D. Pahoyo, U.S. Navy*

The damaged interior of Auxiliary Machine Room 3, 3 May 1988. *Photographer's Mate 2nd Class Rudy D. Pahoyo, U.S. Navy*

Cdr. Paul X. Rinn, captain of the *Roberts,* receives the Legion of Merit from Adm. William J. Crowe, chairman of the Joint Chiefs of Staff, at a pierside ceremony in Dubai on 3 May 1988. *Courtesy Paul Rinn*

(Left to right) Chief Engineman (SW) George A. Cowan, Electrician's Mate 2nd Class Edwin B. Copeland, and Chief Electrician's Mate (SW) Robert C. Bent received the Bronze Star with Combat V for pulling Chief Gas Turbine Systems Technician (Mechanical) Alex Perez from the ship's burning main engine room. Pierside in Dubai on 3 May 1988. *Courtesy Paul Rinn*

The decorated officers of the *Roberts* (listed alphabetically) included: Lt. Cdr. John R. Eckelberry, Bronze Star with Combat V; Lt. Robert L. Firehammer Jr., Navy Commendation Medal with Combat Device (NCM/CD); Lt. Bradley G. Gutcher, NCM/CD; Lt. David Llewellyn, NCM/CD; Ens. Kenneth J. Rassler, Bronze Star with Combat V; Crd. Paul Rinn; Lt. (jg) John Sims, Bronze Star with Combat V; Ens. Robert B. Sobnosky, NCM/CD; Lt. (jg) Michael L. Valliere, Bronze Star with Combat V; and Lt. Gordan E. Van Hook, Bronze Star with Combat V. Pierside in Dubai on 3 May 1988. *Courtesy Paul Rinn*

The decorated chiefs included (left to right): Chief Mess Management Specialist (SW) Kevin J. Ford, NCM/CD; Chief Engineman (SW) George A. Cowan; Chief Electrician's Mate (SW) Robert C. Bent; Senior Chief Boatswain's Mate (SW) George E. Frost, Bronze Star with Combat V; Chief Gas Turbine Systems Technician (Mechanical) (SW) David J. Walker, NCM/CD; Cdr. Paul Rinn. Pierside in Dubai on 3 May 1988. *Courtesy Paul Rinn*

The decorated sailors of *Roberts'* crew (listed alphabetically) included: Electrician's Mate 2nd Class Edwin B. Copeland; Engineman 1st Class (SW) Mark T. Dejno, Purple Heart; Signalman 1st Class (SW) Charles R. Dumas, NCM/CD; Mess Management Specialist 2nd Class Scott W. Frank, NCM/CD; Boatswain's Mate 1st Class (SW) Richard L. Fridley, NCM/CD; Hull Maintenance Technician 1st Class Gary W. Gawor, NCM/CD; Boatswain's Mate Seaman Bobby Gibson, Purple Heart; Signalman 1st Class (SW) Serge E. Kingery, NCM/CD; Hospital Corpsman 1st Class James E. Lambert, NCM/CD; Quartermaster 2nd Class (SW) Daniel J. Nicholson, NCM/CD; Hull Maintenance Technician 2nd Class (SW) Timothy Regan, NCM/CD; Rinn; Electrician's Mate 1st Class (SW) James E. Whitley, NCM/CD. Pierside in Dubai on 3 May 1988. Several more commanders subsequently received awards as well. *Courtesy Paul Rinn*

The *Roberts* was carried from Dubai to Newport, Rhode Island, aboard the semi-submersible heavy-lift ship *Mighty Servant 2*. Here, the frigate is ready for off-loading in Narragansett Bay on 1 August 1988. *Photographer's Mate 2nd Class (SW) Jeff Elliott, U.S. Navy*

A crane lowers the *Roberts*'s 310-ton replacement engine room module into the dry dock at Bath Iron Works' repair yard in Portland, Maine, ca. 1 December 1988. *Author's collection*

Passage to Hormuz

O ut in the Atlantic, the ships from Newport were soon joined by the guided missile cruiser USS *Wainwright* (CG 28), out of Charleston, South Carolina, and yet another frigate, USS *Jack Williams* (FFG 24), sailing from Mayport, Florida. Together, the quartet of warships—by happenstance, all four were products of Bath Iron Works—made up Destroyer Squadron 22 (DesRon 22). Their thirty-five-day journey to the Persian Gulf would require the transit of one ocean, three seas, three gulfs, three straits, and a canal. The time would be spent wisely, in preparation for the hazards that would confront them from their very first day in the Gulf.

The commodore of DesRon 22 was Capt. Donald A. Dyer, a gravel-voiced man with a dead-calm manner. He called himself the Redman, after the brand of chewing tobacco he kept in his cheek; even over the scratchy bridge radio, you could practically hear the juice dripping. No one ever heard the Redman get excited. Rinn had gotten to know Dyer during squadron workups off Puerto Rico. He found the commodore as demanding as he himself—though Dyer's controlled demeanor contrasted with the occasional explosion from Rinn. And the commodore did not hesitate to take the high-spirited skipper down a notch when necessary.

It had happened once during a large fleet exercise. The *Roberts* had passed a busy and successful couple of days, firing off a pair of missiles and completing numerous other assignments with the ship's usual competence and efficiency. Pressed for time to reach his next assignment, the captain sent a message to Dyer's staff, asking what the commodore intended for his ship and asking permission to depart. As time ticked away with no answer, Rinn jumped the chain of command and sought approval from the staff of the admiral who was running the exercise. This breached naval protocol. In his low voice, the commodore chewed

Rinn out over the radio, and followed it up the next day in writing. "Juniors 'request' the assistance of their seniors, keep their seniors informed in a timely manner, think ahead, and are ready for flexible response," Dyer wrote. "Asking you 'your intentions' is my prerogative. Change your tone."[1]

The episode set Rinn back on his heels. "Here I thought we were going to get praise for the good things we were doing," he said later. Instead, the message was: *you're getting too big for your britches.* Rinn conceded almost immediately that he'd acted unprofessionally, and when the *Roberts* pulled into Mayport for inspections, he sent the commodore a meek blinking-light signal: "Quietly reporting for duty."

Dyer laughed. "I just needed to get you back in the box," Rinn recalled him saying. "You were running around doing great stuff, and it was clear that you had gotten to the point where you thought you were invincible, and you were going to get yourself in trouble."[2]

As DesRon 22 made its way across the Atlantic, Dyer kept his four ships on their toes by pitting them against one another in various drills. Glenn Palmer particularly loved the no-notice gunnery contests. The radio would squawk, "Quickdraw, quickdraw, quickdraw, bearing 270, main gun," and the game would be on.

Deep in the *Roberts*'s superstructure, gunner's mates hastened to load their 76-mm gun. Topside, the lookouts and officer of the deck snapped their heads around to ensure that the target area was clear. Down the ladder in CIC, the tactical action officer and his subordinates checked the radar screens, requested the captain's permission to fire, and let fly. Palmer's team, always good, got better. By the time the squadron passed through the Strait of Gibraltar, the *Roberts* could put five rounds downrange in twenty seconds—a very quick reaction.

But gunnery, the defining measure of a warship in an earlier era, had long ago surrendered its primacy among a ship's combat skills. Calls for naval gunfire were all but nonexistent these days. By contrast, the management of information was a crucial, round-the-clock occupation. Captain and crew sorted through a flood of oft-conflicting visual reports and electronic data to figure out what was going on around them—establishing and maintaining situational awareness, as the military called it. The task had grown more complex with the introduction of radio networks that shared sensor data between ships. A blip that appeared on one frigate's radar screen automatically appeared on every other warship on the net—in theory. In practice, the computers had a hard time figuring out when two ships were looking at the same aircraft. So sailors spent a lot of time on the radio with their counterparts in other ships, trying to figure out which blips were real. DesRon 22 practiced all the way across the Atlantic. "My job, basically the whole way over, was getting proficient at it," said Rick Raymond, the sheet-metalworker-turned-operations-specialist.[3]

Raymond and the others also learned a brand-new word: *deconfliction,* the process invented to keep Iraq's aircraft from shooting U.S. warships. After the *Stark* incident, American naval officers had visited Baghdad to develop a set of radio calls to ward off approaching Iraqi pilots. And when a missile-laden Mirage lifted from its air base, U.S. radio operators passed the word from ship to ship down the Gulf, like lighting signal fires along a mountain range.

Yet Dyer also endeavored to keep the mood light and the crews loose. "Give the skipper a haircut on the forecastle," the Redman rumbled over the bridge-to-bridge circuit one day. On four American warships, sailors tumbled over themselves to roust their barbers, run an extension cord out onto the deck, and set clippers buzzing around their captains' heads.

The *Roberts* sonar operators were practicing new skills as well: mine hunting. There would be little call for their award-winning sub-hunting talents on this deployment, for no subs were known to operate in the shallow inland sea.[4] But in the past year, Gulf crews had spotted more than a hundred mines, drifting alone or laid in fields. So the sonar operators had been trained to fire the ship's machine guns at the floating weapons, and on the way over, they practiced shooting empty fifty-five-gallon drums rolled from the flight deck. "SBR has dropped so many simulated mines for targets, we now speak Iranian at meals," Rinn quipped in one message to Aquilino.

Amid it all, normal training on the *Roberts* went on as usual: fire-and-flooding drills, man-overboard drills, collision drills. Sometimes it seemed like most of the day was spent at general quarters—GQ, the crew called it. Everyone learned to carry their lifejacket and gas mask as they moved about the ship. "GQ was likely to happen every day at all kinds of hours," said Chris Pond, the newly arrived hull technician. "Day? Night? You never knew."[5] It was the same rigorous schedule that Eric Sorensen had helped launch almost two years earlier—with each new watch, a new exercise.

THE REWARD FOR the two-week Atlantic voyage was a four-day stop in Palma de Mallorca, a sunny Spanish island town crowded between mountain ridges and attractive beaches.[6] It was the first glimpse of Europe for most of the crew, who swarmed ashore to take in the sights and grab a beer. The cooks restocked the pantry with local goods; bags of bread mix overflowed onto the serving line. Chief Dave Walker departed on an unusual errand: rounding up one of the island's pygmy goats for delivery to the *Jack Williams,* whose skipper had made some sort of crack about the *Roberts* crew "eating goat."[7] (Walker later denied finding one, which does not explain the photos of a goat aboard ship.)

But the sailors paid for their liberty fun when they ran into a January storm halfway through the Mediterranean. For three days the frigate bulled its way through ten-foot waves that burst over the forecastle and splashed the bridge. The incessant rolling sickened the *Roberts*'s young sailors and left even old salts a bit green around the gills. "There were a couple of mornings getting up, where I'd wake up feeling okay, climb down from my third-up rack, and put my feet on the floor," recalled Joe Baker, the fireman. "The ship would twist, and that would be it. I'd run to the head, puke, and start my day."[8] At night, Baker and his shipmates tried to wedge themselves into their racks by stuffing boots under the foam mattresses. But the fireman couldn't even trust sleep for solace. One night he dreamed he was looking aft down Main Street, the big passageway between the hangars. He watched the helicopter on the flight deck as the ship tilted back and forth, back and forth. Eventually, the helo fell over the side and disappeared. Then the whole ship turned over. "I remember that dream like it was yesterday," Baker said. But the fireman's sea legs eventually arrived. "Suddenly, you're walking down a passageway and the ship is forty-five degrees over, and you're just walking, and don't notice," he said.[9]

The squadron ground on through the storm. Fuel was getting low, and they were scheduled for a rendezvous at sea with the oiler USS *Seattle*

(AOE 3). The navy relied on underway replenishment, or "unrepping," the ability to take on fuel without putting into port, to furnish a great tactical advantage over the Soviet navy, which had never quite gotten the knack. Even in fair weather, the maneuver had its risks. The receiving ship approached the larger oiler from behind, slowed to match speeds, and settled into a parallel course. Grunting and yelling, sailors dragged lines and hoses across the hundred-foot gap, all the while keeping a wary eye on the distance between the hulls. The Bernoulli effect created a low-pressure zone in the steel canyon, and ships that drew too close could be sucked into a collision.

Given the thirty-five-knot winds and lashing seas, Dyer wasn't sure unrepping was even possible, but Rinn, to the dismay of his crew, volunteered to give it a shot. There was more than a mite of bravado in the gesture, but there was also a tactical need. The *Roberts*'s thirsty gas turbines had burned their way through two-thirds of the ship's fuel, reducing reserves to a level no frigate skipper likes to see. The crew understood the reason for going after the fuel, but the curses that followed the call to refueling stations showed just how little enthusiasm they had for it.

"Everybody was freaking," Fire Controlman Preston remembered. "'God, we're gonna die, man, we're going to die,' I remember guys saying. I was back there on a tending line, and it was nasty—raining and cloudy and cold. That big ship wasn't moving much, but we were bouncing all over the place. I remember saying, 'Oh God, don't let us collide with that thing.' I've seen pictures of what happened when ships collided, and it's not pretty."[10]

Rinn swung his ship around behind the *Seattle* and conned the frigate straight ahead into position off the oiler's starboard side.[11] The crew cursed and held their breath. The sailors got a pilot line across, but could not get the heavy probe to follow.[12] Rinn eventually conceded defeat, but he remained proud that the commodore had allowed him to try.

A few days later the squadron arrived at the far end of the Mediterranean, and the *Roberts* led the squadron through the Suez Canal. Dyer, embarked aboard the *Simpson*, sent Rinn a pat on the back. A signal lamp blinked in Morse code across the blindingly blue water: "You do nice work, Paul."[13]

THE *ROBERTS* FINALLY got the fuel it needed during a pit stop in Djibouti, a port city on the Horn of Africa that had long been used by the French as a base for naval operations in the Middle East. As boatswain's mates tightened the mooring lines and hauled fuel hoses aboard, John Preston and some mates wandered onto the pier for a look around.

A small crowd was picking apart a bundle of used rags the engineman had tossed over the rail. Brightly colored T-shirts—reds and blues and oranges—went quickly; green and brown clothes were left behind in the hot sun.[14] A small boy was hawking souvenir trinkets, so the fire controlman pulled out a one-dollar bill. The young merchant's eyes went wide, and he dug in his pockets and produced a little pile of coins and notes. "What are you trying to do?" Preston asked, and then realized that the dollar was more than the kid could change. The sailor told him to keep it. Stranger still was the sight of cattle being hoisted aboard a nearby ship by their necks. He watched as the animals made horrible sounds and expired in midair. Back under way, Preston chalked up his short visit to Africa as a turning point: his ship was far from home.

The captain of the *Roberts* was beginning to get that feeling as well. As the frigate sailed up the Yemeni coast, Rinn had received a sobering message from an old friend, now the captain of a minesweeper in the Gulf. U.S. forces were starting to find mines in the main shipping channel, the message said. If the *Roberts* were unlucky enough to discover one, the preferred course of action was to call the commander of the navy's Middle East Force and hope there was an explosive ordnance disposal (EOD) team available. You could also shoot a mine, the message said, but far from detonating the device, bullets usually just pierced its buoyancy tanks. The weapon would sink, still live, into the shadows of the shallow sea.

On 11 February, one month after departing American waters, DesRon 22 squadronmates anchored off Fujairah, a United Arab Emirates port city on the Gulf of Oman. Four U.S. ships were waiting for them: three frigates and a cruiser heading home. *Roberts* paired off with USS *Elrod* (FFG 55), and for three hours, the frigates' officers shared charts, documents, and advice. After a relatively calm January, the situation in the Gulf was turning for the worse.

Iran was starting to flex long-dormant aerial muscles. Many of its U.S.–built aircraft, purchased during the shah's reign and grounded after the revolution by a U.S.–led embargo on spare parts, were returning to the skies, thanks in part to the White House's Iran-Contra shipments of war materiel.[15] In early February a Phantom fired two missiles at a Liberian tanker in the Gulf, the first such attack in more than two years. They missed. But days later, Iranian pilots shot down three Iraqi fighter jets over the southern Gulf.[16]

There were no deconfliction protocols to keep Iranian forces from firing accidentally on American warships. For that matter, the deconfliction agreement with Iraq was hardly foolproof. On 12 February an Iraqi Tu-16 Badger streaked toward the USS *Chandler* (DDG 996), ignoring the destroyer's increasingly frantic wave-off calls. The skipper put a Standard missile on the rail, set the CWIS to auto-fire mode, and, as a last-ditch warning, popped a pair of defensive flares that burned white-hot arcs in the night sky. The Soviet-built bomber veered away—and fired two missiles that streaked off to explode somewhere in the darkness. Had the Iraqi been aiming at the *Chandler* and its convoy before it veered off? No one knew. For U.S. warships in the Gulf, the implications were clear: every airborne radar blip should be considered armed and dangerous.[17]

The *Elrod* passed along more than charts and advice. The *Roberts* took aboard Stinger antiaircraft missiles and two junior sailors trained to launch the shoulder-fired heat-seeking weapons. Stingers had gained fame in Afghanistan, where the mujahideen had used them to bring down Soviet helicopters. In the Gulf, they might provide a last-ditch shield against air attack.[18] The *Roberts* also took on rolled mats made of Kevlar, the bulletproof synthetic fiber. Like most small warships, *Perrys* carried little armor, and the rug-sized mats were hung around various vital equipment spaces to provide a thin but welcome layer of protection.[19]

Rinn was grateful for everything the *Elrod* could provide. When the turnover was complete, the ships weighed anchor and moved off, each crew bidding the other farewell from the rails. Then it was time for DesRon 22 to split up. Dyer passed out awards for the transit to the Gulf, pronouncing *Roberts* the winner of the gunnery and shiphandling contests as well as "Top Hand," the best overall performer. He bestowed a

Redman Tobacco ball cap upon Palmer, who cherished it as a prized possession. Dyer also sent a cap to Rinn, who secretly believed his crew deserved the other two titles as well, and was being denied them to salve the feelings of the other ships' crew members.[20]

On 13 February the *Roberts* arrived in the Earnest Will convoy assembly area, which encompassed miles and miles of open water in the Gulf of Oman. Commercial and naval ships of every nationality and every description milled about, some searching for their assigned escorts, others seeking shelter in any group they could find. Wags dubbed the area "the K-Mart parking lot."[21]

The *Roberts* dropped anchor for the night just a few hundred yards from a Soviet *Udaloy*-class cruiser, spitting distance in naval terms. The next morning, the cruiser's helicopter buzzed the frigate. Several U.S. sailors waved; the Soviet pilot returned the gesture. Preston, on deck, entertained the fleeting thought that the superpowers had spent billions of dollars and rubles for nothing. But a furious Rinn leaned out from the bridge wing and yelled at the .50-caliber gunners, who jumped to point their weapons at the enemy aircraft.[22] It was time to get serious. Two years of exercises would not compare in danger and stress to the frigate's first day in the Gulf.

SIMPLY GETTING INTO the shallow sea was a dicey proposition. The two-hundred-mile Strait of Hormuz was a classic naval choke point. The waterway squeezed past the Iranian mainland, narrowing to thirty-six miles as it made a hairpin turn around the Omani Peninsula. Its inbound and outbound shipping channels were narrower still: only two miles wide, separated by a two-mile "median strip."

A trip through the strait took a ship past Iranian air bases and naval stations, radar installations and powerboat havens. Perhaps even more ominous was the "Silkworm envelope," the swath of water covered by Iranian missile batteries. A Chinese copy of the Soviet radar-guided Styx, the Silkworm could sink a warship from forty miles away. Iran had never launched one in the strait, and the Reagan administration had publicly vowed to wipe the batteries from the earth if they did. But in the northern Gulf, a Silkworm had blinded the American captain of the *Sea Isle City*. And the Iranians had proven they didn't need missiles to wage their naval war. The burnt-out ship carcasses that lined the strait offered silent testimony to that.

In the early hours of 14 February 1988, the *Roberts* rounded up the two reflagged Kuwaiti ships that would form its convoy. One was MV *Townsend,* a 294,700-ton oil products carrier; the other, a 46,700-ton liquefied natural gas ship renamed *Gas Princess.* They were soon joined by the *Chandler,* which was fresh from its nerve-rattling encounter with the Iraqi Badger. Together, they formed the convoy designated EW88011, the eleventh Earnest Will escort mission of the year.[23]

They would not go alone into the strait. Overhead, an E-2 Hawkeye surveyed the airspace with its dorsal radar saucer, while an EA-6B Prowler electronic attack jet sniffed for the telltale emissions of enemy missiles. Some miles away, A-6 Intruder attack jets and F-14 Tomcat fighters circled over the Gulf of Oman, standing by to render aid.

To deal with any small Iranian ships, the convoy would have the temporary aid of a pair of Mk III patrol boats, the sixty-four-foot mainstays of barge operations at the Gulf's other end. A pair of oceangoing tugboats would lead the way, trolling for mines with half-inch steel cables festooned with bits of gear. Guided by small fins, the cables stretched behind the tugs in a fifty-yard "V" that trailed some feet below the surface. Their steel blades, rigged with explosive charges, were designed to snip a mine's tether, allowing it to bob to the surface and be destroyed. The navy had hired the tugs from the Kuwaiti Oil Transport Company in the wake of *Bridgeton's* mining. The ersatz minesweepers had found no mines at all in nine months, and their plodding progress limited the convoy's speed through the strait to about eight knots. Nevertheless, no convoy commander liked getting under way without them.[24]

Just before dawn, the *Roberts* fired up both gas turbines and went to general quarters. Down in CIC, the radar operators took note of their surroundings; there was an Iranian frigate lurking off the nearby Ras Shuratah shoal, and an Iranian C-130 airlifter on patrol far ahead.[25] The warships shepherded their reflagged charges past the lighthouse on Didimar, the canted hunk of rock that marked the beginning of the Strait of Hormuz. The transit would take nine hours.

In a small space behind the pilothouse, fire controlman John Preston hunkered down among the cases of electronic radar equipment and stared at the new Kevlar mats on the bulkheads. This was his regular general quarters station, a cramped and air-conditioned space where he fixed the occasional balky piece of gear. It was a fine place to ride out drills, close enough to the bridge to eavesdrop, but Preston usually longed to be in CIC manning a console instead of stuck up top playing Maytag repairman.

Not this time. For once, Preston was relieved to let someone else do the job. The lives of all his shipmates might well depend on the fire controlman on duty. "It may have been a cowardly reaction to the massive responsibility of protecting the ship, but I also knew that I would be sitting on those consoles later on and would have my share of worries," he wrote.

But by the time the convoy emerged in the Persian Gulf, Preston decided the trip wasn't any better in the radar shack: "Staying at general quarters for half the day, puckered up, thinking a Silkworm missile might have your name on it."[26]

Action soon picked up. The ships' aerial escort headed back to their aircraft carrier in the Arabian Sea. Not coincidentally, the *Roberts*'s radar soon picked up a pair of aircraft barreling south from Iran. In CIC the electronic-warfare operator bent to his scope. His computer digested the planes' electronic emissions and spit out a verdict: two hulking F-4 Phantom fighter jets.

The *Roberts*'s CIC team had practiced this scenario a hundred times. They had shot down scores of ghosts in the Point Loma simulators and had honed their skill against U.S. Air Force fighters off the coast of Massachusetts. Now, for the first time, it was real. The air traffic controller issued the standard radio call: "Unknown aircraft, you are approaching a U.S. Navy warship. Divert your course immediately." He received no response.

Rinn sent the ship to general quarters. The deep synthetic *bong-bong-bong* of the GQ alarm sent sailors scurrying around the ship, pulling on brown flash hoods and tucking pants into socks. Within minutes, the ship was ready for battle.

The captain ordered a missile readied for action. On the forecastle, the ten-ton launcher performed its mechanical dance, whirling to accept the white Standard missile that whisked onto the launch rail. Then the captain told the tactical action officer to illuminate the Phantoms with tracking radar. This was the modern naval equivalent of brandishing a sword.

Like many warships of the day, the *Roberts* carried two kinds of air-defense sensors. The long-range SPS-49(V)5 antenna revolved on its mast just abaft the pilothouse, sweeping a powerful electromagnetic beam through a dozen circles a minute. The ship's 1970s-era computer gathered up the faint echoes from an airborne fuselage and displayed range, speed, and heading. But for altitude data, and for the frequent pulses required for accurate gunnery, the ship carried two short-range tracking sensors: an egg-shaped pod atop the pilothouse and a stubby dish amidships. These radars pulsed several times a second, fast enough to guide a missile or the 76-mm shells from the ship's gun. To shoot down a plane, therefore, an operations specialist found it with the air-search radar and then locked it up with a tracking radar. A fire controlman would confirm the lock, and, upon the captain's order, depress the weapons-release button.

Every pilot of a jet-age fighter knew when he'd been painted by fire control radar. Cockpit instruments sounded gently when brushed by search beams, but beeped urgently when hit with tracking frequencies. The noise told the pilot that a fire controlman's thumb hovered over the missile-release button.

The Phantoms closed to a distance of twenty-one miles, just seconds away by missile flight. Then they veered off. The *Roberts* and its wards sailed on into a gathering thunderstorm.

Later in the night, the frigate's radar operator called out another contact. A single aircraft approached from the north. As before, radio calls went unanswered. But this time, the plane's emissions mystified the electronic-warfare operator.

For the third time in a day, the ship went to general quarters. Rinn studied the radar screen and ordered a missile onto the rail. "Lock him up," he told the tactical action officer. But the electronic warning that had turned away the Iranian F-4s had no effect on this mystery plane. Ignoring the radar blasts and the urgent calls from the *Roberts*'s air traffic controller, the aircraft bore in from the north.

Once again, a fire controlman's finger waited near the release stud. Rinn continued to issue orders through the tactical action officer, as CIC doctrine prescribed and as the *Roberts* had always practiced. But the captain moved over to stand behind the enlisted man's shoulder. Rinn wanted no misunderstandings and no accidents.

The *Roberts* was allowed to fire if fired upon, but could not take the first shot without authorization from Middle East Force headquarters in Manama, Bahrain. Rinn told a radioman to call in. When the command ship answered, the *Roberts* requested permission to fire. "Wait one," the answer came back.

The green blip of the mystery plane drew closer to the center of the radar operator's round screen. Seconds ticked by. The captain weighed his options. Shoot blindly? Or risk sharing the *Stark's* fate?

The radio crackled again. "That's an American aircraft," the Middle East Force radio operator announced.

The frigate held its fire as the plane approached. An awful moment passed. The plane rumbled overhead and continued south.[27]

The aircraft turned out to be part of Eager Glacier, the CIA's secret effort to gather intelligence on Iran using U-2 spy planes, small business jets, and even helicopters.[28] Every U.S. warship that arrived in the Gulf was supposed to get a secret message describing the operation, but the *Roberts* had not yet received it. The spy plane's pilot had detected the frigate's radar, but decided to handle things by calling his boss, who called his boss, and so on up the chain of command until the message started coming back down through the navy. The decision nearly cost the intel pilot his life.

"That guy was lucky," said Raymond, the operations specialist. "I will never forget the look on Commander Rinn's face: 'Oooo, that was a close one.' He was happy we all did our job. And he was, I think, just as nervous as everybody else was—pride and nervousness at the same time. Everything worked fine.

"After that, we watched everything more closely. It could be monotonous, especially to a young crew, but now, everybody paid a lot of attention. This was not the Med or the Atlantic."[29]

For those who had somehow failed to get the picture, the ship's executive officer, Lt. Cdr. John Eckelberry, spelled things out in the Plan of the Day, the photocopied sheet of schedules, reminders, and instructions that got tacked up in the ship's workspaces every morning. "From now on, we are minutes or seconds from combat," the XO wrote. "Each man on SBR is responsible for his own battle gear." This included helmet or hat, long-sleeved shirt or jacket, life vest, gas mask and filters, and flash hood. "Keep it with you or at your GQ station. You may wear it on your hip or keep it with you as you work and sleep." And don't forget ship's policy on personal cassette recorders, Eckelberry reminded them: only one ear at a time, and never on watch.[30]

The *Roberts* captain and crew had passed a test—hardly their first, and certainly not their last. Their first day in the Gulf showed just what kind of steel nerves would be required in the next few months.

CHAPTER EIGHT

In Harm's Way

The *Roberts* had been scheduled to go on to Kuwait with the convoy, but a change of orders turned it around and sent it hustling back out of the strait. It was part of duty in the Gulf: plans changed, and not infrequently or with much notice. The frigate headed to the Gulf of Oman's "K-Mart parking lot," where it met up with the USS *Coronado* (AGF 11), a command ship dispatched from San Diego for duty as the Middle East Force (MEF) flagship. Under cover of darkness, the frigate shepherded the converted amphibious landing ship into the Gulf. An Iranian P-3 Orion—a slow, deadly U.S.–built patrol plane—came nosing southward, and the *Roberts* hit it with a blaze of tracking radar. "Have a nice day," the pilot radioed, turning away.[1]

The U.S. ships tied up at Bahrain, and the next day Rear Adm. Anthony A. Less helicoptered out to the frigate. Less had taken charge of U.S. operations in the region only a month earlier, but he was no rookie. From September through December 1987, Less had commanded the *Missouri* battleship group in the Gulf and the *Ranger* carrier group just outside it.

The MEF commander thanked the *Roberts* crew for delivering his command ship, but he had a more serious purpose as well. He described the missions they could expect over the next four months and the rules for carrying them out. Less informed his listeners that Gulf duty offered two basic types of operations. One was escorting convoys, and they already had some experience with that. The other was patrolling specific areas. In the waterway's northern reaches, the frigate would protect the special-operations barges that were tamping down Iranian attacks. To the east, it would track the Iranian warships and powerboats that swarmed near the Hormuz bottleneck. In the center—well, nothing much had happened in the Gulf's belly since the *Iran Ajr* had been caught laying mines there.

Less moved on to the rules of engagement. The *Roberts* was there to protect U.S.–flagged ships and enforce their right of free passage in international waters. Attacks on U.S. shipping were to be repelled, by deadly force if necessary. But assaults on foreign ships were a different matter. The rules forbade firing to defend anything without an American flag. This guidance came down from the White House, which was hip-deep in conflicting regional policies yet still hoped to avoid open hostilities. These rules could put U.S. sailors and aircrews in helpless witness to assaults on unarmed mariners. Even the rescue of foreigners was discouraged, though *Elrod* had wangled permission to take aboard two dozen survivors of a Christmas Day gunboat attack.

But Less noted that there was a gray area between shooting and standing idly, and he pushed his skippers to explore it. There was little the U.S. ships could do about Iraq's air attacks on unarmed merchants. But a clever and determined captain might harass Iranian forces without drawing undue international attention. The admiral summed up the situation like this: "Hey, guys, we're at war, the threat's always there. We'll support you to the hilt. In the meantime, protect your ship, protect your crew. Make sure we stifle and stymie anything that's going on in this area. You've got radars, you've got systems, you're looking at ships that are less than friendly. Don't let 'em lay mines; don't let 'em attack friendly shipping. The rest of the time, you're going to get assignments on what ship you're escorting and where you're going. Carry out your duties. That's essentially it. You're big guys now; pay attention."[2]

Rinn was delighted with this policy. He interpreted it as "distract and bother, but don't get the U.S. Navy in an embarrassing position." Like most American skippers, the captain of the *Roberts* regarded his Iranian counterparts as murderous bullies. It gave him great pleasure to think of breaking up an attack and "ruining an Iranian skipper's day." He and his ship had done this once already.

IT HAD HAPPENED during the *Coronado* mission. Somewhere west of the Sirri oil fields, the *Roberts*'s surface radar picked up an interesting pattern of blips. Rinn had ordered his SH-60 helicopter into the air for a closer look, and within a half hour, the aviators confirmed his suspicions: an Iranian frigate was stalking a U.S. tanker.

Rinn left the *Coronado* in the care of a nearby British destroyer, fired up his gas turbines, and headed off to investigate. Presently, the Iranian ship appeared over the horizon; the *Roberts* closed the gap. A lookout identified the ship from the name painted on its stern: *Alvand.*

The *Alvand* was one of Iran's four *Sa'am*-class frigates. Built for the shah by British shipwright Vosper, the 311-foot *Sa'ams* were the most potent warships in the Iranian fleet. Each of the 1,540-ton vessels packed a 114-mm naval gun on the forecastle, a pair of 35-mm machine guns, and a triple-canister launcher for Sea Killer antiship missiles.[3] Like the *Perry* frigates, the *Sa'ams* were swift, nimble ships propelled by gas turbines. The *Roberts* would soon become intimately familiar with their capabilities.

By the looks of things, the Iranian captain was maneuvering to fire on the tanker. The *Roberts* pressed on, pulling to within a mile or so of *Alvand*'s stern. The Iranian seemed to hesitate, and then punched his own engines. The *Roberts* turned with him, and a dogfight in two dimensions was on.

The ships turned this way and that, jockeying for tactical advantage. It was a form of contention as old as triremes and as modern as the jet turbines that screamed in the frigates' engine rooms. Each commander strove to keep his ship where his weapons could strike the enemy, while keeping the enemy from doing the same.

Advancing technology had not rendered this a simple game, and naval warfare remained as much an intellectual challenge as a duel of horsepower and caliber. Though captains no longer sought the wind for motive power, the sea still harbored rocks and shoals and currents. And the shipboard introduction of electronics and rocketry brought their own constraints. An effective ship turned to keep its radio masts from blocking its fire-control radar beams and maintained sufficient distance from its prey to allow a missile to arm in flight. The wind itself was far from irrelevant. A stiff breeze could affect the accuracy of gunfire and missiles. It could even turn defensive antimissile flares, whose magnesium cores burned at thousands of degrees, into a hazard for an unlucky ship.

For more than three hours the ships wheeled around each other, matching wits and machinery. Their chessboard was measured in miles, yet at times the two crews were just a few hundred yards apart, their machine gunners nearly eyeball to eyeball. In this duel the *Roberts* enjoyed a distinct advantage over the *Alvand*. The American ship could hit targets in most of a 360-degree circle, thanks to its forecastle-mounted missile launcher and 76-mm gun amidships. But the Iranian ship had a far narrower field of fire, because the U.S.–led arms embargo had deprived it of missiles.[4]

Around 7:30 PM, the Iranian captain decided he'd had enough. The *Alvand* broke off and retired to the northeast. The tanker, a Greek ship named *Tandis,* sailed on unmolested. The *Roberts* rejoined the *Coronado* and escorted the command ship safely to Bahrain.

Rinn was exultant. Turning away high-speed jets was tense, but beating the pants off another skipper—well, that was just plain fun. "No easy kill tonight," he wrote to his brother. "Crew on a high—captain's got balls!!"[5]

The *Roberts'*s first tangle with an Iranian warship had gone well. But it would not be the last, and eventually, the Iranians would come after the *Roberts* two at a time.

THE ISLAND OF Abu Musa sits near the main shipping channel in the eastern Gulf, where the three-square-mile chunk of rock dominates the entrance to the Strait of Hormuz. Iran's Pasdaran paramilitaries had seized the disputed island early in the war—it was also claimed by the United Arab Emirates (UAE)—and established a radar station and harbor facilities for more than a dozen armed Boghammar powerboats. Aided by radar pickets on two oil platforms to the west, the speedboat crews had little difficulty homing in on slow-moving merchant ships.[6] When the tanker war heated up, the waters around Abu Musa became perilous.[7]

Less was doing his best to fix that. He kept a warship or two on patrol in the area, where they could track Iranian ships, assist the convoys that passed by, and break up attacks. The admiral dispatched the *Roberts* to Abu Musa—and, unknowingly, toward a rematch with *Alvand.*

The frigate's first patrol mission began with a poor omen. Once clear of the harbor, Rinn had his gunners fire a few rounds from each of the ship's guns. It was an old habit, intended as much to clear liberty-induced cobwebs from sailors' heads as to ensure the guns were working. The

25-mm and .50-cals worked fine, rattling slugs into the water, but the 76-mm main gun jammed. "Lousy time for gun casualty," Rinn wrote.[8]

The gunners' mates investigated, pulling cowlings from the complicated mechanism that drew the two-foot shells from a rotating magazine. One of the guide rails had bent. There were no spares aboard. Someone summoned Chief Dave Walker from his haunt in engineering. Walker was no expert on the 76-mm gun, but he had a knack with broken machines, and he climbed up to have a look. After some inspection, he fetched a towel rod from the chiefs' quarters and carefully bent it to mimic the damaged part. When he put it in place, the shells rode into place like clockwork. The jury-rigged solution broke all sorts of regulations, Walker acknowledged later, "but we were in the combat zone, and it had to be fixed."[9]

Once on station near Abu Musa, Rinn made a beeline for an Iranian oiler named *Bushehr.* The five-thousand-ton oiler served as mother ship to Pasdaran powerboats and as a picket in the shipping channel. The *Roberts* approached the larger ship, allowing the Iranians to study its gun and missile launcher through binoculars. He wanted the Iranian captain to think hard before starting anything violent. "Now we know each other," Rinn wrote to his brother.

Some hours after dawn, the radar operators on the *Roberts* spotted a warship beyond the northern horizon, and Rinn sent the Seahawk for a closer look. It was the *Alvand,* and its skipper was apparently still smarting from his recent encounter with the *Roberts.* As the SH-60 hove into view, the Iranian commander silenced his radios and radars, turned his bow toward the American frigate, and accelerated to twenty knots. Rinn sent his crew to general quarters and cranked up his own gas turbines. The warships approached each other in a forty-knot game of naval chicken.

The *Roberts* painted the *Alvand* with both fire control radars, and Rinn sent a radio message for good measure: "Unknown vessel, this is a U.S. Navy warship. Divert your course. I intend to stand on." The Iranian hung in for several minutes, and presently the *Roberts's* forward lookout could distinguish the water creaming at *Alvand's* bow. But the Iranian skipper lost his nerve at three miles' distance, veered off, and disappeared over the horizon. Rinn let him go.

But the *Roberts* was waiting for the Iranian ship the next morning, thanks to a bit of detective work by the radar operators. At the suggestion of XO Eckelberry, the combat team had dug through the ship's electronic memory, looking for patterns in the *Alvand's* behavior. They discovered that the Iranian captain began each day's patrol at dawn in the same place. The *Roberts* mounted a stakeout. When the *Alvand* appeared at 5:30 AM, the U.S. warship began to shadow it from the horizon.

The work paid off a few hours later. The *Alvand* closed on an unescorted tanker and radioed orders to heave to and prepare to be boarded. This kind of thing happened every day, and the situation could go several ways. Sometimes the Iranians would send a whaleboat over to search the target ship for Iraq-bound arms and military equipment. But sometimes the radio call was just a ploy: once the merchant stopped, the warship opened fire.

The *Roberts,* whose crew had been monitoring the conversation on the bridge radio, accelerated toward the tanker and frigate. The *Alvand* warned the U.S. warship to stand clear, and when Rinn ignored the warning and stood on, the Iranian bugged out to the northeast. Score one for Detective *Roberts.*

The American frigate was just getting warmed up. A few days later, the teleprinter in the ship's radio room rattled with reports that a trio of Boghammars and a *Sa'am* frigate had been spotted in the Hormuz strait, headed southwest toward Abu Musa. Rinn doused his running lights, shut down his radars, and set out to hunt. By 4:30 AM, the U.S. ship had settled about three nautical miles off the Iranian frigate's quarter. It was a perfect tactical position: near enough to keep an eye on his quarry, distant enough for a Standard missile to arm itself in flight. "Got him!" Rinn crowed to his brother. "No higher honor!"

For half a day, the *Roberts* stayed glued to the tail of the *Sahand.* The Iranian captain changed course several times in hopes of shaking his American shadow, but to no avail. Around 3:00 PM, his patience snapped. He hauled his frigate around, pointed his bow southeast, and headed for the *Roberts* at twenty-eight knots. The duel was on: guns and gas turbines at five miles. Rinn cranked up his engines and veered to meet his adversary. The Iranian frigate approached, its bow riding a bloom of white water. The *Sahand's* skipper seemed to be made of sterner stuff than his colleague aboard the *Alvand,* and the gap between the ships closed to less than a mile.

Rinn waited, waited—and then turned sharply to starboard. The *Roberts* heeled hard, letting the *Sahand* speed by. The U.S. frigate kept turning, rudder straining against the sea, until a full circle put it back on the Iranian's tail. *Sahand* jinked north and then cut back hard to starboard, crossing the bow of the *Roberts* and heading east. Rinn took his ship northward and then doubled back to face the *Sahand.* The Iranian turned northeast across the *Roberts*'s bow once more, and the American frigate barreled through its foe's dissipating wake. The *Sahand* captain finally ran out of ideas. He gave up and steadied on a northeast course. The *Roberts* settled back into its trailing position.

Rinn was ecstatic. "This moment [is] one of the most exciting I've had in the Navy," he wrote.

Around 8:00 PM, Middle East Force called the *Roberts* off the hunt, instructing the frigate to drop back over the horizon and track the *Sahand* by radar. The message praised the ship's work and included a word of warning against being too provocative.[10] Rinn shrugged. "Tomorrow is another day," he wrote. The next time *Roberts* tangled with *Sahand,* the U.S. crew would need help.

By the first day of March, Rinn was starting to worry about fuel. The high-speed duels with *Alvand* and *Sahand* had burned off oil by the ton, and the *Roberts* had just wrapped up a quick escort mission, ushering a single reflagged tanker through the strait. The big tanks in his engine room were down to 42 percent, raising the uncomfortable possibility that the frigate might get into a tussle it couldn't finish.

Rinn sent a message to the *Coronado* asking for advice. "Hope they are paying attention," he wrote his brother. "I'm starting to worry. Prolonged surface engagement or bad weather could be problem."[11]

Two hours past midnight, *Roberts* crew members spotted *Sahand* about fifty miles off Abu Musa. The Iranian seemed to have learned from Rinn's playbook: he extinguished his ship's lights and radar, made a twenty-five-knot rush toward the American ship, and painted the *Roberts* with fire-control radar. This guy was definitely more aggressive than the *Alvand.*

The radar pulses tripped the electromagnetic sensors on the *Roberts*'s mast, touching off an alarm in CIC. The electronic warfare team bent to their computers, which identified the Iranian emission: it was the guidance system for the Italian-built Sea Killer, a sea-skimming missile with a fifteen-mile range. This was a bit unexpected. *Alvand* had carried no missiles; was *Sahand* better armed? The *Roberts* replied by returning the favor, locking up *Sahand* with tracking radar of its own. But it began to look like this engagement was going to involve more than dueling radar beams. Rinn ordered the 76-mm gun readied for action. Two-foot rounds moved from a rotary tray up the screw feeder. The ships sped past each other and began to jockey for position. So far, so good.

The engagement took a new twist when *Sahand* broke off to pursue a container ship that had appeared in the channel. The frigates were some miles apart at this point, and over the radio the *Roberts* crew heard *Sahand* order the ship to stop. The merchant was registered in the Iraqi port of Basra—not a good omen—and the *Roberts* was, for the moment, too far away to help. Rinn had his radioman call for help.

An answer soon arrived from the French frigate *Montcalm,* some fifteen miles distant. The U.S. and French crews had met a few days earlier when they dropped anchor and exchanged small groups of sailors for dinner. Rinn and a few officers spent a fine evening on the foreign ship, enjoying crusty bread and trading tactical tips. Now, *Montcalm* heeded the U.S. frigate's call—and just in time.

The French warship appeared on the horizon just as *Sahand* lowered a whaleboat to the water. Clearly, a boarding party was headed over to the container ship. *Roberts* and *Montcalm* firmed up their plans via flashing light signals and closed on the Iranian from different directions. Rattled, the skipper of *Sahand* recalled his whaleboat and sent the merchant on its way. The allied warships steadied up about three miles off the Iranian's stern, one to port, the other to starboard. *Montcalm* kept up the tail for a few hours; *Roberts* dropped back to eight miles' distance and stuck there for a day. *Sahand* stopped no more ships.

Two days later, with fuel reserves down to 39 percent, Rinn got the order he was looking for: break off and go fill 'er up. The message specified no tanker for the rendezvous—simply a time and a location: off the tip of the Omani Peninsula, just fifty miles from the Iranian coast. That was odd.

The frigate presently dropped anchor at the appointed place. A thick mid-afternoon haze settled over the water. Not long afterward, the bridge-to-bridge radio crackled. "This is MV *Yusr*," said an accented voice. "I come along your port side now, *Roberts*." A small black-hulled tanker with a beige deckhouse and red stack glided into view. Inflatable Yoko-hama bumpers dangled along its sides.

"Any idea who these guys might be?" Rinn asked Eckelberry.

"No, sir," the XO responded.

The captain of the mystery tanker maneuvered his big ship expertly alongside the smaller frigate. The U.S. sailors exchanged lines and hoses with the mariners, who looked Asian, perhaps Chinese. As the hazy sun faded into the sea, 124,000 gallons of F-76 flowed from tanker to warship. When it was done, the tanker skipper collected a navy voucher from the *Roberts,* plus a dozen FFG 58 ball caps for his crew, and his ship slipped away into a starless night.

"Why," Rinn wrote to his brother, "do I feel like a chapter out of *Lord Jim?*"[12]

WHEN KEVIN FORD had a spare moment or two, he documented what he could of the deployment with his bulky video camera. The ship's chief cook and unofficial videographer, Ford had recently wrapped up a tape to send home to the *Roberts* families in Newport. His first video production featured scenes from the Mediterranean and the Suez passages and some footage from the Gulf. After an introduction by the captain, the tape cut to Ford himself. A compact, broad-backed figure with a straightforward look and a wisp of a mustache, Ford led the camera-man around the ship, describing things in a Rhode Island accent. He pointed out a shipmate who was patrolling the deckhouse in bullet-proof vest and rifle. "Ya see that sailuh, all dressed up like a soljuh? He's gahding the ship, making sure no bad guys come aboard while we're all out here."

The twenty-seven-year-old Ford was about as young as a navy chief could be. A native of East Providence, he had enlisted the day after he turned eighteen, seeking adventure and military service. He chose to become a cook—in navy argot, a mess management specialist—because he liked the hours. Cooks stood no duty watches and, on large ships at least, worked just three or four days a week, albeit in fifteen-hour shifts. But Ford was far from lazy. Possessed of a cheery acumen and a can-do attitude, he rose through the ranks as fast as the navy would let him take the advancement tests, and donned the khaki uniform of a chief after just nine years.

On the *Roberts* Ford ran a team of twelve cooks, plus the junior sailors lent to the kitchen as busboys. Together they served their roughly two hundred shipmates three meals a day—plus plenty of post-midnight snacks to boost morale during long nights. Ford also developed a knack for picking up extra jobs around ship: besides videographer, he was a member of the damage control training team and a line captain during underway replenishment.

Belowdecks, his camera found a mess cook in a T-shirt, who grinned, flexed, and laid a kiss on a bulging bicep. Another muscular fellow in a yellow lifejacket told the camera, "We're all out here doing okay. We can't wait to get back." A tall sailor with jug-handle ears looked up from a book. "I don't have anybody who really knows who I am," he said, in a matter-of-fact tone.

The video wound up with shot of Rinn in a thin olive sweater out by the exhaust stack. "It's February 28, 1988, and we're on Abu Musa patrol in the southeastern part of the Gulf. It's been a hotspot for the past two months, with about twenty ships coming under attack by rocket-propelled grenades. We've been on patrol for seven or eight days here, and I'm happy to say I think we've been instrumental in preventing any attack being conducted in the area." Ford edited the tape on his camera and mailed it off to Newport.

ONE REASON THINGS had gotten worse around Abu Musa was that the violence had largely been quashed in the northern Gulf. In fact, no merchant had come under fire there since November, and the credit belonged largely to the secret forces of Operation Prime Chance. Like cops shooing street thugs from the neighborhood, the army helicopters and navy patrol boats had forced the Iranian raiders to ply their deadly trade elsewhere.

But the unsteady peace was shattered on 5 March. Not long after midnight, the *Roberts* bridge radio crackled with dispatches from USS *John A.*

Moore (FFG 19), a frigate on patrol near the barge *Wimbrown VII.* A pair of Iranian speedboats was approaching, *Moore* reported. The frigate tried to warn them off with radio calls and then put two 76-mm shells into the water in front of the boats. The Boghammar drivers just poured on the speed. They whipped past the warship at forty-four knots, opening up with chattering machine guns. The frigate returned fire, sending nearly a hundred rounds after its nimble antagonists. The boats soon faded from radar, and the frigate gathered up bits of wreckage, but it was far from clear that the boats had been sunk.[13]

The *Moore's* skirmish was the first exchange of naval fire in the Gulf in three weeks, and Admiral Less quickly dispatched six of his sixteen ships to squelch the fighting. The *Roberts* was headed northwest at full speed. Rinn found the *Moore's* captain understandably exhausted but confident that he'd performed well.[14] The next morning, Less sent the *Moore* to Bahrain for a rest and put Rinn in charge of protecting the barges. "SBR's got the bag!" he wrote his brother. "Things are getting interesting."

The attack on the *Moore* came by sea, but the skies around the barges were even more full of peril. They seethed with warplanes. The geography of the northern Gulf funneled Iraqi strike jets southeast to their watery hunting grounds and drew Iranian fighters hungry for air-to-air battle. To the *Roberts,* every one of them might as well have had "frigate killer" painted on its nose.

The first night—6 March 1988—set the tone for two tense weeks. At three in the morning, a radar operator called up from CIC: "Iraqi Badger inbound, speed 330 knots, altitude 200 feet, CPA four miles." The last bit stood for "closest point of approach." The plane, a Soviet-built medium bomber, would pass within four miles of the *Roberts*—much too close for comfort. Rinn sent the ship to general quarters. The alarm bonged throughout the ship. Sailors rolled from their bunks and rushed to their stations. A Standard missile slid onto the launcher rail, and gunners switched the CIWS from manual to automatic.

The air traffic controller in CIC radioed the Badger pilot, warning him to divert his course or face deadly consequences. The Iraqi pilot was just nineteen miles away—a handful of seconds of missile flight—when he acknowledged *Roberts's* command and veered south to miss the frigate by less than a dozen miles.

At 5:30 AM the alarms sounded again, and a weary crew scrambled to GQ stations. This time it was a trio of Mirage F1s, screaming toward the ship at 385 knots, right down on the deck. They closed to twenty-three miles before turning away.[15]

And there was one more development. Sometime in the night, the *Roberts* had welcomed aboard a mysterious pair of small black helicopters. The call to flight quarters confounded sailors who knew that the ship's own aircraft was tucked snugly in its hangar. The mystery only deepened as two choppers approached the ship, their landing skids barely clearing the waves. Rotors whirring softly, the aircraft climbed up to land on the flight deck, both squeezing onto a platform that barely accommodated a ten-ton Seahawk. The pilots disembarked, and the deck crew tucked the tiny helicopters into the frigate's starboard hangar.

The new shipmates remained a mystery to most *Roberts* sailors, who knew them only as some sort of special-ops army aviators. They wore their hair long. They slept by day and flew at night, low and fast over the black water, night vision goggles clamped to their helmets. The *Roberts* was accustomed to running without lights, but went super-dark whenever the army guys had a mission. Sometimes the black helos took off with a load of rockets and landed with empty canisters. "A buddy of mine, Ron, asked them what they did one day," recalled Mike Tilley, a junior engineman, "and he said, 'Mind your own fucking business.' Just like that, point-blank. Ron said 'Sorry.' The guy said, 'No problem; just don't worry about it.'"[16]

The soldiers were, in fact, five pilots and four mechanics from the army's 160th Aviation Group (Airborne), the elite unit formed after the disastrous attempt to rescue U.S. hostages from Tehran in 1979. They flew AH-6 Little Bird helicopters, small and agile craft armed with 7.82-mm mini-guns and 2.75-inch rockets. They operated at night, lights out, with their landing skids just six feet above the waves. "You'll know you're too low when you get wet," their pilots told one another. They were nicknamed the Night Stalkers, and they were part of the secret Operation Prime Chance. Even aboard a warship, their identity was strictly need-to-know.[17]

For the next ten days, *Roberts* patrolled the waters around the barges. The crew dubbed the area Badger Alley. In just the first week, watchstanders warded off a dozen Iraqi Badgers, two Blinder bombers, and fourteen Mirage fighters. Iran's air force generally kept its distance, but the frigate's radar operators spotted Iranian C-130s, F-4s, F-14s, P-3s—even Bell AB-212 helicopters. And the frigate was doing some hunting of its own. During the day, the *Roberts's* Seahawk swept the area by sight and radar. At night, the army helos emerged from the hangar, lifted from the flight deck, and flew off to do their thing.

Rinn described the feeling a few weeks later. "The type of operation that we do over here is one of the most demanding physically and mentally that you can do . . . I think the saving grace and tribute to these guys is that we survive in that environment and do our jobs—fully aware all the time that we can go from a semi-relaxed environment to an absolutely hostile one ready to fight. It never goes away; it can't go away. That's our job."[18]

The job was always toughest on the midwatch. By longstanding naval custom, midnight duty lasted until four in the morning. The pilothouse was darkened, its fluorescent lamps extinguished, the better to keep eyes sharp for the unknown dangers beyond the ship's skin. Black came in shades and texture: obsidian sea, dusty sky, plastic instrument panels. Bulkheads and windscreens faded into the surrounding night.

Here and there, light pricked the void: the red letters of gauges, the running lights of ships, gas flares atop unseen derricks. From time to time there were streaks of tracer fire and the quick blooms of antiaircraft shells. Far off, lightning flickered, the tocsin of a coming thunderstorm.

A dozen watchstanders went about their business in near-silence, just the way Rinn wanted it. Lookouts screwed binoculars to their eyes. The watch quartermaster studied his charts for shoals; the officers bent to the rubber visor of the surface-search radar, or eyed the spectral green images of night vision goggles. Any blip on the radar screen could be an armed ship, boat, or aircraft looking for things to shoot. The idea was unnerving enough during the day, when human sight could help sort things out; at night it could rattle the coolest crew.

A radar operator called out a contact: an Iraqi Badger, inbound. The radio operator warned the pilot off, but the jet was less than thirty miles away when it finally turned to port. Under a brilliant quarter moon, the bridge crew watched a missile flare beneath the jet's wing. The rocket motor ignited, transected the dark sky, and hit its target. Flames rose above the silhouetted shape of a tanker, well short of the horizon. The helmsman drove the ship onward, leaving a trail in the Gulf's pale green bioluminescence, tracing endless fourteen-by-seven-mile boxes in the dark water.

Fatigue dogged the bridge watch. They might have grabbed an hour's sleep before coming on duty, but each had worked a full day before dusk and would work another after dawn. And yet the watch demanded closer attention at night; darkness concealed the dangers of the enemy, and the sea. Even more than in daytime, the sailors on the bridge cradled their shipmates sleeping below. So the watchstanders drained mug after mug of coffee, watched the passing Gulf traffic, and, bored, half-wished for something to happen. They indulged in wry, clipped conversation, or nibbled on welcome gifts from the galley: a late-night plate of chocolate-chip cookies or an early batch of breakfast rolls. From time to time the radio squawked, breaking the quiet with a burst of static. Most of the messages were fully routine, the expected traffic in a crowded sea. But every so often a high manic voice would break from the speaker: "Hee hee hee! Filipino monkey!" No one knew who the caller was, or what he meant by his strange message. It became part of the background, just another reminder that the ship was in foreign waters.

Ennui mixed with apprehension; the resulting brew could make standing watch just a bit giddy. Mike Roberts recalled taking the signalman's watch one night. "It was black as hell out," the petty officer said,

and the bridge was dark like the chart table light was out. I stood there trying to adjust to the dark, when some anti-aircraft tracers silhouetted a gang of guys over at the chart table. The whole bridge crew was just standing there, silently, staring at the chart. I went over to see what it was all about and found that the previous watch had very carefully penned a "W" in front of OMAN. We all just stood there and quietly stared at the word for awhile. Then, without saying anything, we just split off and went back to our stations.[19]

The quartermasters, who tracked the ship's position in neat pencil lines, wore through one chart, and then a replacement. The bridge watchstanders drummed their fingers and waited for their relief.

Day or night, the rest of the crew had their own problems. Most could be chalked up to the Gulf climate: hot, humid, and dusty. Sand and dust shrouded radio masts and radar antennae, clouding the frigates' electronic eyes. Airborne grit dust clogged the seals on the big SPS-49 radar, which leaked big globs of muddy oil down onto the sailors manning .50-cals on the deck below. The engineers wrapped cheesecloth around air intakes and changed it almost daily. Frustrated aviation mechanics struggled to clean the dirt from the crevices of their aircraft. Even the warm water played havoc with a ship built to fight in the cool Atlantic Ocean. It took more time and fuel to distill hundred-degree seawater into drinkable fluid, and algae built up in the intakes. Water-cooled systems fared poorly, including the frequency converters that turned 60Hz electricity into the 400Hz variety required by the ship's weapons.[20]

"The hot sticky days turned into hot sticky weeks," Preston wrote. "Every day I was glad we had discovered Freon. Without air conditioning, I would have died in the Persian Gulf."

The pace and the conditions wore on everyone. People lost weight; Ford, despite his hours in the kitchen, was twenty pounds slimmer by mid-March. The officers had it particularly bad. Their assigned duties, plus drills, plus watchstanding, plus taking care of their sailors yielded far too little rest.[21] "You don't get eight hours' sleep. You get four or five here and there, but you find you do without a lot of sleep," Glenn Palmer said. "There's a lot of tension, there's a lot of pressure, and you just sort of live on a high."[22]

Commanding officers sometimes got even less sleep than their subordinates. A running joke among skippers held that command tours generally lasted eighteen months because you just couldn't stay awake much longer than that. And Rinn was one of those captains who loved to prowl his ship at all hours, surprising engineers at 3:00 AM or just sitting in the dark on the bridge, fostering the perception that The Skipper Never Sleeps. But in the Gulf, this propensity, combined with the hectic pace, frequently left Rinn exhausted. One morning, just after dawn, he started a letter to his brother. "This place is crazy," he wrote, and fell asleep atop the bed's undisturbed covers, still wearing his uniform khakis.[23]

Rinn tried to get by with catnaps but occasionally fell asleep standing up.[24] Eckelberry finally stepped in after the captain chewed out the bridge watch for failing to alert him to a radar contact. "Sir, we did call you—three times," the XO said. "You've got to cut that out." Abashed, Rinn apologized to the watchstanders. He admonished them not to let him slumber through anything again. "If that happens, send somebody down. Drag me out if you have to. God, don't be intimidated."[25]

His officers preferred their captain to simply get more rest, and so they plotted to keep his unconscious hours undisturbed. Someone rigged his cabin door with a "traffic light," a brass box the size of a soap bar that glowed green for awake, red for asleep. Only Ens. Rob Sobnosky dared disobey; the CIC officer had orders to wake the captain whenever a strange ship approached. The rest of the wardroom dubbed him "Red Light."[26]

The conspiracy eventually gathered the entire crew, who began passing the word whenever Rinn put his head down. The announcement "set condition Circle Zebra," a play on damage control conditions, went around the ship via sound-powered headsets. The idea was to keep things quiet—dog the hatches gently, easy on the course changes, no loud maintenance. CIC watchstanders used the door near the sonar console instead of the one that opened next to the skipper's cabin. It was some weeks before Rinn discovered his crew's well-intentioned conspiracy of silence.[27]

AMID IT ALL, the ship kept up Sorensen's training routine: every four hours, a new watch, a new team on duty, a new damage control drill. The mock situations were as realistic as possible; from time to time the engineers would bleed smoke from a generator into a space so the firefighting teams could practice in obscured conditions.[28]

"There's nothing worse than having the duty late at night, and your section leader has a bug up his butt to do these drills," said Jim Muehlberg, an electronics technician second class. "And you wind up doing a fire drill at midnight. And you've got the four to eight [AM] watch."[29]

But even all the drills, all the work, all the time at battle stations couldn't fill all the hours at sea.

Official working hours ended at 5:00 PM, after which came dinner. At 6:00 PM, the ship broadcast its very own nightly news program, live and quite unrehearsed from the broom-closet workspace of the ship's interior communications technician. Kevin Ford, who handled the sports roundup, traded wisecracks with fellow newsreader Senior Chief Storekeeper Earl Crosby Jr. Even with all the joking around, the closed-circuit program was the crew's main source of information about the world beyond their hull.

Sailors with no pressing tasks might hang out for a few hours on the mess deck, where a television showed selections from the videotape library: hundreds of movies, sitcom episodes (*ALF*), and TV dramas (*L.A. Law*). There was usually a game of hearts or Monopoly going, or just knots of sailors sitting on plastic swivel-seats and shooting the bull. Some of the crew wrote letters home, or answered mail from the two grade-school classes the ship had adopted as pen pals.

Mail was the sweetest escape aboard ship, a breath of the faraway familiar. "When mail call goes down, the work day just about ends," said Dick Fridley, a boatswain's mate first class. "You let them get their mail. You don't bother them. You let them go where they want to go and then relax and listen to their tapes and watch their videos. . . . That's when they're spending their time with their families."[30] But tinfoil packages of cookies or cling-wrapped fudge were shared, lest unfortunate things befall the addressee.

For more urgent matters, there were telegrams. On 1 April a message arrived from Newport, addressed to Glenn Palmer, reporting the birth of his fourth child. The combat systems officer was overjoyed to hear that mother and infant were doing fine—and yet the separation made it the worst moment Palmer had endured since leaving home. Mercifully, perhaps, duty soon distracted him. "Right after it got there, we had a helicopter that came close to the ship," he recalled, "and I was right back on the console in the combat information center."[31]

In late March a pair of *Roberts* engineers had taken pen in hand to write to the editors of the *Wisner News Chronicle,* a Nebraska newspaper. The small-town paper had become regular reading in the engineering spaces, thanks to a shipmate whose mother had taken out a subscription for her son. The *News Chronicle* featured headlines like "Persons Interested In Housing For Elderly Should Contact Clarence Schmitt," and had become a crew favorite, passed around until the graying pages were torn, grease-stained, and soft as rags.

"Dear Editor," the two engineers wrote,

We are currently serving aboard USS Samuel B. Roberts *in the Persian Gulf. One of our shipmates, David Claus, is from Pilger, and receives your paper almost every "mail call." All of us enjoy reading it, because it helps us "escape" the gulf for a short time. We are engineers and concern ourselves with keeping the ship moving and the lights turned on. So for us, things can quickly become boring and routine rather quickly, but after reading several of your newspapers, we feel that we are becoming part of your community. We are also waiting for the next editions. (Go Lady Gators!) I'm sure you can understand our meaning by us being eight thousand miles from home.*

Our deployment is only half over, and it seems like an eternity, but the Navy has given us port visits in Palma, Spain, a quick stop in Djibouti, East Africa, then on to the Persian Gulf, where we have had liberty in Bahrain. While in the gulf, we have seen things like Iraqi aircraft, and Russian ships and aircraft, along with that of our allies. A sister ship to us found an Iranian gunboat drifting. We had it in tow for a few hours, until we passed it to another American warship.

Things here for the most part are quiet, and we believe we aren't in any real danger as long as we do our jobs and remain alert. If anyone would like to write us (or send cookies) we would be more than happy to write back. Thank you for your time.

> *Sincerely,*
> *GSM2(SW) Randy Tatum and HT2 Ted Johnson*[32]

Many found escape in exercise, pumping iron on the ship's weight machines or riding the stationary bike. Out on the flight deck, Chief Engineer Gordan Van Hook and Gas Turbine Chief Dave Walker led daily calisthenics—"snipercise," they called it. You could even jog on the miniature airfield if you could endure a left turn every ten paces.

And an enterprising crew could carve out time for fun, even in a war zone. Every month or so, Ford's cooks set up barbeque stands on the flight deck—"steel beach picnics," the crew called them. "Just being able to eat back there, relax, listen to music, talk to people you haven't seen in a couple days—it just relaxes you," said Fridley, the boatswain's mate.[33]

Mike Tilley, in particular, knew how to take relaxation to the limit. When one steel beach picnic was declared a no-uniform zone, the young seaman showed up without a stitch of clothing. The engineman striker from Missouri had a knack for trouble. During precomm duty in Norfolk, he'd been cited for having an altered identification; when the ship visited the Bahamas, he'd helped set adrift someone's dory. Rinn had no time for troublemakers, but there was something about the junior sailor that showed promise, and the captain had let him off with some stern words. And when Tilley joined the burger line au naturel, Rinn just laughed— and had a chief send him below to get dressed. "We're in an environment where twenty-four hours a day we have to be ready," Rinn told a visiting reporter. "We can get by with a barbecue even though we're in a tough situation, but everybody has to know that within two or three minutes they've got to get that barbecue over the side and into their battle station."

In early March, cryptic missives began appearing in Rinn's cabin.

I walked in my cabin one day and there's a note stuck to my mirror that said, "Beware the Ides of March." And every time I went to the bridge, there was a note on my chair that said, "Beware the Ides of March."

So I said, "What the hell is going on around here?" It's not a lot, but it's there, and I'm getting the sense: who's screwing around with me? It's the XO or someone, and I have no clue. I'm not going to go and ask, "What the hell's going on?"

But I think I did bring it up in the wardroom at lunch one day. Lunchtime at the wardroom was a great social event for me, and the rule was, I would never discuss work, talk business. And if I did, I would apologize and say, "I'm sorry." So I asked one day, "Does anybody know what's going on?" and they said, "No, no."

So, lo and behold, we're on the bridge one day and five Iraqi Mirages go by. We've got a live missile on the rail and we're doing twenty-five knots, and the Iraqis go by and we track, and they do what we tell them to do, and they go away. Eleven-thirty, lunchtime, and everybody goes down to the wardroom. I'm on the bridge, and the XO says, "Captain, are you coming down?"

"Start without me, I'll be there."

Ten minutes go by, and the intercom rings, and they say, "Captain, are you coming?" I said, "Yes, start without me."

Five minutes later, it rings again. "We've got something special."

And so I said, "Okay, I'm coming." Nobody ever bothered me like this so—stupid—I get up and I go down to the wardroom.

We're twenty-five miles off the Iraqi coast, we're running around with live missiles on the rail, we're in modified Condition Zebra, we are a full-up round ready to fight—and here's my entire wardroom in togas. Hail Caesar! They've got wreaths around their ears. I took one look and I started laughing so hard I fell over one of the chairs and onto the floor.

Later on, they said, "We were sure glad you laughed when you came in that room."

It was tremendous. That was the kind of attitude about them. It was a really good bunch of guys.[34]

On 18 March the *Roberts* relinquished its northern patrol duties and its coterie of army aviators and headed southeast for a well-deserved port visit in Bahrain. It would be the crew's first liberty since entering the Gulf, and it would be a blessed relief from hidden mines, hostile speedboats, and missile-flinging warplanes. Rinn celebrated with his first full night's sleep in weeks.

The frigate tied up next to a garbage scow at Sitrah pier in Manama, and sailors streamed over the brow. For many, the first stop was the phone booths pierside, where three-minute calls to the United States cost a wallet-scorching eleven dollars. Then they hit the whitewashed desert town, savoring beer and pizza at the navy canteen, haggling for souvenirs in the souks. They bought hammered gold jewelry by the ounce, rugs from afar, and the traditional Arab headgear that sailors called the "tablecloth and fan belt."[35]

Fire Controlman Preston purchased a gold Seiko watch for his girlfriend, Shelley, and tried to relax. The long weeks on his CIC console had tied him in knots. He'd heard shipmates express frustration with the rules of engagement and talk about how they wished their ship could be free to fight back. Once in a while he'd even voiced such sentiments himself. That scared him.

"What was I turning into?" Preston wrote later. "I know I just wanted to go home, just like everyone else on the ship did, and if that meant being involved in all-out combat, then let's take our chances and possibly set a new order in the Gulf." Preston had to consciously remind himself on watch that he was "still a rational, logical, human being and that by my actions I could mess up everything some high-paid civilian and military decision makers were trying to do over here."

It didn't seem to do much good to try to talk about the pressure. He'd tried, once or twice, to describe what it felt like to sit at the missile console as an armed aircraft bore in. He wanted his shipmates to feel the fear, the exhilaration, the anger of knowing just how close the *Roberts* had come to "kill or be killed." But no one wanted to hear it, or if they did, they blew it off like it was nothing. "Maybe it was their way of coping with something they had very little control over. I stopped telling people after a while," Preston wrote.

But with ten weeks to go in the Gulf, he wondered whether he was going to keep it together. He worried that "I was going to flip out and maybe shoot when I wasn't supposed to, or worse, not shoot when I should have."[36] He could not have known that the *Roberts*'s patrols would end much sooner than that.

ON 22 MARCH the *Roberts* weighed anchor, test-fired its guns, and headed back to the war zone. The frigate was slated for several weeks of convoy duty, starting with the mission designated EW88018.

Over the three-day weekend, violence had flared again. Iraqi warplanes had bombed two Norwegian supertankers, killing 90 percent of their sailors, and Iranian forces had hit another seven merchants.[37] Even the weather had turned nasty. The *Roberts* headed into a desert *shamal,* battering eastward through fifteen-foot waves as sailors fell from their bunks and DC gear skittered from its racks.[38]

The convoy was already assembling in the Gulf of Oman. By the time *Roberts* arrived in the K-Mart parking lot, the USS *Reuben James* (FFG 57) had corralled the merchants: *Gas Princess;* the 290,000-ton supertanker *Middletown;* and—rarity of rarities—an honest-to-God unreflagged American ship, the 36,000-ton tanker *Courier*.[39]

The five-ship group got under way on 25 March, accompanied as usual by various ships and aircraft. Two minesweeping tugs, *Hunter* and *Striker,* led the way. Next came the *Middletown,* a double-hulled giant that stood the best chance of absorbing a mine without fatal consequences. *Courier* trailed it about a mile back. Last in line, as far away as its captain could be persuaded to stay, was the *Gas Princess.* Its spherical tanks held liquid natural gas at minus-260 degrees Fahrenheit, giving *Princess* the look of a seagoing banana split. But no one laughed; the potential energy bottled up inside was equivalent to that of a small nuclear bomb.[40] The *Reuben James* brought up the rear, ready to shoo off any Iranians who tried to sneak up from behind.

The tugs led the convoy through the strait and then broke off; a pair of fighter planes far above returned to the carrier *Enterprise* in the Gulf of Oman. But the convoy retained several uninvited participants: four merchants, none under U.S. flag. They tagged along, huddling close, hoping to sail through the danger zone under the convoy's protective wing. Some of the ships sported real American flags; others merely ran up the crew's best attempts at vexillogical forgery. Rinn had become accustomed to maritime hitchhikers flying red-white-and-blue banners with four stars or ten stripes.

They would jump in the line, and you were supposed to tell them to get out, but it was difficult to do. What were you going to do? They would ignore you.

I think everyone over there driving a destroyer or a frigate was very much averse to what the Iranians—and later the Iraqis when you got further up the line—were doing, so we tended to tell them to get out, and if they didn't, not do anything about it, and escort them. They really didn't cause problems. A lot of times, they'd tag on to the tail end of the formation. Other times, they'd sneak into a gap in the line, which made it even more difficult, and when they got to the point when they could peel off and go to their port, they'd simply turn and go.[41]

When Rinn was the convoy commander, he liked to put the *Roberts* in the middle of the line, where he could be reasonably safe from mines but able to react to any moving threat. The crew kept a live missile ready to go, pushed 76-mm rounds up below the breech, and scrutinized the radar screen. Any ship big enough to show up as a blip would get a stern message if it came within five miles: "You're standing into harm's way. We want you to stand clear." When nothing threatened, the *Roberts* would take a spin around the miles-long string of ships, just to reassure the merchant crews that their U.S. Navy sheepdog stood ready to drive away the wolves.

"The hardest part of the mission is that you have to stay ready 24 hours a day. There's no time, really, to let your guard down," Rinn told a trio of reporters who came aboard for a few days as part of the Pentagon-run media pool. "I'm never going to allow my ship to be shot at and hit." The *Stark*'s fate, he added, "is not lost on us."[42]

But there were always surprises. One day, the *Roberts*'s Seahawk spotted a twenty-one-foot boat headed for the convoy. When it repeatedly ignored radio calls, the frigate prepared for a confrontation. But from what the aviators could see, the two mariners on board weren't armed. Maybe they were Revolutionary Guard sailors testing the U.S. defenses, but maybe they were just fishermen in a hurry. So the pilot descended, and as the rotor blades whipped the seas into a furious chop, the little boat turned away and headed for Iranian waters.

Three days and 550 miles after setting out, convoy EW88018 reached its destination off Kuwait. As usual, each tanker captain sent over a token of thanks, a bottle of scotch or some such gift.[43] *Roberts* dropped anchor in thirteen fathoms over a bottom of shell and mud, and waited for an oiler to refill its tanks.[44]

Over the next two weeks, the frigate escorted five more convoys. Some missions went without incident. Others, such as EW88023, did not. On 7 April the *Roberts* and the *John A. Moore* picked up four tankers off Bahrain and were ushering them toward the mouth of the Gulf when two Iranian warships converged on the group from the north. One was a *Sa'am* frigate; the other an aging U.S.–built, steam-powered *Sumner*-class destroyer. Both were painting the convoy with fire-control radar.

Rinn described it later as an "immediate problem." The *Roberts* had to get between the convoy and the Iranians, while staying positioned to fire on both of them with missiles or guns. Moving matchbooks on a tabletop to retrace the curving paths of the combatants, he described the engagement:

> I cannot wait on this. I have to take the initiative or they will definitely outfox me.
>
> I had on two occasions watched the British escort convoys, and had seen Iranians get inside of them and just run roughshod over them, run all through the formation, and they were powerless to stop them. So I maneuvered up very quickly and crossed the formation, and came after the Iranian [frigate] who was to the north. He needed to break off, or I was going to engage him. I brought a missile up immediately. He questioned my right to do that, and I told them they were both illuminating their fire control radars on me, and I said, "I'm going to give you a five-minute warning to disengage and move away."

About three minutes later, the Iranian frigate turned away, heading north.

> As soon as he did, I turned toward this [destroyer] guy and told him immediately that I was going to engage him if he didn't disengage—keeping an eye on the *Sa'am* frigate the whole time. It was a very bad situation, and I think this whole evolution was done at about twenty-eight to thirty knots. We were moving very fast.
>
> The second ship seemed much less interested in getting into it. As soon as I turned—he was an older ship—he turned and started moving [westward].
>
> The beauty of that was, his missile launchers were all forward. On this first ship, his launchers were aft, maybe. When the second ship turned, his illuminators were blocked. I could tell as they went off, they were incapable of engaging. As number two headed south, the guy I was more concerned about was the gas

turbine ship, because he was faster than me—forty-knot-capable—and could turn right back around. So I turned and came back at him.[45]

For two hours the *Roberts* kept its sights on both Iranians. Rinn had planned his attack, should either one swivel guns or missiles to fire: take out the destroyer, which was a few miles distant, with a trio of Standard missiles with fragmentation warheads; then go after the nearer *Sa'am* gunfire. It didn't come to that; two hours after the engagement began, the Iranians backed off and disappeared over the horizon.

ON 14 APRIL 1988 the *Roberts* dropped off the two tankers of EW88025 and headed back south, following the convoy track in reverse. The frigate was slated to rendezvous and refuel with the oiler USS *San Jose* (AFS 7) in mid-Gulf and then would head back north for barge escort duty. Rinn dashed off a note to a Charleston-based friend asking him to order birthday flowers for Pam.

The ship was halfway through its deployment: three months gone, three to go. In the past ninety-four days, it had spent eighty-nine days at sea and had completed eight convoy assignments.[46] The crew was weary but still on top of their game, and they were proud of the accolades their ship had received.

Weeks earlier, the crew had submitted its entry for the squadron Battle E awards. The list of plaudits and accomplishments was rather breathtaking:

- November 1986: navy shipbuilding inspectors call *Roberts* best new FFG to date.
- May 1987: highest damage-control scores ever recorded by Norfolk testers.
- June–July 1987: best ship in two years at Guantánamo Bay, with best passive antisubmarine warfare scores ever seen.
- August 1987: best missile firing in FleetEx 4–87.
- November 1987: aviation inspectors find no problems, a first for a frigate.
- January 1988: deployed five months ahead of schedule.

The package noted various *Roberts* dispatches that had been forwarded to all Atlantic Fleet ships, and the memo that had been added to the Newport course for prospective commanding officers.[47] It went on for pages, and may have been a bit of overkill.

But when the results arrived in early April, they were everything Rinn and his crew were shooting for. For the October 1986–March 1988 battle efficiency awards cycle, *Samuel B. Roberts* earned Mission E's in eight categories: antiair warfare, antisubmarine warfare, antisurface warfare, electronic warfare, engineering, and three others. Only one other of Surface Group Four's sixteen ships equaled that accomplishment.

Best of all, *Roberts* had won the squadron's Battle E, beating out seven other frigates.[48] The awards were public acknowledgement of the *Roberts*'s excellent performance, and set the frigate among the fleet's elite. Van Hook's engineers lost no time affixing a poster-sized red "E" to each side of the ship's stack.

Aquilino sent his warm regards and wished them well in the second half of their deployment. "Congratulations on reaching 'Humpday,'" the commodore wrote from Newport. He noted that the *Roberts* families were preparing for the traditional celebratory dinner that marked the halfway point. Organized by several crew members' wives, it was set for the evening of 14 April in the officers' club at the naval station. Among the featured attractions would be Ford's first videotape, which had just arrived in Rhode Island. "It's downhill from here," Aquilino wrote.[49] He could not have been more wrong.

A FEW DAYS earlier, the *Roberts* had passed through the central Gulf, the lone warship assigned to the two tankers of EW88025.[50] North of Bahrain, they passed a group of American mine hunters at work. This was somewhat alarming.

The mine threat seemed to have receded since the minesweepers were rushed to the region in the wake of the *Bridgeton* attack. Mines had damaged or sunk seven ships in 1987, but there had been no incidents at all in 1988. The sweepers could take partial credit; they had found a mine on their first day of Gulf operations and had since cleared several dozen devices from three fields. An equal share of credit belonged to the forces that kept the black spheres from going in the water at all: the barge crews, Eager Glacier spy planes, army aviators, navy warships.

And yet the threat remained. Every week or so, a merchant sailor or naval lookout found a lone mine drifting with the current or anchored in place. Three such mines had been spotted in a recent ten-day stretch. The *Roberts*'s own helo had spotted a drifter as the ship made its way toward the mysterious refueling off Oman. *Iran Ajr* was at the bottom of the Gulf, but everyone knew how easy it was to turn almost any ship into a minelayer.

So what was going on in the central Gulf? Rinn had received no warning about mines nor a recommended Q-route—a swept and safe course. He put in a call about it to Middle East Force, but received no reply. Long after it might have helped, he learned that the minesweepers were responding to a CIA report of Iranian mines in the vicinity.[51]

CHAPTER NINE

Mine Hit

Perched on his metal chair, Bobby F. Gibson leaned into the slip-stream. The sun was lowering behind the nineteen-year-old lookout, and the seaman peered through the light afternoon haze.

The *Roberts* was running at twenty-five knots, about as fast as it could go on one turbine. The ship was hurrying toward a rendezvous with the oiler *San Jose,* which would top off the frigate's fuel reserves. For the moment, there were no tankers to herd, no armed raiders to ward off in this calm central region of the Gulf. There was time, it seemed, to enjoy a moment's calm and a cooling breeze that belied the eighty-seven-degree air.

But when Gibson raised his binoculars, the lenses showed a floating object, and then two more. Perhaps the dolphins were back? But the black shapes were just sitting there on the surface, a few hundred yards off the starboard bow. He studied them in the magnified circle of the binoculars. There were protuberances on their round tops. The lookout pressed a button on his sound-powered phones and spoke into the mouthpiece.

Down in the captain's stateroom, Rinn was reviewing menus with Kevin Ford. The chief cook had planned a steak-and-lobster dinner for the following night, a small celebration of the deployment's halfway mark. The phone rang, and Rinn pulled the heavy handset from its bracket. It was Lt. Bob Firehammer, the officer of the deck. He had taken Gibson's report, then ordered the helmsman to stop the ship. Firehammer began to tell the skipper about the floating objects. But Rinn could already feel the ship shuddering to a halt, and he hung up before the lieutenant could finish. Two quick right turns, and he was scaling the ladder to the bridge. *It's not mines,* the captain told himself. *It's sheep floating upside down, or trash bags.*

Rinn took up binoculars and focused them through the windscreen. The shapes were perhaps six hundred yards away. They were shiny. Unencrusted with marine growth. Horned. "Holy shit," he said. "Those *are* mines."

The bridge, always quiet, had gone silent. The sounds of wind and waves drifted through open hatches. Deep within, a gas turbine spun idly, its humming diffused to the edge of consciousness. Someone scratched a pencilled note; it was 1639, what civilians call 4:39 PM. The ship's position was 26 degrees, 22.5 minutes north; 52 degrees, 18.4 minutes east, halfway between Qatar and Iran.

Out on the wing, Dan Nicholson bent to the big-eyes, the spindle-mounted binoculars built to identify ships on the horizon. The quartermaster examined the black spheres through the two-foot barrels. *Whoa, this is real—big time!* Nicholson thought.

Beside him, a shutter clicked. Tom Reinert, the chief gunner, was snapping photos through a telephoto lens. Someone whispered, wondering whether the ship should try to sink the mines with gunfire.[1]

Reinert already had it sorted it out. You could shoot mines a mile or more distant with the 76-mm deck gun. Out to a thousand yards or so, you'd use the 25-mm chain gun, and the .50-caliber machine gun if they were really close. *These look like candidates for the .50-cal,* the gunner thought.[2]

Rinn called down to CIC. Fire Controlman 1st Class Matt Shannon was flipping through his radar modes, trying to pick the mines out of the surface clutter for a gunnery fix. Van Hook was standing watch as tactical action officer. "Get on the radio to *Coronado,*" Rinn told the chief engineer. The Middle East Force had explosive ordnance teams to deactivate or destroy the mines; they would also warn the rest of the fleet to stand clear.

Then Rinn paused to think. His ship didn't seem to be in immediate danger. It had stopped short of the line of the three visible mines. His options were nevertheless limited. He could not simply freeze the ship in place. For all the virtues of gas turbines and auxiliary propulsion units, they did not turn the frigate into a hovering helicopter. Nor was the anchor much help. A ship moored at sea moves with the wind and water like a tethered balloon, not a car with a parking brake. In any case, Rinn dared not drop the anchor for fear of setting something off.

The longer the ship hung around, the greater the danger would become. With sunset less than two hours away, spotting other mines would soon become all but impossible. Worse, the frigate would be a sitting duck for warplanes and surface craft. No, sticking around was hardly an option.

So, which way to safety? The visible mines were sitting off the starboard bow, and the way directly ahead appeared to be clear. But it would be folly to move forward, or even to try a sharp turn to port. Moored mines, when laid correctly, float below the water's surface. Who knew why these three were riding so high? Maybe their anchors were sitting on top of some underwater boulder. Maybe whoever dropped them off eventually found the proper length for the mooring cables. The rest of the string—or strings—could well be underwater.

This was truly disturbing, Rinn thought. *We may not be on the periphery of these things. We may be in the middle of them.* That alone was enough to scuttle the idea of shooting their way out. Even if the visible mines blew up or went to the bottom, there was no telling where the others might be. There was also the danger of sympathetic or noise-triggered detonation. It occurred to Rinn that for all the courses the navy provided to prospective commanding officers, none addressed the problem of withdrawing from a minefield. In the end, only one choice made sense: back up. The captain stepped onto the bridge wing and leaned over the port railing. The ship's wake pointed stick-straight toward the northwest horizon. It would be no easy thing to retrace that path, which was already fading into a faint bubbly scum.

Backing a single-screw, single-rudder frigate was more complicated than it sounded. Water flowed unpredictably around the blunt stern, and a backing ship could easily wander off course. Rinn had long known about this sticky spot in the frigate's operating envelope. During the long days off Cuba last summer, he and several of his officers had experimented with backing techniques, practicing while the Gitmo instructors were elsewhere. Now he would put his findings to the test.

The next move was all but automatic. Rinn lifted the silver microphone and thumbed its button. The 1MC loudspeaker system carried his words to every compartment in the ship. "This is the captain. We've spotted some mines," he said. "I want everyone to set Condition Zebra [maximum compartmentalization] and go to your general quarters stations." There would be no GQ alarm, he said. The dark shapes had the horns of simple contact mines, but there was no way to know whether they could also be triggered by sound, or the approach of a steel hull. "Move calmly and quietly," Rinn said.[3]

TWO HUNDRED SAILORS streamed about the ship, moving forward in the starboard passageways, aft in the port ones, dogging hatches, tugging at their clothing, reporting to their stations. The call had roused Signalman Mike Roberts from the television in the crew's berthing space and filled him with instant dread. The absence of the battle-stations alarm was eerie enough, but the skipper *never* called GQ himself.[4]

Rinn's call pried Lester Chaffin from his rack, where the electrician's mate first class was sifting through family snapshots and looking forward to the evening meal. A native of Huntington, West Virginia, Chaffin had abandoned a grocery-stocking job to accept the navy's promise of free education and travel. He pulled on a flash hood as he headed for the deck, where he chatted with the leader of Repair Locker 5. To Chaffin, the situation didn't feel much different from other false alarms about an ominous something-or-other.[5]

Chris Pond, who was flushed from the chow line, was less blasé than annoyed. *Another drill,* the hull tech thought. *I'm going to miss dinner.* Rolling down his sleeves and buttoning his shirt to the neck, Pond joined his team at the forward repair locker, Repair 2, under the forecastle. Then the 1MC instructed all hands to fan out around the ship and take extra OBA canisters with them. Pond and a few others wandered forward to the missile magazine.[6]

The call had awoken Rick Raymond a half hour into his post-duty slumber. Like the rest of the CIC team, Raymond had been standing watches in two sections: six hours on, six off. Shaking off the fatigue, the operations specialist-cum-hoseman pulled on coveralls and headed forward to Repair 2. The locker leader, Senior Chief Boatswain's Mate George Frost, was spreading his crew out to reduce the chance of a mine getting everyone at once, and Raymond wound up near sick bay. He walked in to chat with Hospitalman 1st Class James Lambert. The corpsman was still sweaty from a workout on the ship's stationary bike. Lambert was also working on his enlisted surface warfare qualification, so he and Raymond chewed over some test-prep questions.

Down in CIC, Van Hook had spent several frustrating minutes attempting to establish a clear radio link to the *Coronado*. When he finally got through, the Middle East Force staff officers had offered two instructions: "Put your helicopter in the air to keep an eye on the mines," and "don't get any closer to them." Van Hook relayed this up to the bridge. Rinn rolled his eyes at the latter advice, but the first part sounded sensible enough. He called the officer in charge of the helicopter detachment, Lt. Cdr. Tim Matthews, and told him to prep the Seahawk for launch.[7]

The word was passed to set flight quarters, and sailors assembled in the hangar and flight deck. Hull Technician 2nd Class Ted Johnson turned out in the bulky silver flame-retardant "hotsuit" of the crash-and-rescue team. Johnson squatted on a toolbox in the port hangar, chatting with one of the enlisted aircrew. On the other side of the hangar door, the helo crew ran through the preflight checklist.

In the radar shack behind the bridge, John Preston perched on a bench, straining at his sound-powered headphones for clues about the situation. The fire controlman grasped for soothing thoughts. *Everything is going to be all right, because we're on the mighty* Samuel B. Roberts *and Commander Rinn is going to save the day for us again.* He longed to stick his head out of his windowless room for a look around, and thought about the engineers far below in their cramped machinery rooms: *I wonder whether this is what they feel like.*[8]

DAVE WALKER, THE ship's gas turbine chief and all-around Mr. Fixit, was heading forward for some chow after his four-hour watch when the GQ call came. Walker turned around and went back to Central Control Station (CCS), the ship's engineering nerve center.

The other engineers were already prepping the ship for battle, twisting knobs and punching buttons on the floor-to-ceiling control panels that divided the space. The panels, covered in dials and gauges and switches, stretched from the yellow-flecked linoleum up to the cable runs above. They sent electronic commands to equipment around the ship, and described conditions in blinking lights.

Most of the equipment they monitored was in the four main engineering spaces under Walker's feet, noisy and crowded compartments where sailors wore earplugs and hollered to make themselves understood. Engineers called them the "main spaces," or simply "the hole."

The forwardmost was Auxiliary Machine Room 1 (AMR 1), which held a pair of fuel tanks and one of the frigate's four diesel-powered electrical generators. Immediately aft of AMR 1, and twice its size, was AMR 2, which held two of the big generators, plus fuel pumps, air conditioners, and two of the ship's five fire pumps. Next came the main engine room. This was the biggest space in the frigate and yet one of its most packed, thanks to a capacious pair of fuel tanks and the truck-sized soundproofed enclosures that held the gas turbines. Finally, there was AMR 3, which held one generator and the ship's freshwater distillers directly below Central Control.

Walker watched as Gas Turbine Systems Technician 1st Class Michael Wallingford manipulated the main propulsion panel. One deck down, the starboard gas turbine rumbled to life. Walker flipped a switch, sending throttle control to the helmsman on the bridge, and then lifted a heavy brass-rimmed handset. "Bridge, CCS. Second turbine's up; you have program control."[9]

Behind Walker and Wallingford was another tall panel, lined with L-shaped circuit-breaker handles like a stand of fiddlehead ferns. It sketched the state of the ship's electrical grid in lights and indicator gauges. Two of the four generators were already online, pumping out a thousand kilowatts apiece. But general-quarters doctrine prescribed one more, and so Chief Electrician's Mate Robert C. Bent was working through the start-up sequence for generator number one in AMR 1.

As the hulking diesel powered up, Bent watched the tachometer needle, which tracked the engine's shaft speed. The needle shot past the red line, a light flared, and an automatic safety override shut the engine down at 1,800 rpm. That was odd. Walker sent Electrician's Mate 1st Class Jim Whitley to investigate. Bent flipped switches to bring up generator number four instead.[10]

Then the chief electrician called Electrician's Mate 2nd Class John Kolynitis, who was in the auxiliary propulsion room waiting to lower the outboard motors into the water. Bent told Kolynitis to seek higher ground after the pods were in the water.

That sounded like a good idea to Walker. On the fifth deck, the lowest one, you could look past your boots to the half-inch steel skin of the ship. With mines about, it only made sense to get everyone up to higher ground. Walker rotated a switch and spoke into the 2JV, a sound-powered communications circuit. The 2JV carried his voice to the sailors in the engine room and machinery spaces. "Why don't you all come up from the lower levels," he said.[11] Those few words would save lives.

Walker rechecked his panels, then picked up a phone and told CIC that the frigate's engineering plant was ready for battle. *Okay, we all know something bad's out there, and we're all here in this nice little steel room,* Walker thought.[12] The minutes ticked by.

ELSEWHERE IN THE main spaces, the rest of the engineers had taken their stations. Directly below Bent in AMR 3, Engineman 1st Class Mark Dejno had watched his own control panels as the chief electrician brought diesel generator number four to life. Three spaces forward, a trio of men had assembled in AMR 1. One was Gas Turbine Technician 2nd Class Randy Tatum, who had recently written to the Nebraska newspaper. Another was Mike Tilley, the wisecracking junior engineman from Missouri, and the third was Fireman Joe Baker, who had just pulled on shorts and T-shirt for a bit of weightlifting when the GQ call came. As Baker skinned back into dungarees, a familiar ball of fear had gathered in his gut. He'd felt it back in Newport, that first day aboard ship, when he'd learned that the *Roberts* was destined for the Gulf.

On Walker's order to evacuate the lower levels, the three men climbed up a ladder to the refrigeration deck. The sailors perched on steel cans, keeping up a stream of chatter to hide their nerves. "Our ship doesn't hit mines; that's what happens to other ships," someone said. The smell of frost and cold cardboard drifted from a walk-in refrigerator. Baker remembers a moment of calm after the banter ran out—"still, like the moment the sun peeks over the horizon on a cool spring morning," he wrote.[13]

Down in the main engine room, Gas Turbine Systems Technician 3rd Class Dave Burbine had answered the call to general quarters by snaking his way down a ladder and squeezing between the gas turbine modules. The twenty-three-year-old from Westerly, Rhode Island, settled onto a tiny platform and donned sound-powered phones. Wedged under the upper-level grate, below the waterline, and between two hot and humming steel boxes, Burbine's seat was about as claustrophobic a duty station as the *Roberts* offered. Adding insult to inconvenience, the job was redundancy personified. He manned a small joystick that could control the pitch of the ship's sixteen-foot propeller, but he'd be called upon only if both the bridge and Central Control lost their ability to do it.

When Walker passed the word to move up a level, Burbine was only too happy to comply—not because of any particular foreboding, but rather because hours of drills had rendered him thoroughly sick of perching on the small square of metal. He set down his headphones and clambered to the upper grate, where he met fellow gas turbine tech Fireman Wayne Smith. Amid the roaring blast of a cool-air vent, the engineers leaned against compressed-air reservoirs and watched the massive reduction gear turn slowly beneath their feet.[14]

Chief Alex Perez stood at the engine room's local control panel, about twenty feet farther into the compartment. An expert in the care and feeding of the frigate's big turbines, the thirty-eight-year-old from Los Angeles led Burbine, Smith, and a few other junior engineers with ready knowledge and a firm touch.[15] Perez checked on his guys, making sure they were up on the grate, and surveyed his panel, which indicated a fully functional propulsion plant.

All preparations made, Perez had a moment to think of his wife, Mary. A month earlier he had waved to Kevin Ford's camera, offering a hand-lettered sign—"Hi, Mary!"—and a fleshy smile under a bushy mustache. Now she was starting her day back in Rhode Island, tending preparations for the evening's Halfway Day dinner. Presently, Perez thought he heard a faint rasp, metal scraping on metal.[16]

FOUR MINUTES AFTER Rinn called general quarters, all stations reported ready. It was time for a choice. Hold steady? Move? The fates of two hundred lives and an American warship rested on his decision. Centuries of naval tradition and the command star on Rinn's right breast said the choice was his alone. Two thoughts came to him, shining clear and bright:

he could drive that ship as well as anyone, and his well-trained crew could handle anything he could. He pondered a moment more, alone, seeking no counsel. He made his choice. *I gotta get out of here.*

He picked up the 1MC again. "I can see our wake," he told the crew. "I'm pretty certain we can back down." The captain dispatched officers to back up the enlisted lookouts. Firehammer went out to stand on the starboard wing, opposite the captain, while Eckelberry and the junior officer of the deck, Ens. Michael Infranco, headed aft to the hangar roof. It was time to move.

Rinn ordered the auxiliary propulsion units (APUs) deployed and angled to power the ship aft. Several decks down, Electrician Kolynitis toggled a switch, and the pods dropped into position.[17] The captain told the bridge helmsman to put the rudder hard left and ordered engines back one-third. This turned the shaft at ten revolutions a minute—just enough, he hoped, to keep a wash over the rudder and the stern in place. Then he ordered power to the APUs, and the ship began to move backward.

Less than ten minutes had elapsed since Gibson, the forward lookout, had called up to the bridge to report the first sighting of mines. Now the *Roberts* was backing away from danger, with trusted shipmates keeping close eyes out for new black, bobbing forms. Rinn was not terribly worried. After all, he reckoned, they had spotted the one out front, and stopped with hundreds of yards to spare. *We're going to get out,* he thought.[18] He was wrong.

DESIGNED IN 1908 for Tsar Nicholas II, the M-08/39 naval mine remains a marvel of cost-effective weaponry. It consists of a three-foot black sphere perched atop a heavy cylinder, like a tennis ball on a tin can. The sphere contains 253 pounds of the high explosive called trinitrotoluene, or TNT, and flotation voids to make it buoyant. The squat cylinder holds 360 feet of mooring cable and a 700-pound slug of iron.[19]

Laying an M-08 is a relatively simple matter of taking a depth sounding, setting the cable length, and sliding the mine overboard. The iron anchor settles on the sea floor, and the buoyant sphere floats up to the end of its tether. Tide and current notwithstanding, the ball floats about a dozen feet beneath the waves—deep enough to be invisible, shallow enough to strike a passing ship.

The buoyant globe is studded with five triggering devices, called "Hertz horns" after their nineteenth-century German inventor. Each is roughly the size and shape of a fat sausage and holds a glass ampoule of battery acid. When one of these lead-foil horns is crushed against a ship's hull, the acid drains into a wet cell, whose electrical charge ignites a detonator, which touches off several hundred pounds of trinitrotoluene.

The material products of a TNT explosion are humdrum: nitrogen gas, carbon monoxide, water, and soot. Ounce for ounce, the pale yellow solid releases less energy than burning gasoline or even sugar. It is the blinding speed of its combustion that does the violence. When TNT detonates underwater, it disassociates within milliseconds into a bubble of gas. This bubble displaces water, sending a shockwave racing away at supersonic speed. The bubble, heated to thousands of degrees and pressurized to thousands of atmospheres, expands just behind the shockwave, driving water before it like a battering ram.

This one-two punch—shockwave followed by bubble—alone can cripple a ship. But under certain conditions, the punishment can go on for several more seconds. If the gas bubble doesn't pierce the ocean surface, it will collapse under the sea's weight and then re-expand to deal a new blow. In a shallow sea like the Persian Gulf, the shockwave may bounce off the channel floor and return to strike again. Even if a ship survives the initial shocks, this whipping action can break its keel, as a terrier snaps a rabbit's neck.

And finally, if the gas bubble finds an outlet—say, a hole in a battered hull—it vents. The weight of the surrounding seawater forces the superhot vapors through the opening, like a burst steam pipe letting loose with the fires of hell itself.

NO ONE SAW the mine that got the *Samuel B. Roberts*. This particular weapon had been laid with more skill, or perhaps luck, than the three visible off the bow. The mine's anchor sat on the silt floor, some 250 feet down. Its steel tether had unreeled just enough to keep the buoyant sphere below the Gulf's opaque surface, riding just a bit higher than the frigate's sixteen-foot draft.

Nothing happened for the first few seconds after the warship backed over the black sphere. The frigate's hull sloped down from the stern, reaching its full draft about one-third of the way toward the bow. As the ship moved backward, the mine missed the rudder, screw, and the skeg that stiffened the aft part of the hull. The mine may have been pushed off momentarily by the stern's "bow wave"; it may even have bumped the ship a few times without hitting any of its five triggers.[20]

But luck for the *Roberts* ran out about 4:50 PM. A lead-foil horn crumpled against a half-inch hull plate. Chemicals mixed, generating an electrical charge. An eighth of a ton of TNT violently transformed into heat and vapor and soot. The shockwave hit the ship at frame 276—two-thirds of the way down the 445-foot hull, as measured from the bow—and just four feet to port of the centerline.[21] The blast lifted the entire ship at the point of impact, and the stern rose a few feet more than the bow. The stress was more than the keel could endure.

The keel and the main deck were the source of a frigate's structural strength. Bound together by relatively light bulkheads and stringers, they gave the ship the longitudinal stiffness of a seagoing I-beam. This structure, which had ridden unbowed through a Mediterranean gale and a Gulf *shamal,* could not cope with the lightning-fast loads imposed by the mine blast. For a moment, the frigate flexed around the point of impact. The main deck acquired a slight convexity, like a far-off hilltop or the curve of the earth. Then the ship flexed back. Bow and stern snapped up. The motion cracked the aluminum deckhouse in three places. Six feet of hangar came loose from the main deck.

The shock rippled through the ship. It cracked the mounts for both fire control antennae, dumped cooling water into a radar equipment cabinet, broke the ship's photocopier, and shattered the sneeze guard on the mess deck's salad bar. Directly above the impact point, the main deck bent, and stayed bent. The keel failed entirely: at the hull's lowest point, a twelve-foot section of HY-80 steel beam curled away like a pipe cleaner. And yet the mine had just begun to wreak its damage on the ship.

The gas bubble came hard on the heels of the shockwave. It is unclear which one pierced the hull plates. It was the bubble, however, that enlarged the hole to the size of a delivery truck and injected scalding vapors into the ship's main engine room. A fireball filled the space, instantly converting millions of dollars of precision-engineered machinery into flaming junk. The gas turbines came off their mountings, flooding their enclosures with fuel. The blast tore open a pair of ten-thousand-gallon fuel tanks and a trio of oil sumps. An aviation-fuel line vaporized, spewing its volatile contents around the space. Atomized diesel and other petroleum distillates sprayed about, bursting into flame as they touched down on red-hot steel.

Still expanding, the fireball blew out the rubber gasket that surrounded the propeller shaft in the aft bulkhead. Scorching gases rushed through the two-foot, ring-shaped gap, filling AMR 3 with a wall of flame. The blast opened seams and punched basketball-sized holes in the forward bulkhead as well. But the rest of the hull plates held tight, sealing the force of the explosion inside the engine room. The pressure continued to grow as the gas bubble, still heated to hundreds of degrees, sought release.

A second later, it found an escape route. A rent opened in the starboard exhaust plenum, the five-foot-wide duct that carried the waste products of turbine combustion up four decks and into the atmosphere. The bubble forced its way into the duct. Superhot gases vented up through the ship, setting fires along the way, and burst out of the exhaust stack. The result was a hundred-foot eruption of fire and lagging and the flaming detritus of a wrecked propulsion plant.[22]

Far below, the engine room was now open to the sea. Seawater rushed through the twenty-five-foot hole. In seconds, the ship's largest space was flooded to the waterline. The water flowed aft through the shredded shaft gasket, filling AMR 3 almost to the overhead. Then it sluiced forward through the riddled bulkhead and began to flood AMR 2. Within minutes, some eighteen hundred tons of seawater sloshed in the ship's belly.[23] This put a dangerous new load on the main deck. Every passing wave caused it to flex, like a soda can bent and rebent. Eventually, it might come apart, and if that happened, the ship would break up and sink.

Sorensen had taught his sailors that the *Perry* frigate was a three-compartment ship, but he had secretly wondered whether that was still true after all the extra weight that had been added over the course of the class's design. Now, with the loss of the keel, the three-compartment claim was even more suspect. With two large spaces gone and a third filling up, no one knew how much more the ship could take.

In a heartbeat, a single low-tech weapon had roughly halved the structural strength of a U.S. Navy warship. Many hours would pass before the crew of the *Roberts* realized just how fragile their ship had become.

ON THE BRIDGE wing and weather decks, the stunned crew gaped as the fireball burst from the ship's exhaust stack. The plume of smoke and fire stabbed into the air above the radio mast. The blast had ripped shards of metal and insulation from the guts of the ship, coated them with fuel, and set them alight. Now fist-sized chunks of flaming debris plunked down all over the ship. Others landed in the water, surrounding the hull with hissing wisps of steam. Small fires flared on paint, hoses, canvas, and the tarry nonskid walkways.

The forecastle dipped and then surged upward, vaulting Bobby Gibson from the lookout's chair. Airborne for an instant, he could see only water and forecastle. Then the deck rose up to meet him, and he landed hard on his neck and shoulders.

On the bridge wing, Rinn was dumbfounded. "The ship just blows up underneath me. A totally different sound than anything I'd ever heard, as if the ship got dropped from a ten-story building. Not a 155-mm [artillery shell] explosion, not a bomb going off, just *baahhm*. Everything shook, and in a totally different way. The whole stern lifted up. A huge fireball came out of the stack, and I thought, 'Damn, we blew up an engine.' Or the helo. I don't think anybody thought we hit a mine."[24]

Someone pulled the 1MC handset from its mount, hit the aircraft crash alarm, and announced to the crew that the helo had hit the deck. Nicholson stared at a black-and-white video monitor. It clearly showed the SH-60 on the flight deck, rotor blades still spinning away. It took the quartermaster a moment to realize what was actually going on. He grabbed the handset and corrected the previous call: "Mine hit, mine hit. The ship has hit a mine!"

Coming out of the signal shack, Signalman Roberts felt automatically for a list—a tilt in the deck. There was none. He looked over the side. A sea snake went by. If it came to abandoning ship, there were plenty of lifeboats aboard, rolled into canisters the size of fifty-five-gallon drums and primed to inflate automatically when dunked in water. Roberts hoped fervently that he would not have to put their seaworthiness to the test.[25]

The explosion was the loudest sound Ted Johnson had ever heard. The hangar deck bucked, flipping the hull technician into the air like a rag doll. He crashed to the rough nonskid deck, his fall cushioned by his bulky fire suit. Black smoke belched from the midships bulkhead. The blast had ruptured the exhaust duct that carried fumes from the gas turbines up from the engine room to the stack. The smoke filled the hangar and then ceased as the gas turbines ground to a halt far below. Johnson checked the sailors around him and looked out to the helicopter. It looked okay, but its blades were spinning down and the engine seemed to be off. He'd never seen an aircraft knocked out before, and he decided it wasn't going anywhere soon. So he picked himself up and headed below to Repair Locker 5. Somewhere, there were fires to fight.[26]

In sick bay the blast jolted everything into the air. Aspirin bottles and bandages went flying. In the first split second, Rick Raymond thought it was the ship's gun going off. Then he noticed that he, the corpsman, and everything else in sick bay were airborne. "That's when we realized we hit a mine," Raymond wrote. For a moment, everyone just looked at each other. What happened? What comes next? "Then I said, 'I gotta go,' and went running down the passageway to grab a hose."[27]

In the mess room, time slowed to a crawl for Lester Chaffin, who found himself drifting upward and then falling slowly to the deck. Time returned to its normal pace as he picked himself up and felt gingerly for broken bones. He was fine, but the ship was clearly in trouble. The jolt had shattered the glass sneeze-guard on the salad bar, and shards lay on the blue linoleum. More ominously, smoke was beginning to waft through ventilation grates. As electrician for Repair Locker 5, Chaffin's job was to check the equipment in AMR 2 for flames and cut power to anything that had caught fire. He pulled open the engineering hatch and slid down the ladder. To his dismay, the lower deck was already filling with black seawater. Chaffin found fellow electrician Whitley already on the scene, so he grabbed a firefighter's oxygen mask and tried to enter the main engine room. But the hatch was jammed, and he headed back to the repair locker, shaken by the chaos.

Chris Pond recalls the ship being picked up, shaken, and slowly let back down. The 1MC squawked. "Check for damage and report to DC Central," someone said, his voice cracking. "I think we just hit a mine."

Pond and three others raced aft along the port side, skidding to a halt outside the hatchway to the mess room. Tendrils of vapor were seeping out from inside. He received permission to investigate and grabbed a hose. Stepping through the haze, he spotted its source: it was harmless steam, rising from the food-warming trays in the galley.[28]

IN CENTRAL CONTROL a grating sound had drawn Walker's eyes to Bent's. Then *wa-WHAM!* The explosion threw everyone in CCS into the air. To Walker it felt like the worst car accident he'd ever been in. He picked himself off the deck, and his eyes flew to the engine gauges. The temperature for the gas turbine modules was skyrocketing. Fire! The chief hit switches to fill the turbine enclosures with the flame-suppressing Halon gas. Nothing happened. Within seconds, the enclosure sensors were reporting temperatures beyond two thousand degrees.

Then the propulsion control console died, all seven feet of it. From below the waist to the overhead, lights went out, gauges fell to zero, and indicators slumped behind glass shields. Walker spun around to the electrical control panel. It, too, was mostly dead, though some lights still flickered. *What the hell was the matter?* The consoles were designed to survive a total power failure; they were hooked to a battery pack in the main engine room. No juice from the uninterruptible power supply system meant there was something going seriously wrong under their feet. "Holy shit," said Walker, Bent, and Wallingford, more or less simultaneously.

Without the control consoles, the CCS team was blind. They had spent thousands of hours mastering prescriptions for confronting hundreds of engineering emergencies. They had proven at Gitmo and since that they could diagnose almost any problem by studying the panels and could fix many of them by manipulating their controls. But those troubleshooting recipes proceeded from the assumption that the panels would provide vital information and control. They had never trained for a scenario in which their central diagnostic device disappeared.[29]

FIVE HUNDRED POUNDS of high explosive had detonated within twenty yards of Alex Perez's seat. Faster than thought, superheated gases filled the main engine room and vented up the stack. The sea rushed in through the truck-sized hole in the hull, rising to the upper-level catwalk in an eyeblink. The gas turbine enclosures became cockeyed islands in a burning oil slick. In an instant, Perez's well-ordered engine room had become a dark and surreal hole lit by flame.

Perez missed his one-second introduction to hell, because the initial blast knocked him out and flipped him off the catwalk. He plunged into a maelstrom of black water. Somehow, he bobbed to the surface. When he regained consciousness, the chief found himself under the upper-level grate—the very thing he'd been standing on a moment ago. He was trapped by mangled railings and compressors and other gear. Only a few inches of space remained between the burning water and the grate. When he gasped for breath, a superhot mist of smoke and burning oil and seawater scorched his lungs. "One minute I was sitting at the console and the next, it was all dark and I was down below," Perez said later. "I thought I was lost. It was all dark, and all I could see was the fire from the burning engine. I thought I was going to drown." Fighting the pain from his damaged throat, he began to yell for help.[30]

TWO OTHER ENGINEERS had already gotten out of the engine room. The blast had surrounded Dave Burbine in a roaring bonfire, the loudest thing he'd ever heard. The engineer had a dim glimpse of lower-level machinery embedded in the overhead, and he vaguely wondered whether the reduction gear's sheer bulk had saved his life. He grabbed Wayne Smith by the shirt, dragged him out the hatch and across a passageway, and stepped into Central Control.

The injured engineers' appearance momentarily quieted the growing pandemonium in the engineering space. Everyone turned to stare at them. Burbine looked down at himself. His fuel-soaked dungaree shirt was in tatters. Chunks of raw flesh were hanging from his arms. He could barely see, and when he ran his fingers through his hair, it came off in clumps. "I'm hurt bad," Burbine told Walker.

The chief stared back. Gobbets of flesh were peeling off a burned face that looked like it belonged in a horror movie. It took Walker a moment to recognize the young petty officer he'd known for five years.

Burbine remembers Walker telling him to take a seat on a nearby table, and everything would be okay. So he sat, dribbling fuel over engineering logbooks. He had a queer sensation of air pockets in his pants, so he took them off and watched the skin bubble on his charred legs. There was no pain. The chief remembers putting it a bit differently: "Dave, there's not a fucking thing I can do for you right now, so just get in the corner and shut up." Walker felt like everything was happening at once. Smoke from the engine room was wafting through the door. None of the closed-circuit communications to the bridge seemed to be working.

Engineman Dejno, who had been standing watch in AMR 3, limped battered and burned into Central Control. He reported that a wall of fire had swept through the auxiliary machine room, followed by a wave of water that had filled the space nearly to its overhead. That meant there was fire and seawater a few feet directly below the engineers' feet.

Other damage reports were trickling in by voice and by sound-powered phone. Behind the propulsion panel, in the corner called DC Central, a petty officer was drawing symbols onto laminated deck diagrams, assembling a grease-pencil map of the damage. The reports seemed to confirm what Walker had guessed: the main engine room was inundated, flooded nearly to the upper deck, gone. That likely meant that the gas turbines were out of commission. It also meant the ship had lost the flasks of high-pressure air that restarted the ship's electrical generators. That was bad news indeed.

The list of things Walker thought he knew was as dismaying as it was short. The ship was on fire and dead in the water. The electrical control board still stood dark and mute, and the power grid seemed to be going south in a hurry. The number one generator was dead, thanks to the mysterious automatic override just after the call to battle stations. Number four was underwater in AMR 3. Number two had died soon after the blast, the victim of sheared and short-circuited cables now sitting in saltwater. Number three struggled gamely on. But the electrical demands of an entire wounded ship would soon overwhelm it. Walker knew this: if he lost those generators, the ship was doomed.

Fingers flying across his panel, Electrician Bent tripped bus breakers and twisted remote governors, trying to save what was left of the dying power grid. It was no use. Five minutes after the mine blast, the ship's electrical system browned out. All over the *Roberts,* the lights went dark. Radios shut down. Fans stilled. Pumps stopped. The ship had a backup lighting system that was supposed to activate if the power failed. But generator number three was still putting out a feeble current, good for nothing—but just powerful enough to keep the emergency lights from clicking on.[31]

An unaccustomed silence filled the spaces. Throughout the hull, there were only the shouts of sailors and the noise of equipment being dragged from repair lockers. And every so often, an unearthly metallic groan came from deep within the wounded frigate.

ON THE BRIDGE, Rinn was looking for answers. Fiery debris was drifting down around the ship. Electrical power had died. There was nothing on his instrument panels to tell him what happened. There was nothing that told him what needed to be done. But his mind raced with questions. *How many casualties do I have? How bad are they? What's damaged? What's the status of the engineering plant?* Just about the only thing he knew for certain was that the sun was going down, and pretty soon they were going to have to save the ship in the dark.

Injury reports started coming in. A handful of crew members were down, hurt, burned. There was a fire in the stack. It looked like the superstructure was cracked in several places. Someone called up to say the main engine room had totally flooded. That didn't sound right to Rinn. How could the biggest space on the ship flood so fast? Another call, this one from the flight deck, reported that the helicopter had taken some sort of damage. Fluid was pouring out of one of its engines. Rinn donned sound-powered phones and called Palmer in CIC. *How are my combat systems? What have we got?* The answer came back: *We got nothing, really. No surface-search radar, no radios.*[32]

The captain told the combat systems officer to cut the radar out of the ship's power system so it wouldn't drag on the grid as the engineers worked to bring it back up. If they couldn't get electricity back, the ship was going to sink whether it came under attack or not. Still, this turned the frigate from a sitting duck into a deaf and blind one. The *Roberts* crew members' knowledge of the ship's surroundings shrunk to the horizon. They lost track of the *Sa'am* frigate that had been lurking some thirty miles to the north and the Iranian P-3 that had dogged them all the way from Kuwait. Neither ship nor plane had acted threateningly, but the lookouts had spotted antiship missiles under the P-3's wings. Without the radar, there was no way to tell whether the pilot had turned to attack.

No one even knew where any friendly ships were. Those they had escorted to Kuwait were far behind; those they were rushing to meet had started their day at the Gulf's mouth. Not that it mattered much; no one was going to come help them in a minefield.

FLASHLIGHT IN HAND, Robert Bent picked his way forward from Central Control, heading for AMR 2 to see what he could do about the generators. Like his captain, the chief electrician was viscerally attuned to the vibrations and noises of his ship. A ventilation fan that cut out for a moment could wake him from sleep. When the ship's power died, Bent felt as if his own heart had stopped. A ship without juice was a dead ship. As he left Central Control, smoke in the U-shaped passageway stopped him short. It was pouring from an engine room hatch popped open by the blast. A noise like an animal's cry drew his attention.

Bent stepped through the hatch and pointed his flashlight through the acrid haze. The cramped engine room had become a phantasmagoria of tortured metal painted in flickering firelight. Glowing embers pocked blackened surfaces. He played the light through the grating beneath his feet, where he should have seen his panel's batteries and other gear. Instead, black water lapped a foot below his boots.

Following the cries, Bent found Gas Turbine 2nd Class Larry Welch not far from the hatch. The engineer was disoriented and badly burned. Bent reached to help his shipmate, and Welch's blackened skin sloughed off in his hands. Taking a better grip, Bent helped his shipmate stagger out of the engine room and aft to Repair Locker 3.[33]

Meanwhile, twenty feet farther into the engine room, Alex Perez's strength began to ebb.

IN THE REFRIGERATOR deck above Auxiliary Machine Room 1, the explosion came as a deafening roar. The shock flung Baker, Tatum, and Tilley into the air, but they landed on their feet. Even the steel cans they'd been sitting on settled softly back onto the deck. For a moment, the sailors stared at each other, befuddled. Then their training kicked in. A breath of smoke drifted up through the hatch, and the three men pulled emergency breathing devices from wall racks. Tatum, the senior man in the space, got everyone moving.

Baker headed off to check the nearby electrical switchboard, while Tatum and Tilley descended the ladder into AMR 1, a low-ceilinged space about thirty feet square. The door to generator number one had popped open, and smoke drifted from ventilation ducts in its enclosure. The big engine inside sat idle; this was the one that had oversped and shut down just moments before the mine hit. Air conditioning whirred in the vents. The loudspeaker barked; someone reported that the mine had hit someplace aft, and that the ship was on fire. The two engineers knew their duty: start that generator.

The entire engineering department had practiced a mass conflagration scenario just the previous week, and Chief Bent had drilled it into their heads: if you lose touch with Central Control, make sure you get your generator back online. Fire pumps, drainage systems, ventilation, all depended on electricity. In an emergency, the ship needed all the juice it could get. Redundancy was key; who knew what was going on with the other generators?

Tatum hollered up through a hatch to Gas Turbine Systems Technician 2nd Class Tom Wagner, who opened the circuit breakers on the local switchboard. Wagner stripped his board, isolating generator number one from the ship's electrical grid for startup, and disconnected everything except the lights.

Meanwhile, Tilley squeezed into the soundproofed enclosure that surrounded the generator. The machinery inside left little room to move; the generator was powered by a turbocharged, intercooled sixteen-cylinder Detroit Diesel engine the size of a Volkswagen minibus. The engineman spotted the reason for the earlier malfunction: a cracked control plug in the engine's mechanical governor. Tilley figured he could manage the speed of the hulking diesel manually, but he wanted confirmation from Central Control. "My mind went blank. Would it run without that part? Of course it would, wouldn't it?" the engineman recalled.

Tatum tried four times to call CCS, but the 2JV line was dead. Seconds later, the lights dimmed and went out. Tatum and Tilley scrabbled for the square yellow flashlights called battle lanterns. In the darkness, Wagner yelled down to flip their sound-powered phone's rotary switch to 5JV, the electrician's circuit. Tilley called back, telling him to pass the word to Central Control that they were going to restart the engine. The phone buzzed. It was Walker, telling the other switchboard operators to strip their own boards. If Tilley managed to get his generator going, the chief didn't want the grid going down again because of damaged cables and electrical shorts.

Tatum and Tilley played their flashlights across the generator's control panel. Under normal circumstances, they would kick-start the giant diesel with a push of a button on the panel. That would turn the engine over with a blast of high-pressure air from compressors in the main engine room. But the panel was as dead as the fluorescent tubes above their heads. They punched the start button anyway, more out of desperation than anything else. No dice.

Tilley was about as junior an engineman as the navy had, but he knew the next step, and he did not particularly want to take it. Each diesel had a backup air flask for just such a situation. To use it, an engineman wedged himself into the enclosure and pushed a plunger to open the air passage. Engineers called it the "suicide start." "You have to stand on top of it and push down on the plunger," Walker recalled. "Of course, you're on this sixteen-cylinder great big huge turbocharged intercooled diesel, and it's the last place you want to be at."

Tilley yelled back up to Wagner, asking him whether he could start the engine with a cracked governor. "If I go in there and push the button, is it going to just run away on me? Am I going to get a piston upside my head, or is it going to be okay?" he recalled.

Wagner passed the questions along to CCS.

"Tom said, 'I can't do it; we're not supposed to do it this way!'" Walker recalled. "I said, 'Just fucking do it.' I had to get power back to the ship."

Wagner passed the word to Tilley, who took a deep breath and said, "Okay, fine."

Flashlight in hand, Tilley opened the door, walked in, and shut it behind him. The enclosure was about twenty feet by ten feet, with an overhead he could reach up and touch. The gray engine block loomed in the darkness. Tilley climbed up onto it, avoiding the cables and tubes that kept the beast running, and worked the air and fuel valves.

The junior sailor put his hand on the plunger, and winced. It had to be done, he told himself. His ship had struck a mine, fires were burning somewhere, and the electricity was out. He did not know about the floods that were swallowing the other three engineering spaces. But he knew this: he had to start this engine, or his ship and everyone on it might die.

Tilley pushed the manual override button and brought the plunger down. Air rushed past his face. The engine roared to life. The sailor tensed as the noise built around him—and began to relax when the rpms settled at their customary howling pitch. The manual governor was holding. He opened the enclosure door and hollered up to the switchboard operator.

Wagner checked his gauges. The generator was pumping out alternating current at fifty-seven cycles per second, three short of the sixty hertz the ship needed. He yelled back to Tilley. The engineman looked around for a wrench to adjust the governor. The nearest toolbox was just a few feet away—in a padlocked workbench. Tatum broke off the lock with a single blow.

Tilley turned an adjustment bolt until Wagner was satisfied. Then the switchboard operator flipped a switch, routing power into the grid. The lights came back on. Ten minutes had passed since the mine blast.[34]

CHAPTER TEN

Rising Water

In DC Central, Ens. Ken Rassler could begin to read a rough outline of the ship's condition in the grease marks scratched on his deck charts. To Rassler, Sorensen's successor as damage control assistant, the picture wasn't particularly encouraging.

Ten minutes after the blast, the *Roberts* was dead in the water, its gas turbines damaged beyond recovery. The engine room was flooded to its upper level, AMR 3 to the overhead—spaces that totaled nearly one-fifth of the ship's length. The amount of seawater already inside the ship would cover a tennis court to a depth of sixteen feet. More was coming in every second. There were fires in both compartments, and probably in other spaces as well. Smoke was pouring from the exhaust stack. The deckhouse had cracked in two places, and the aft end of the helicopter hangars had come loose from its foundation on the main deck.

Thanks to Tilley, Rassler was no longer doing his job in the dark. But three other generators were still offline. One of them was inundated in AMR 3, along with a pair of fire pumps, desalinators, and water chillers that cooled internal spaces and combat systems. The other two generators were in AMR 2, where the seawater was several feet high and rising.[1] If the ship were to survive, someone would have to stop that flow.

Around the corner in Central Control, Walker was trying to resurrect his electrical control panel. He had been delighted when the power came back on, but juice was useless unless he could route it to fire pumps and whatever else needed it. For that he needed a working console. The chief turned to Wallingford, who had taken Bent's place as watch electrician. The younger man was flipping switches, trying to bring the dead panel back to life.

"Chief, it's all fucked up," Wallingford said. "What do you want me to do?"

"Wally, I don't give a fuck what you do, but you better get that thing running again."

"You got any ideas?"

Walker looked around. He hoped the console wasn't actually damaged, but rather had simply been cut off from its electrical supply when the engine room flooded. His eyes landed on the floor buffer, a fluffy-footed instrument the sailors loved to hate.

"Yes," Walker said. "You see that buffer over there? Cut the fucking cord off that buffer."

The chief explained his idea: take a fifty-foot length and strip the leads, producing a long extension cord. Next, find a connection to the panel's power supply by severing its cable to the now-useless battery pack. Twist the buffer cord and battery lead together. Now you've got a console with a handy plug-in cord. Start trying 120-volt outlets until you find one that works.

"We can do that?"

"Fucking right we can do that," Walker said. "Nobody's down here to tell us we can't." Moments later, lights rippled across the electrical control console.

It was one small step, but Walker's head was still spinning. The damage was far beyond anything he'd seen before, beyond even the sadistic imaginations of Gitmo instructors. The chief paused, unsure. His eye fell on a red, well-thumbed three-ring binder, and he pulled it from the shelf. This was the master light-off checklist, the MLOC, or "em-loc." It listed the sequences of steps that would get the ship's systems running, enumerating in endless detail just how to start the power plant—in short, it was a recipe book for bringing a ship to life. Walker had used it and its cousins thousands of times, every time he readied a ship to leave its pier.

Amid the chaos of a crippled ship, the binder was a lifesaver. As Walker scanned its pages, his mind cleared. To get the radars to work, he needed to get air conditioning back online. Air conditioning required compressors and dehydrators. Those required electrical power, which required generators and switchboards.

The chief took a few moments to organize his plan and then began to dispatch his shipmates on repair missions.[2] Within just a few minutes, both of the generators in AMR 2 were back online. Number two came up first; after a quick repair job on a malfunctioning circuit breaker, number three started pumping out electricity as well. Soon one, then two, then three fire pumps started up. Fifteen minutes after the mine blast, seawater began to flow into the hoses atop the deckhouse.[3]

BENT HAD LEFT Central Control a few minutes earlier, just after the power came back on. Smoke was still drifting into the space from the engine room hatch, and the electrician had stepped across the passageway to close it. But as he moved to seal off the doorway, he heard another call for help.

For a second time, Bent ventured into the smoky engine room. The explosion had shattered every lightbulb in the space, so he picked his way onto the catwalk with his flashlight. He followed the yelling, and realized with a shock that a shipmate was trapped under the floor grate. It was Perez, badly burned but still struggling for his life.

Bent could see the chief's oil-soaked head and hands through the grate. He dropped to his knees and tugged at the metal lattice. It did not budge. He searched for the bolts that anchored the grate to its metal frame, looking for exposed nuts that might come off with a wrench. To his dismay, he found only J-shaped bolts that could not be loosened from above. Bent knew he needed more help.

Leaving Perez, the electrician hurried to Repair Locker 3. He rounded up Chief Engineman George Cowan and Electrician's Mate 2nd Class Ed Copeland. The crowbar was gone from the locker, but they grabbed an armful of other tools and headed back to the engine room. They flicked on battle lanterns, the battery-powered lamps that resembled small yellow lunchboxes, and began to attack the grate. Nothing worked. Their bolt cutter's jaws could get no purchase on the smooth metal loops of the J-bolts. The three rescuers passed a succession of wrenches to Perez—all the wrong size. They tried a few ineffective whacks with a sledgehammer. And the fuel-drenched surroundings were hardly the place to use the blowtorch. "We were scared the place was going to blow. You could see the burning embers, hear all kind of weird noises," Bent said later.

Copeland began to move down the catwalk, peering through the smoke, kicking at the grates. A few steps past Perez, he felt something give. He rammed a screwdriver under one of the J-bolts and yanked on it. It moved. He called to Bent and Cowan, and the three men tugged the grate free.

Now Perez had an escape route, an odyssey of three yards. He would have to duck under the fouled seawater and swim through catwalk supports and cableways to get to the opening. It would have been no easy task for an uninjured man, and Perez was badly hurt. Second-degree burns covered some 40 percent of his body. His eyes were filled with diesel fuel. In the initial fall, he had bruised a lung and fractured three vertebrae.

Perez took a deep and painful breath and dropped beneath the surface. Feeling his way through the submerged wreckage, the chief pulled himself hand over hand toward his shipmates, who beckoned with their battle lanterns and bellowed encouragement.

Eternal seconds dragged by. Then Perez surfaced. His three rescuers pulled him from the water, wrapped their arms around him, and helped the injured chief hobble toward Repair Locker 3.[4] Their shipmate had endured a quarter of an hour in burning water. His injuries were far more severe than the ship's corpsman could treat. If Perez were to have a chance at survival, he had to get off the *Roberts*.

ON THE BRIDGE, damage reports were coming in faster. Water was pouring through the fractured engine room bulkhead into AMR 2. There was a report of seawater in AMR 3, the aft machinery room—again, the words were something like "totally flooded"—and Rinn still couldn't bring himself to believe it. But some minutes after the blast, the captain was beginning to add up the clues that arrived from around his battered ship. He imagined the hole in the hull, picturing it about the size of a home stereo. He was off by about two orders of magnitude, but his visions helped. He began assembling a mental picture of the ship and its systems and its people. *If that's what happened, here's what we can do about it . . .*

At least the muster reports were reassuring. Every single member of the crew was alive, even the sailors in the engine room, which seemed like some kind of miracle. And word was also arriving of the DC efforts starting up around the ship. Hose teams were moving out inside the ship and atop the superstructure, some following the leads from Rassler and the CCS engineers, others simply reacting to the flames before their eyes. In the main storeroom, aft of AMR 3, a shoring team was sawing up beams to hold the rear bulkhead steady. Down in AMR 2, a patching team was attacking the leaky bulkhead. But there was still too much Rinn didn't know.

When word arrived from Central Control that the power had stabilized, the captain ordered Palmer to turn the surface-search radar back on and told him to get working on the fire control radar. A few minutes later, Palmer reported that fire control was back up as well, and the ship could once again track targets.[5] Rinn told him to call the pilot of the Iranian P-3. "Make him understand that if he comes near us, we're going to shoot him down," he said.

It was far from clear whether *Roberts* could back up that threat. Palmer ordered the gunners to power up the 76-mm mount, and the automatic feeder loaded rounds without a hitch, which was a good sign. But there was no easy way to diagnose hidden damage, the kind that might cause the gun to blow up if fired. Moreover, the 76-mm turret and the fire control radar sat on opposite sides of the crack in the superstructure. Shooting from a misaligned radar would be like aiming a rifle at arm's length. Could the ship actually hit anything?

This, and a thousand other questions, told Rinn he needed to see things for himself. It wasn't an easy decision. In battle, a skipper generally belonged on the bridge or in CIC, where target data flowed and where a captain could communicate with his crew and to his own commanders.[6] But the current problems had far more to do with things inside the ship, so the radars and other sensors were useless. And the reports coming over the sound-powered phone could tell him only so much. Rinn told the .50-cal gunners on the bridge wing to keep a sharp eye on the horizon, gave the deck to Eckelberry, and headed below.[7]

In CCS, Walker told Rinn that the main thing he worried about was the short circuits that might kick another generator or two offline. Without high-pressure air—the flasks had been destroyed in the main engine room—there might be no way to get them back up and running. On his way out, Rinn stopped by Burbine, who was shivering from his burns. "Captain, are we going to be okay?"

"We're going to be okay," the CO told his shipmate. "We're going to get you out of here."

Back in CIC, Rinn put in a call to the *Coronado*. He'd radioed the Middle East Force flagship once already since the mine blast. The conversation had been brief, because he didn't have much to say: *We've hit a mine, no reports of any deaths, damage to the ship unclear.* This time Admiral Less came on the line. The news that *Roberts* had stumbled onto a minefield had reached the Middle East Force commander as he'd walked in the door of his small house outside Manama. His chief of staff reported that Rinn was about to start backing down the *Roberts*'s wake. "He's the captain," Less responded, "and that sounds as if that's as good as you can probably do in a situation like that." The admiral had raced back to the *Coronado* through sun-baked city streets.[8]

Now, some twenty minutes after the mine detonation, Less asked for a status report. Rinn told him things were not looking particularly good. The engine room was gone and there was flooding in AMR 3. But he said all his primary combat systems were operational, and the ship was ready to defend itself.

But, Rinn told the admiral, he was going to need medevac helicopters, and fast. The *Roberts*'s SH-60 had been knocked out, and there were more burn cases than the ship's corpsman could handle. The clock was ticking on the Golden Hour, and people were going to go into shock.

Less told him help was on the way, in the form of the amphibious transport dock USS *Trenton* (LPD 14) and its marine helicopters. Rinn rogered and hung up.[9]

THE FIGHT TO save AMR 2 had begun within minutes of the mine blast. The phone buzzed in Repair Locker 2, and Senior Chief Frost, the locker leader and ship's senior enlisted sailor, picked it up. While he talked, Rick Raymond and other members of Repair 2 waited in the starboard passageway. *Is there another mine out there, ready to explode?* Raymond wondered. The half-inch hull plates had never seemed so thin.[10]

Frost hung up. The call was from DC Central, which needed someone to confirm a report of flooding in the auxiliary machine space. The job properly belonged to Repair Locker 5, but most of that team was already up on the deckhouse laying out hose and getting ready to fight the stack fire. Others were rescuing Chief Perez; still others had been injured in the blast.

Frost sent five of his men down to check it out. The team was led by Kevin Ford and included Rick Raymond, Mess Specialist 1st Class Scott Frank, Radioman 2nd Class Gary Jackson, and Dick Fridley, the boatswain's mate first class. They scooped some DC gear from their locker—mallets, wooden plugs, wedges—and headed out. They trooped through the mess room, swung open a soundproofed door, and headed down a ladder.[11]

Thirty feet long, AMR 2 was one of the bigger spaces on the ship, a two-deck compartment only slightly smaller than the engine room. Much of the space was taken up by the soundproofed enclosures that held generators numbers two and three. There was plenty of other gear as well: chilled-water circulators, fuel filters, and most crucially, two of the ship's fire pumps.

The upper deck looked okay to Ford and his team, so they headed down a second ladder. They expected to see the ochre-painted bilge stringers several feet below the deck plates. Instead, there was only black water, six inches under their boots. But the sight of flooded bilges could not compare with the shock of seeing water pouring from holes in the aft bulkhead. The steel plates that separated AMR 2 from the inundated main engine room had buckled inward. Water was pouring from a half dozen cracks and punctures. Several holes were the size of basketballs. This forty-five-foot stretch of battered steel, obstructed by pipes, equipment, and the two generator enclosures, would become the front line in the battle to save the *Roberts.*

Raymond stepped past the pumps and panels that protruded like islands from the flooded bilges. He took aim at a two-inch split seam, wrestled a wooden wedge into the gushing water, and began pounding it into place with a mallet. This was standard DC technique; Raymond had done this dozens of times in the Buttercup. But the steel bulkhead responded in a way he'd never seen in the simulator. It split again, opening a new gusher about a foot above the original hole. The words of an instructor came back to him: "It only splits like that when there's a ton of water behind the bulkhead." *Just how bad is it in here?* Raymond wondered.[12]

Next to him, Ford was wrestling with another hole. The awkward, cramped space made his job far tougher than anything the simulator had ever thrown at him. The punctures and splits were obscured, hidden behind water pipes, fuel valves, and electrical junction boxes.

Raymond lay down atop an electrical distribution panel and reached down behind it to get to another leak. When he got up, Jackson was staring at him. "I didn't want to tell you, but that thing was smoking," Raymond recalled Jackson saying. "I was just waiting for you to get electrocuted."

Soon, there was more bad news from the number two generator enclosure. The blast had shoved the aft bulkhead upward, opening splits as it bowed. Water was spurting onto the diesel's engine block.

The sailors hammered away, but the wooden plugs weren't working. In desperation they looked around for other materials, softer ones that would be less likely to cause new holes. In other ships they might have found rags floating up from the bilges, but the *Roberts* was kept too clean for that. So they began to tear off their clothes—chambray shirts, white hats, even their coveralls—and stuffed those in the holes. The water spit some of them right out, but others stuck.

It was several minutes before anyone outside AMR 2 knew how bad things were getting in the ship's second-biggest space. Damage control doctrine called for one man in the repair party to don a pair of sound-powered phones and keep in touch with DC Central, but Ford and his team were too busy for that. It was too noisy for the phones anyway; the sailors were shouting just to hear one another. The big diesels were still roaring along, their soundproof doors open while Ford's team battled the flooding. The aural assault of thirty-two cylinders was almost too much to bear.

Nevertheless, a steady stream of shipmates was soon flowing into AMR 2's crowded space. At first they had joined Ford's team at the aft bulkhead and lent a hand in plugging the leaks. But the chief cook soon found that the extra pluggers were more trouble than they were worth; everyone kept tripping over one another in the narrow spaces between the equipment.[13] But there was certainly plenty else for them to do. Lt. (jg) John Sims, the main propulsion assistant, had arrived to help direct traffic. He assigned some sailors to ferry status reports to DC Central. Others

he asked to fetch equipment: wooden and metal shoring beams to buttress the damaged bulkhead, gas-powered pumps and drainage hoses. It
was time to start getting some of the rising seawater out of the bilge.

Within minutes, several sailors had rigged a pair of eductors, the two-
foot pipelike devices that used pressurized water to generate suction. The
supply hoses ran from nearby fireplugs; the wastewater hoses snaked
up two levels from the bilge, across the mess deck, and out to a discharge
fitting in the hull. But the eductors required water pressure to work—
and at that moment, none of the ship's fire pumps was operating. Two
of five were underwater; the others had shut down with the electrical
brownout. The sailors waited anxiously for the Central Control engineers
to restabilize the electrical grid.[14]

They did not wait long. The eductors and hoses had been rigged no
more than a minute when one fire pump, then the other, hummed to life
just ten feet from the aft bulkhead. Seawater filled the *Roberts*'s eight-
inch fire mains, branching into the feeder pipes that carried it to dozens
of fireplugs around the ship. The water pressurized the hoses of the fire
teams who waited atop the deckhouse. Dials showed the pressure at 150
pounds per square inch, right on target.

In AMR 2, water flowed into eductors. Their intakes burped and
began to suck dark liquid from the bilges. Fifteen minutes after water had
begun to flood the engineering spaces, the *Roberts* crew was starting to
pump it off the ship. But all the eductors on board wouldn't keep the
water from rising if the DC teams couldn't get some patches on the gushing holes. Ford realized that none of the hard patches they had been
forming were going to work. And the shirts and coveralls were simply
too small to stanch the flow. He needed something bigger. What, on a
ship, was big and soft?

The cook had an idea. He picked a couple of the extra guys, told
them to go get pillows and mattresses. And he added a kicker, intended
to take the edge off the rising tension: Ford told them to go get the bedding off their chiefs' racks.

The sailors returned several minutes later with broad smiles and several blue foam mattresses. Raymond emerged from the generator enclosure, folded one of the six-foot cushions in half, and carried it back in.
He pushed the three-foot foam square at a corner leak and wedged it into

place with a four-by-four-foot beam. Water was still flowing vigorously down the bulkhead, but at least it wasn't splashing on the diesel. Raymond rounded out the patch with a couple of pillows someone had carried down the ladder. It wasn't pretty, and it didn't even stop the leak, but it fixed one problem, and that was progress. But seawater was still coming in faster than they were pumping it out.[15]

AFTER RINN GOT off the phone with Admiral Less, the captain decided it was time for a look at AMR 2. He waded through the fire hoses that crisscrossed the mess deck and headed down into the machinery space. On the lower level, the captain stepped off the ladder into shin-deep water. *Oh, fuck, this is worse than I thought.* He could see that Ford and his team had done plenty already. Two big blue mattresses were pinned against the leaky bulkhead by steel shoring beams. Other holes were plugged by various bits of uniforms, boards, and even an entire toolbox. Two eductors were pumping away. But there was still plenty of water coming through.

Two sailors came by in their skivvies, having sacrificed their coveralls to the damage-control effort. Both were overweight; the captain recognized them as members of the ship's weight-loss program. "You guys look pretty shitty with your clothes on, but this is almost unbearable," he told them.

Rinn found Ford. The situation didn't look so good, the captain said. "That's nothing," said the cook, and led Rinn into the generator enclosure. Raymond's patch was keeping the seawater from spurting onto the diesel engine, but the wall was soaked.

"They've clearly got their work cut out for them," Rinn recalled,

and I think it's important that they know the gravity of the situation. I gather them together, not taking a lot of time, but a moment.

I said, "We've lost the main engine room, we've lost AMR 3. We can't lose any more spaces. We're going to hold GSK [General Store Keeper, the ship's largest storeroom], I hear. But you've got to hold this bulkhead. If you don't, we're going to sink, and we're going to sink very fast, and you guys are going to die right here. Simple as that. The bottom reality is, if you're going to bail, do it now, because I need you here."

The most amazing thing was, here I am telling these twenty-year-old kids that their reality was, this could be your last five minutes on the face of the earth, and you can die right here. It's going to be pretty awful, to die in this stinking space. Not a one blinked, not a one said anything, not a one said, "Shit, that's terrible; I've got to get out of here and save myself."

Almost to a man, with Ford, they looked at me and said, "We got it. You get out of here; you've got other things to worry about. We're not going to lose this space. We're going to save it."

I was incredibly buoyed by that.

Ford told the captain to give his team twenty minutes; they'd have things under control. "Okay, you got it," Rinn told him. As the captain turned to leave, the strains of rock music caught his ear. In the din of the diesel and the yelling and the watery rush, there was also a boom box, perched on a refrigeration unit, blasting out tunes by the rock band Journey.

Halfway up the ladder, Rinn turned around. Raymond thought he looked worried. But for just an instant, the captain felt lighthearted. The music reminded him of a joke that had started after his teenage daughters visited the ship. *The captain fears no man,* the sailors said, *but what he really fears is that he'll come back to the house one night and see one of us in a Trans Am in his driveway with a Journey tape playing and his daughter in the front seat.*

Rinn smiled. "Even in this situation, your choice of music sucks," he told the room. The sailors laughed and the captain left. He wondered whether he'd see them again.

CHAPTER ELEVEN

Ship's on Fire

The DC effort atop the deckhouse had begun while the mammoth fireball was still dissipating into a charcoal smudge on the late-afternoon sky. Flaming debris fluttered down to the deck, and sailors soon stamped the pocket-sized blazes into extinction. But there was clearly a more serious fire to fight. Dark fumes boiled from the stack and wafted up from cracks in the deck. Somewhere in the steel maze beneath their feet, flames were spreading.

The response by the sailors atop the deckhouse, mostly signalmen and quartermasters, was all but automatic. Treading paths worn in countless drills, they flaked out hoses into long canvas lengths on the deck, screwed them into knee-high fireplugs, and attached the heavy brass nozzles. Signalman 1st Class Chuck Dumas and other petty officers directed traffic as junior sailors set up fire parties. Within a few minutes of the blast, a pair of hose teams was ready to go: nozzleman, two hosemen, plus three or four helpers behind. A team leader gave the signal to charge the hose. Someone turned the valve on the fireplug. Nothing came out.

What was the problem? No one knew. But they had seen this before, in drills. When a fire hose lost pressure, it often signified a gash or leak in one of the ship's fire mains, the eight-inch copper-nickel pipes that carried water from fire pump to fireplug. Someone in the repair party would go find the leak and turn the nearest cutoff valve, closing the pipe as a surgeon might clamp a bleeding artery. The hose would be connected to the nearest plug that still had pressurized water, and the battle against the flames would go on.

The *Roberts* sailors soon determined that there wasn't a working fireplug aft of the mast, but they found pressure farther forward. Willing hands unscrewed fittings from dry plugs, broke out more hoses, and began daisy-chaining them forward in fifty-foot lengths. In moments, someone opened the tap on another fireplug, and the nozzleman drew on his control ring. A stream of cooling liquid arced over the ten-foot lip of the stack and disappeared into the smoke.

The pressure wasn't great, because of the missing fire pumps and the long draw through 1 1/2-inch hoses. But it was a start. A minute later another hose team opened up on the blaze.

Then the water flow slowed to a trickle and stopped once more. Someone yelled back from the pilothouse: the electricity was out, and the fire pumps with it. The stream of smoke emanating from the stack became a flood of boiling black vapor. The deck plates grew warm beneath their boots.

The power returned as suddenly as it had vanished—thanks to whom the firefighters did not know—and the fireplugs began once again to operate. But the pressure was even worse than before. Somewhere, something was definitely wrong with the fire main system.

But there was more than one way to skin this cat. Two decks down, on the quarterdeck, groups of sailors under the direction of Chief Sonarman John Carr connected hoses to a pair of P-250 gas-powered pumps. One pump drew seawater from the port side; the other from starboard, and both sent it up to the hose teams two decks above. At about four gallons a second, the pressure was weaker than a fireplug's, but it was all they firefighters had. They resumed their work, playing the relatively light flow of water over a stack fire that was clearly getting worse.[1]

GUNNER REINERT HAD hustled aft from the bridge when the mine went off, stomping a few pieces of flaming insulation into charred fluff along the way. Then he stopped, caught by the sight of controlled bedlam before him. His junior shipmates were throwing themselves into the damage control effort with impressive abandon. *Looks just like a drill,* he thought.[2]

Twenty minutes after the blast, the topside firefighting effort was going full bore, dumping dozens of gallons of seawater down the stack each minute. But the smoke was only getting thicker. Reinert tried to picture the fire's progress through the superstructure. By this point, he figured, the heat must be spreading from the engine room through the ship's steel beams and plates—but to where? He looked down at the cracks in the deck. One of them extended all the way across the top of the deckhouse, snaking past the covered voids that descended to the engine room, exhaling hot gray fumes along its entire length. The fissure was less than a dozen feet from the 76-mm gun turret. Suddenly, Reinert began to worry.

The munitions stacked in a warship's magazines can be as dangerous to their own crew as to their targets. Exposed to the heat of a shipboard fire, they can explode. The United States lost several ships in World War II when bombs and shells cooked off. The navy failed to absorb these costly lessons, and cook-offs killed scores more aboard the aircraft carriers *Enterprise* and USS *Forrestal* (CV 59) in the 1960s. Those disasters had at last galvanized efforts to create heat-resistant munitions, and so the shells and warheads aboard the *Roberts* were designed to keep their cool.

But Reinert wasn't taking chances. Descending to the main deck, he stopped by the torpedo magazine. It contained the ship's Mk 46 torpedoes—each eight feet long, thicker than a telephone pole, and tipped with ninety-six pounds of high explosive. The magazine also held Zuni rockets brought aboard for the army helicopters. Zunis had a bad name in the navy; earlier versions had caused both of the carrier fires.[3]

This mag should be safe from the fire, Reinert reasoned. A thwartships passageway separated it from the fires boiling up through the exhaust plenum. But when he laid a hand on the aft bulkhead, the aluminum was warm. He sent for buckets and mops, and sailors to wield them. His instructions were brief: swab the warm bulkheads with cool seawater, and don't stop until everyone else puts the fires out. It would be a nerve-wracking job, standing fire watch amid deadly weapons, but someone had to do it.

The chief headed up one deck to the 76-mm magazine. The space backed up to the exhaust plenum, and he expected warm bulkheads. But when he undogged the hatch, plastered with red and gray warnings, the air itself was warm, and his nostrils picked up a whiff of smoke. Reinert looked around. The magazine held hundreds of two-foot shells stacked vertically in metal racks. The blast had knocked two racks loose from their mounts. He stepped past the gun's rotary feeder, a massive cylinder that dominated the space. Dark wisps wafted through a three-inch rent in the aft bulkhead. The chief laid his knuckles on the metal plate. It was not merely warm; it was hot.[4]

Mops and swabs would not fix this. The obvious move was to evacuate the shells from the magazine, but that decision had to come from the commanding officer, and the sooner the better. Reinert sent word to DC Central and waited for the response. The wall thermometer registered one hundred degrees.

Rinn hated to give up his most flexible weapon, but it was far from clear that the gun could still shoot accurately, or safely, or even at all. And he knew that if the shells cooked off, the battle to save the *Roberts* would come to a quick and unsuccessful end. The captain passed the order back to Reinert: toss the shells overboard.[5]

The chief sent for help—lots of help. As the word flashed around the ship, several sailors converged on the magazine and scrambled to take their places in a bucket-brigade line. The shells, each a fifty-pound cylinder of brass, fuse, and high explosive, were soon moving from hand to hand. Gunners muscled them one at a time from their racks and passed them out the magazine's doublewide hatch. Still cradled in their packing cases, the shells moved around a corner and down a ladder, through yet more arms to the port quarterdeck. One by one, the munitions went over the side and disappeared with a splash.

Inside the magazine, Reinert sweated with his men. He didn't tell them what he had learned from DC Central: that there was no water pressure in the sprinklers. If fire broke out, they would get no help from the automatic system, which had become just another bit of emergency gear knocked out by the mine.

The temperature kept going up: 110 . . . 115 . . . 120.

IN CIC, RINN put in another call to the *Coronado*. When Admiral Less got on the horn, Rinn described the loss of the main engine room and propulsion, the fires, the flooding, the wounded sailors. Less asked, "Considering your situation, what do you think about remaining with the ship?" For years afterward, instructors in Naval Academy leadership classes would ask their midshipman students to ponder that decision. The question is: was the prudent choice to get the crew off the ship before it went down and took them with it? To Rinn, then and later, the answer was crystal clear.

> Was I confident that we were going to save the ship? No. Did I think we had a fighting chance? Yeah. Did I think that was the best decision? Yeah. Was I going to give up my ship? Not a chance. They don't put people in charge of ships in the United States Navy who are going to abandon them.
>
> In fact, it wasn't clear to me that if I gave the order to abandon ship, many guys would have gone. They were sticking around, and they were into it. It's a decision made based on all that I know, but one made based on faith in the crew, and their faith in me.

And as bad as things were, piling into life rafts would make them far worse. The *Roberts* was still in a minefield; the rafts would have been at the mercy of current and winds. There were sharks and sea snakes out there. And who would come rescue them? No, the best option was to stay and fight.

Rinn's reply came back in a flash. "I haven't thought about that at all. I have no desire to leave the ship. We'll stay with the ship and fight it. Right now, I have no other choice. In a nutshell, we're in trouble." It was the last time Less brought up the notion.[6]

"Do you have anything else to pass?" the admiral asked.

"No higher honor," the captain said, and signed off. He headed up to the bridge, where he gathered the nearby officers. "I want you to give me a rundown," he began. "Here's what I already know: we've lost the main engine room, there is flooding in AMR 2, but it seems to be under control; there is flooding in AMR 3."

Rinn stopped. His officers were staring at him.

"We don't have 'flooding' in AMR 3," someone said. "AMR 3 is gone!"

The captain said, "You're telling me my other main engineering space is gone? Are you sure?"

"Yes," they said.[7]

Rinn stepped out onto the bridge wing and looked aft. Smoke was still pouring from the stack and the cracks in the deck. The sun was getting low on the horizon. Something was bothering him, something tickling the back of his mind, telling him he'd forgotten something important.

He decided to take another look around the ship. Down on the mess deck, the floor was covered with glass shards. The sight of the soda vending machine reminded him that the ship was out of drinking water. He told someone from the supply department to open up the machine and distribute the cans to thirsty sailors.

Then Rinn headed aft. As he picked his way through the midships passageway, steaming hot water dripped on his bellcap and flowed down the bulkhead. It was the runoff from the fire hoses two levels above him, heated by the deck plates. Water was pouring into the stack, but also running across the deck, draining through the gaps down into the hull. *This is an odd situation,* he thought. *Water above me, fire below.*

On his previous tour of the ship, Rinn had walked onto the flight deck and pulled aside Boatswain's Mate 2nd Class Kim Sandle. A member of the flight-quarters team, Sandle had nearly been decapitated by the helo's flexing rotor blades during the mine blast. Rinn had a vital task for the serious young sailor. The ship's number, 58, was painted on the side of the ship about four feet below the flight deck and—under normal conditions—about nine above the waterline. The ship was riding low, and Rinn had told Sandle to watch the number. He wanted to know just how bad things got.

Now the captain pulled the nearest phone from its hook and called the poop deck.

"Where's the water?" he asked Sandle.

"I don't know," the boatswain replied.

This ticked Rinn off. *I gave him a direct order and he can't tell me where the water is?*

"The reason I can't tell you the relationship of the numbers to the water," the petty officer said, "is because they're underneath the water, Captain."

This was surprising. *They said there wasn't any flooding in the main storeroom. Is there water in some space, some void I don't know about?*

"Sandle, how bad is it?"

"Captain, if I get down on my hands and knees on the poop deck, I can put my hand in the water."

Rinn looked down at his shoes, wet with seawater.

Something came back to him. It was a lesson as old as the *Normandie* and as recent as the *Stark,* concisely stated in Eric Sorensen's little blue DC handbook: "One of the hazards of fighting a fire aboard a ship is that it is possible to sink the ship while putting out the fire."

Rinn realized with a shock that his damage control teams were putting ton after ton of seawater into the skin of his heavily damaged frigate. *We're sinking ourselves!*

The captain charged back up to the bridge. It was 5:23 PM, about thirty-five minutes after the explosion. He ordered the quartermaster to make a note in the deck log: the captain orders the cessation of firefighting efforts aboard the ship.

Before the sentence was two seconds out of his mouth, Rinn felt a hand clamp onto his arm. It was the XO: "Can I talk to you on the bridge wing?"

Eckelberry waited until the pair was out of easy earshot of the rest of the bridge team. Then he said, "Have you lost your mind? What are you doing?"

Rinn said, "No, we don't have to worry about the fire. In a little while, we're going to be underwater and the fires won't matter anymore. We've got to stop putting water into the skin of the ship. We've got to hold back on that until we can get control of the flooding."

Eckelberry relented, rogered, and stepped back inside. Soon, the word was going out over the 1MC: stop fighting the fires until further notice. The ship's survival depended on the damage control team down in Auxiliary Machine Room 2.

AMR 2 WAS beginning to look like the mine had blown up the ship's laundry instead of the engine room. Along with a small pile of mattresses, there were pale blue-striped sheets and pillows, plus random items of clothing. But more orthodox damage control gear was also making its way down the ladders. Ford and his team were especially grateful to get metal shoring beams. By placing one end of the adjustable beams against something sturdy, they found they could extend the other to—finally—hold soft patches in place. When they ran out of extendable beams, they called for wooden four-by-fours and handsaws. The results weren't the textbook examples of shoring they'd completed in Guantánamo training, but things were moving too rapidly for perfect carpentry.

Somewhere in the madness, someone had noticed that diesel number three was running out of lube oil. The fluid cooled the diesel; without it, the engine would soon overheat and fail.[8] There wasn't time to diagnose the ailment; they settled for symptomatic treatment. The sailor rigged up a hand pump and hoses, connecting the nearby lube-oil tank to the diesel's filling port, and took turns cranking away at the pump. Joe Baker, who had found his way down into AMR 2 after Tilley got his diesel running, took one of the first shifts. The diesel's appetite for lube oil had turned voracious. Gallon after gallon of oil flowed from the tank to the engine, propelled by the arms of one sailor after another. It would be hours before they discovered that the diesel wasn't burning the oil; it was just flowing out a crack in the bottom of the engine block.

Light smoke wafted through the air; more hoses and eductors came down the ladder. Ford and crew raced to set them up. About a half hour after the mine blast, they got one of the perijets working, which was a big help. The suction began to pull water from the bilge.

They had also rigged two P-250 pumps—the extra pair the crew had scrounged up in Newport. Small knots of sailors had lugged them down to the lower deck, and now they were helping to turn the tide. The pumps and perijets were sucking up a combined 750 gallons a minute and sending it overboard through a discharge fitting. But the noise, added to the roar of the diesels, was almost overpowering. Ford dispatched Alan Sepelyak, a junior sailor, to sick bay for more earplugs.

And meanwhile, the team had finally stanched most of the major gushers in the bulkhead. Water was still leaking in, but no faster than it was flowing back out through drainage pipes and hoses. About 5:25 PM, Ford sent word to DC Central that the water level in AMR 2 was six inches below the deck plates and holding there.

Ford, Frank, Fridley, Jackson, and Raymond, with the help of dozens of their shipmates, had kept the *Roberts*'s serious wounds from turning into mortal ones. Now the crew could return to fighting the infection of fire.

AGONIZING MINUTES FOLLOWED Rinn's order to stop pouring water on the fire. The hose teams atop the deckhouse watched the smoke pour unchallenged from the stack. The minutes ticked along like hours.

The deck was getting hot, very hot. Rubber-soled boots began to stick to the metal plates. Some men just stepped out of their melted footwear and left them adhered to the deck as they high-stepped away to fetch new shoes.

One of them, a chubby sailor who'd never managed to pass his damage control test, rushed past Rinn, then stopped and turned around in his stocking feet. "Captain, does this mean I'm DC-qualified?"

The skipper smiled. "No," he said.

"Damn," the sailor said, and hurried on.

About ten minutes passed, and finally the good news about AMR 2 arrived from DC Central. What was more, pumps had been set up near the main engine room and AMR 3, and the water levels had stabilized there as well. The captain lifted the ban on fighting the fires. The hose teams needed no urging to get back to work.

Rinn's mind was still on the weight of the ship. He had ordered some other things thrown overboard. A helicopter engine had already been tossed out and the position marked for salvage later. The water was only 150 feet deep here; divers should be able to bring it up, once the EOD guys cleared the mines. Rinn wondered what else might go. *Maybe we should jettison the torpedoes along with the shells?*[9]

Then he started having second thoughts about the entire notion of tossing ammo overboard. In the first place, it seemed too much like giving up, and that was the wrong signal to send to his crew. And second, if they did save the ship, it was going to be a monumental headache to explain where all the ammunition had gone. The men had already transferred thirty-four rounds, plus one charge designed to clear a jammed gun, from the ship's magazine to the briny deep. Rinn sent word down to Reinert: stop throwing the shells away—stack 'em on the forecastle instead. The gunner passed the word for more men and added them to the bucket brigade. The line of sailors grew, made a left turn on the quarterdeck, and stretched forward through the breakwater to the forecastle. About forty crew members were now working to clear the magazine, one-fifth of the souls on board the *Roberts*.[10]

SOON AFTER AMR 2 reported things under control, Rinn received another bit of good news from Lt. Cdr. Tim Matthews, the senior officer of the *Roberts*'s air detachment: the ship's helicopter might soon be ready to fly.

Matthews had been powering up the Seahawk from the left cockpit seat when the flight deck surged upward beneath him. His instrument panel lit up in red, and the engine shut down. Liquid gushed from the turbine. But when the ship's motion subsided, the helo was still clamped tightly to the deck.

The frigate was equipped with a RAST (Recovery, Assist, Securing, and Traversing) system, a movable winch built to draw helicopters onto heaving decks in bad weather. Matthews liked to use it as a safety belt when his helo was out on deck. This habit had probably saved half a dozen lives. Untethered, the helo could have tipped over. Its spinning rotors could have tilted into the deck and shattered into deadly shards. The helo itself may well have rolled off the deck and into the sea, taking Matthews, his copilot, and the enlisted aircrewman with it.

What actually happened was nearly just as hazardous. The blades had flexed, their tips whirling to within a yard of the deck, narrowly missing Sandle and the rest of the flight deck crew.

The pilot had shut down his battered bird and climbed out. His maintainers surrounded the aircraft, scrutinizing it for evidence of damage. There was almost no conceivable way that a helicopter subjected to such a blow would soon fly. There was too much that might have broken— engines, transmission, flight controls. The working hypothesis on the liquid was that a fuel line had severed, possibly flooding the engine with JP-8 jet fuel. Even the landing gear, which had absorbed most of the shock, might collapse if tested again.

But a half hour later the aviation mechanics gave Matthews a surprising verdict: odd as it sounded, they couldn't find anything that looked too broken to fly. They'd replaced some leaking seals in the tail rotor and tightened the fittings on a pump that was oozing hydraulic fluid, but if the aviation commander wanted to ignore training, instincts, and rulebook, the helo looked good to go.[11]

It was hard to beat a helo pilot for the propensity to see disaster at every turn. The job demanded it. A helicopter, it was said, was less an aircraft than ten thousand parts flying in tight formation. The potential for harm multiplied when such an aerodynamically unstable flying machine operated from a tiny moving platform at sea.

So when Matthews approached Rinn around 5:30 PM, the captain was surprised to hear the lieutenant commander ask for permission to fly. Rinn wasn't initially inclined to approve. If the helo went into the drink, no one could save its crew.

Matthews proposed that he take things in stages: power the helo up. Then try hovering. Then orbit the ship a time or two before finally landing to load the wounded men.

Rinn recognized the risk. But he also had sailors who were going to die unless they could get off the ship. The captain sent the crew to flight quarters and told Matthews to call when he was ready to go.[12]

ECKELBERRY HAD TURNED the bridge into a backup DC Central, plotting the damage control effort on the chart table with the aid of Yeoman 1st Class Paul Hass. It was standard practice to duplicate the engineers' record keeping on the bridge; a second perspective on the problem was always a good idea. But the executive officer had elevated the concept to include occasional broadcasts to the entire crew over the 1MC. These kept everyone informed about the DC effort, where the problem areas were, and most important, who needed help. Eckelberry, for example, had helped round up sailors to empty the 76-mm magazine and had urged otherwise unoccupied sailors to get down to AMR 2 and lend Ford a hand.

Some minutes after the bucket brigade had started sending 76-mm shells to the forecastle, Eckelberry caught the impossibly incongruous sounds of rock music. He stepped out to the bridge wing and looked down. Neat cordwood stacks of shells had begun to take shape between the deckhouse and the missile launcher. Someone had plugged in a portable cassette player and cranked it up. "It was almost comical," the XO recalled. "Ship's on fire, sinking aft, these guys are moving ammunition out of a hot magazine and they've got a boom box playing music on the forecastle. It was one of those things where you stop, and your jaw drops, and you say, 'I'm in Fantasyland.'"

Eckelberry also helped direct the movement of injured sailors to various first-aid stations established by the ship's corpsman, Hospitalman

1st Class James Lambert. A tall, lean man, Lambert was the closest thing the ship had to a physician. Inevitably, everyone called him Doc. Two months earlier, Ford's video camera had caught him in the galley, wearing a deadpan expression and a white turtleneck emblazoned with a red cross. "Here's bread," the corpsman informed the camera, placing a loaf in the automatic slicer, "and it goes in here, and the lever goes down, and here's the finished product: sliced bread. So, kids, if you ever wondered, now you know where sliced bread comes from. It comes from the Persian Gulf."

When the mine went off, Doc Lambert picked himself off the sick bay floor and considered his options. The frigate had two spaces intended as emergency treatment wards: one was far aft under the flight deck; the other was farther forward but surrounded by racks of DC gear.[13] Neither was usable in the current circumstance, thanks to passageways full of smoke and hoses and equipment. So Lambert consulted with Rinn and Eckelberry about setting up a triage area atop the deckhouse, just behind the signal bridge.

It was hardly an ideal location for a makeshift infirmary—two levels up from the main deck and only a few dozen yards from the hose teams that were pouring water on the smoke-belching exhaust fire. But at least it wasn't inside the ship, which looked as if it might sink at any moment. It was also close to the whaleboat. If Matthews and his mechanics couldn't get their helo running, the *Roberts* might have to send its most severely wounded out by motorboat. So Eckelberry got on the 1MC and told anyone with an injury to make his way to top of the deckhouse. Privately, he thought, *We're going to lose some of these guys.*[14]

Lambert had already begun treating several of the hurt men below-decks. In engineering's Central Control, he applied burn salve to Wayne Smith and Dave Burbine, who was shivering uncontrollably despite the blanket wrapped around him. He sent others up to the triage area behind the signal bridge. They were met by Lambert's phone talker, Master-at-Arms 1st Class Stanley Bauman, and Ens. Steven Giannone, a disbursing officer who had arrived aboard during the deployment and become Lambert's medical assistant. Giannone and Bauman took in the new arrivals and tried to make them comfortable.

Forty minutes after the blast, Lambert joined them. He checked on Bobby Gibson, who had been tied to a stretcher and carried up to the aid station. The boatswain's mate had tried to join a repair party after the mine blast had flipped him from his lookout's chair, but the pain had soon debilitated him. Lambert bent over Gibson, sweat dripping from his brow.

Chewing ice chips to keep himself hydrated, Lambert moved from patient to patient, applying Silvadine antibacterial cream, pushing IV needles into their arms, starting drips of Ringer's lactate to replenish their fluids. As his supply of bandages dwindled, Lambert sent a junior personnelman, Charles Morin, and a seaman named Richard Klemme down to his sick bay for more. *Just cut the lock off the medical supplies,* he told them.

Several of the burned engineers eventually arrived. Lambert worked to stabilize them. Severely burned patients are at great risk of shock, and Lambert knew that their chances for survival depended on better care than he could provide on the frigate. But he took hope in the news that the ship's Seahawk might become available for an evacuation flight. Leaving Lt. (jg) Robert Chambers, the ship's electronic readiness officer, in charge of the IVs, Lambert headed down to the hangar to establish a medevac station.

The supply officer, Lt. Bradley Gutcher, had beaten him to it. Anticipating the need, Gutcher had raided the aft battle-dressing station, gathered up all the first-aid supplies he could carry, and hauled them in a blanket to the hangar.[15]

Eckelberry passed the word over the 1MC, and injured men began to show up at the hangar. Several dozen had wrenched their backs and limbs, either in the initial blast or by slipping on the various liquids that were being tracked around the ship: water, fuel, AFFF. Some had gotten oil and smoke particles in their eyes, yet had been unable to bear to use the ship's eyewashes to clear the gunk out. Lambert slit open saline bags and gently cleansed their faces.

Presently, the sailors began to make their way down from the deck-house aid station. Bill Dodson, an electrician's mate third class, was working in the midships passageway when one badly burned shipmate hobbled past. "Everyone was yelling and we were moving ammo around or something. Lots of heavy things. And I looked up to see two people escorting GSM Welch aft to the helo deck. He was naked, and completely burned and bloody. He had a gray blanket draped around him. It was a bad scene, and everyone hushed as he walked slowly by. I couldn't believe he could walk.

"After he went by, I think our efforts took on a new sense of urgency."[16]

Outside the hangar's aluminum roll-up door, an aviation mechanic gave Matthews a thumbs-up as the aviator powered up the Seahawk. The cockpit lit up green, and he twisted the cyclic, willing the aircraft off the deck. It shuddered, lifted, and came to a hover off the starboard quarter.

Rinn radioed the pilot and asked him to circle the ship. Against the setting sun, Matthews could see the orange glow of flames through the deckhouse cracks and sparks floating amid the black smoke that still boiled from the stack.

When the helo set back down, Lambert had picked his first medevac patient: Welch, who had second-degree burns over 40 percent of his body. Volunteers loaded their burned shipmate onto the helicopter.

About 6:15 PM, the Seahawk took off again and bore away into the darkening east. His destination was the amphib *Trenton,* which was making its best speed toward the wounded frigate.

Years later, Matthews told Rinn that as he flew away with the wounded man, he never expected to see the ship afloat again.[17]

Darkness Falls

The sun set at six o'clock. "I swear the sun went down faster that day than I ever saw it," firefighter Ted Johnson recalled. "It got so dark, so fast. And sea snakes, they were everywhere when you looked over the side."

With the new moon just two days away, the coming night would be dark indeed. Lookouts on the bridge wings played searchlights over the water, straining to spot drifting mines. All they saw were the five-foot snakes.

Lester Chaffin figured the ship's moaning had drawn every terrifying resident of Davy Jones's locker to the scene. With a start, the ship's Protestant lay leader remembered that he had neglected to read the evening prayer over the 1MC the previous night.[1]

The damage control effort had continued nonstop for an hour and a half. Belowdecks, electricians checked power connections while engine specialists tended their diesels. Shoring teams worked to strengthen strained bulkheads. Everyone who wasn't passing 76-mm shells from the magazine seemed to be humping pump gear and hoses from place to place or helping their injured shipmates move toward medical aid. The captain moved around the ship, dispensing "attaboys" and drawing inspiration from his crew. On the quarterdeck he watched passing sailors touch the bronze plaque, brushing their fingers across the raised names of their predecessors on DE-413.

Up on the deckhouse the hose teams were still doggedly throwing water on the pillar of spark-flecked smoke coming from the stack, and pouring it through the cracks under their feet. Under the direction of Chief John Carr, the hose teams had begun to add fire-smothering foam AFFF into the water. The flow of AFFF through the permanent reels was intermittent, thanks to uncertain electricity and fluctuating water pressure, so the firefighters had rigged their nozzles to draw the soapy chemical straight from the blue five-gallon drums. From time to time Carr sent word down to Reinert, who interrupted the flow of 76-mm shells to send more blue canisters up to the roof.[2]

The twin needs for firefighting water and drainage had nearly exhausted the ship's supply of hoses and fittings, so much was done with improvisation. Chris Pond yelled to Johnson, "Ted, Ted, I need a two-and-a-half-inch plug and I can't find one! What do I do?"

Johnson responded in true sailor fashion: "Just use a two-and-a-half-inch nozzle and shut it," he said.[3]

Still, the crew was making progress with the stack fire; the smoke from the starboard vent seemed somewhat dissipated. But the hose teams were becoming increasingly frustrated by the on-again, off-again flow of water. Sometimes they would get only five or ten minutes of continuous pressure before the hoses ran dry. AFFF refused to foam up at less than 150 pounds per square inch, and some of the more irritated sailors had taken to pouring the stuff straight from the can into the cracks.[4]

Down in Central Control, Van Hook and the engineers were trying to figure out what was causing the problems with the water pressure. All the clues pointed to a major fire-main leak in the main engine room. The engineers tried various tactics to deduce the exact location of the leak, turning the water on and off, experimenting with various cutoff-valve settings. Unless the damaged pipe could be found and cut off from the others, the firefighters were never going to get the smooth flow they needed.

Finally, a repair team in the still-smoking engine room spotted a bubbling trickle of AFFF under the oily water. That suggested a leak in the fire main's port upper loop. The sailors closed valves to cut the flow to the damaged pipe, crossed their fingers, and applied pressure to the entire system. It worked. Four minutes after they'd shut down the fire main, there was pressure again—at least in the starboard lower loop. The repair crews decided to detour the water around the leak, and began the forty-minute process of rigging jumper hoses to restore pressure in the port upper loop.

Around 6:45 PM, about two hours after the mine blast, the hose teams had one good source of water again. The return of pressure set one hose to jumping. The nozzle had somehow jammed or been left open when pressure went down, and now it whipped around on the deck, spraying water like a spitting cobra. As firefighters backed away from the nozzle-turned-wrecking ball, Lt. Dave Llewellyn pounced on it. Rinn, who happened to be on deck, watched in horror as the heavy nozzle smacked his ship's control officer square on the forehead. "I thought he was dead, but he just shook it off and got up," the captain said.[5]

The pressure stayed steady for a half hour, flickered for a nerve-wracking minute as two teams hunted for another suspected break in the line, and then held steady.

NOT LONG AFTERWARD, a bit of help appeared on the horizon, in the form of helicopter running lights. They belonged to a CH-46 Sea Knight, call sign Nightrider, flying from the *San Jose,* the replenishment ship *Roberts* had been slated to meet that eternity of two and a half hours ago.

Lambert had heard about the inbound CH-46s, but he didn't see how that was going to help. The double-rotored Sea Knights were even bigger than the *Roberts's* ten-ton Seahawk. *That's not even going to fit on the flight deck,* he thought.[6]

Nevertheless, Lambert and his helpers readied eight of their patients for evacuation. The corpsman used a marker to scrawl treatment notes on the sheets of their bedding, a technique he'd picked up during a stint in an emergency room. Headed out were the badly burned Perez, Burbine, and Smith. Gibson, who had been diagnosed with a concussion, would go as well. So would Radioman 2nd Class Doug Thomas, who had become dizzy while moving 76-mm ammo; Gunner's Mate 3rd Class Randy L. Thomas, who had strained his back at the same task; Fire Controlman 3rd Class Jack Paprocki, who had been thrown against the bulkhead of the CIWS control room by the mine blast; and Seaman Recruit Richard A. Bailey, who had been carried to the hangar bay by two shipmates after his legs went numb.

Sonar Technician 1st Class Joseph D. Boyd, "J. D." to his friends, had been fighting the stack fire for hours when a team leader sent him forward to the bridge to rest. It was only when Boyd sat down that he felt the pain in his midsection, a possible hernia. After a quick check from Lambert, Eckelberry told the sonar tech to grab the next helo flight to the *San Jose.*[7]

The *Roberts*'s air traffic controller got on the radio with the Sea Knight and told its pilots to be prepared to evacuate as many men as possible. The pilots replied that they were carrying a large fuel bladder on board. It had helped them make the long trip from the *San Jose*, but it was really more a redundant safety move than a necessity. They asked whether they could leave the bladder with the *Roberts*.

Negative, the *Roberts* controller replied. *We're on fire here.* So the crew of the Sea Knight kicked the flexible rubber tank out the helo door instead. It landed with a splash near the ship and began to float as the CH-46 came in for a landing.

Sandle was in charge of guiding the aircraft to the flight deck. As it approached, the boatswain's mate realized that the deck was fouled by the RAST gear, the harness that had saved Matthews and the Seahawk. Sandle decided to land the helicopter crossways, giving the forty-five-foot-long helo about six inches of clearance on each side of its landing gear. He had seen Sea Knights perform aerial ballet, but he'd never seen one land with so little room to spare. Guiding the helicopter down with illuminated signal flashlights, he stared at its wheels until they touched down less than a tire's diameter from the safety nets at the deck edge. The pilots kept the rotors turning, ready to lift off if the ship took an unexpected roll.

As Lambert and his helpers lifted their shipmates into the big aircraft, one of the CH-46 pilots snapped a photo. That irritated the corpsman. *What the hell are you taking pictures of?* But when he turned around and stepped out of the aircraft, the reason became clear. The ship was lit up like a Christmas tree, every floodlight and spot shining away. All the doors were open, with hoses snaking this way and that. Atop it all, the stack was still belching sparks like a chimney. *I guess that* would *make a good picture,* he conceded.[8]

A little after 7:00 PM, the twin-rotor helo lifted off, bearing the eight *Roberts* sailors toward the *San Jose* and a doctor's care. The aircraft would return in less than an hour with hoses, DC gear, food, and water.

ONE MAN WHO was not aboard the helicopter was Hull Technician 1st Class Gary Gawor, whose knee had been banged up in the blast. Rinn found him perched on a stool in the hangar, a matted red bandage around his leg. The captain told Gawor to get on the helicopter, but the hull tech was having none of it. He had spent two hours directing the flow of DC people and supplies from his stool, and he wasn't about to stop.

"Captain, I'm not leaving," Gawor said. "I got a job to do in this hangar."

Rinn nodded and moved on to the flight deck. He spotted a dark shape in the water off the starboard quarter. It was the discarded fuel bladder, now illuminated by a magnesium flare that floated nearby, burning piercingly bright at thirty-six hundred degrees.

Rinn turned to Ensign Sobnosky. "Rob, what's that?"

"Captain, it's a smoke float," the junior officer replied.

An ensign with an amazing grasp of the obvious, Rinn thought. "I know it's a smoke float. What's it doing in the water?"

"When the '-46 came in, they had a fuel bladder, and when they left with the people, they couldn't carry it, so they threw it in the water."

"Okay. Why is there a smoke float in the water, a *magnesium* smoke float?"

Sobnosky said, "I thought you'd want to know where it was."

This, Rinn told himself, *is not my best day in the navy.*

Then the captain noticed some other objects bobbing alongside the ship. They were 76-mm shells, each still in its plastic wrapping. *God, don't tell me I had to tell these guys to open the damn canisters before they threw the ammunition over the side.*

Rinn decided that minefield or no minefield, it was time to get the hell out of Dodge. He returned to the bridge and spent a few minutes alone with the navigational chart. His engines might be in pieces, but he still had the electric-powered APUs. Rinn checked the load requirements with engineering, then ordered the electricians to start up the port pod. By a process that was far more gut than reason, Rinn picked a southeasterly heading. If the crew thought he possessed some special knowledge or training that had helped him select the course, so much the better. In his best command voice, he told the helmsman to come to three knots and 146 degrees and just keep going.[9]

In the coming days, EOD teams sent to clear the minefield would discover that the retreating *Roberts* had tiptoed past nine other mines.

NEARLY THREE HOURS had passed since the explosion, and all traces of sunlight had faded from the sky. The frigate's decks were flooded with every spotlight aboard—an uncomfortable condition in the Gulf. The ship had been accustomed to working at night with the barest of anticollision lights showing. Now it glowed like a beacon.

Somewhere in the ship, the fire still burned. Smoke was still coming from cracks in the deck superstructure; the crew could smell it everywhere. But where was it? Van Hook decided to take a look inside the gas turbine ventilation system.

Gas turbines required air in prodigious quantities. On a *Perry* frigate, air came in horizontally through a set of louvers on each side of the superstructure and then headed down three decks to the engines. About one-third of the air was used to sustain combustion, the rest to cool the gas turbines. The exhaust went out the back of the module, straight up four decks, and out through the stack.

Grabbing flashlights and breathing devices, Van Hook and Boatswain's Mate 3rd Class Eduardo Segovia headed for the engine intake plenum. They opened a little-used hatch in the deckhouse. Smoke billowed out. They crawled inside. Picking his way through the fumes, past dust filters and deicers and dehumidifying equipment, Van Hook crawled to the vertical shaft. He peered over the edge and looked thirty-five feet straight down into a fiery hell. On his hands and knees in the fire-lit dark, he realized what had happened. The mine had ignited a fire within the gas turbine modules. The sea had eventually inundated the engine room, putting the modules underwater—but the fires roared on in the intakes.

As Van Hook wormed his way back into the passageway, he considered his options. The ship's designers had built Halon dispensers into the enclosures, where the LM-2500s heated their exhaust gases to more than nine hundred degrees Fahrenheit. But Van Hook also knew that the fire-suppressing gas hadn't been released from its tanks. (Later investigation revealed that the blast had cut power to the dispensers' electrical panel.) The enclosures had a pair of small maintenance hatches, but they were under five feet of black oily water and likely jammed to boot. The final assault on the fire would have to come from above.

There was no room for a hose team to work in the cramped plenum, but Van Hook had another idea. The vertical air shafts had a second purpose: they allowed the gas turbines to be winched out of the engine room for repair or replacement. The massive cylinders rose up on rails and emerged between the 76-mm gun and the smokestack.

Back atop the superstructure, Van Hook drew the captain's eyes to the heavy steel plate that covered the starboard hatch. "We've got to attack this through the engine removal port. That's the only way we're really going to get at it," the chief engineer told his commanding officer.[10]

Rinn wasn't immediately convinced. "I don't know, Cheng," he said. "The minute we take that off, there's going to be this huge blast of air going in there, and it's going to explode right back at us."

Van Hook countered that it was unlikely to provide more air than was already coming down the big intakes.

"Okay, go ahead," Rinn said. "Get 'em off." The time was about 7:35 PM.

Van Hook gave the word, and about a dozen crewmen leaped to loosen the seventy heavy-duty bolts that sealed the plate to the deck. In an eyeblink—or so it seemed to the engineer, who was still wondering where they were going to find enough wrenches—the sailors had the bolts off. Chief Firecontrolman Al Jochem stuck a crowbar under the lip.

Jeez, I hope I'm right, Van Hook thought.[11]

When Jochem's crowbar opened a crack between plate and deck, flames boiled up, licking at pant legs and nearly taking eyebrows off. Everyone jumped back, leaving the plate lying askew atop the hole.

"Maybe this wasn't such a good idea," Van Hook announced. "Maybe we should do this tomorrow."

But the fire shrank back after the flare-up, and sailors rushed to pour AFFF-treated water down the hole. Within minutes the smoke changed from black to white, and shortly thereafter it went out completely.

That was the big one.

There were other, smaller fires to be put out. In a final, dying gasp, the stack belched up some hot cinders that fell onto a weather-deck tarp and set it alight. At 8:05 PM, fires reignited in both exhaust plenums. Hose teams quickly smothered the fire and set reflash watches to spray cooling water.

But thousands of tons of steel hold a nearly unimaginable amount of heat. Even after the flame is gone, the danger persists. A few minutes past

9:00, one of the gas turbine modules flashed back into flame. Once again, the watchstanders quickly put it out, and that was the last of the fires aboard the *Sammy B.*

At 9:05, the blazes that had burned aboard the frigate for four and one-quarter hours were, at last, extinguished.

WHEN WORD WAS passed that the fires were out, many of the men slumped straight down onto the deck and fell asleep, drained from four solid hours of adrenaline-soaked exertion. Others found sleep elusive. They wandered the decks, checking on buddies. The damaged hull creaked eerily, a reminder that their ship was fragile and still in danger. Serendipitously calm seas had reduced the stress on the main deck, but even small ripples caused the hull girder structure to flex.[12] Now that the noise and commotion of damage control had ceased, the groans of the damaged ship were inescapable.[12]

The captain ordered the crew into life jackets. He also told everyone to sleep out on deck, a safety-minded order that was generally, though not universally, obeyed. Quite a few sailors snuck down to their bunks for a few hours of well-deserved rest.

The cleanup started within hours of the final victory over the fire. Part of it was pride. Rinn was determined to show the world that the USS *Samuel B. Roberts* was but lightly fazed by adversity. Even before day broke, he was stomping around the hull passing the word: *We're going to look good for the cameras.*

But part of it was the realization that a crew without work is a restless crew. Rudyard Kipling wrote:

When you think of the amount of work a ship needs even after peace manoeuvres, you can realise what has to be done on the heels of an action . . . And as there is nothing like housework for the troubled soul of a woman, so a general clean-up is good for sailors. I had this from a petty officer who had also passed through deep waters. "If you've seen your best friend go from alongside you, and your own officer, and your own boat's crew with him, and things of that kind, a man's best comfort is small variegated jobs which he is damned for continuous."[13]

So Rinn pushed his shipmates—those who weren't utterly exhausted—to start restoring some semblance of order to their battered ship. It was a daunting proposition. Fuel and oil had been tracked the length of the ship. Spent OBA canisters and empty AFFF jugs littered the decks. Red, green, and gray hoses covered the passageways like tricolor spaghetti.

The first order of business was dealing with the tangled mass of hoses. The damage control teams sorted through them, picking out those that could be disconnected, rolled up, and returned to their racks. Some were left in place, in case some undetected hotspot flared up in the night. And the dewatering hoses remained in place; both P-250s and ship's fire pumps kept running at full capacity. But as longer lengths of hose were put in place of spliced-together shorter ones, many of the fittings borrowed from other ships came free.

Within hours, Eckelberry was surprised and impressed to see the damage control lockers beginning to resemble their orderly selves. The DC teams had carefully taken inventory, noted what equipment was still usable, and carefully stowed it away. Neat rows of OBAs all but dared disaster to strike again.

The XO was checking on the new hose configuration when the ship's weary-looking senior yeoman approached him. "Anything else I can do for you, sir?" Paul Hass asked.

"Yeah," Eckelberry replied. "Where's my Plan of the Day?"

A bit horrified, Hass looked at the officer to see if he was kidding, or had perhaps gone a bit crazy. The executive officer was neither. Within an hour, as if a hole had never been blown in the *Roberts*'s hull, a weary Hass slipped the photocopied schedule into its slot.[14]

The sun came up at 6:00 AM. "The dawn meant to me that I was going to live," Signalman Roberts recalled later. "I don't know why, but the dawn meant that time had passed, we were a ways from the mines, and we weren't going to sink. Eddie Segovia took my picture then, and had me take his. I swore I would keep that picture in a prominent place for the rest of my life. So far I have."[15]

Against all odds, there were morning showers. Months ago, the engineers had turned a forecastle void into a freshwater holding tank. Now someone rigged a pump, and sweat-caked, smelly sailors stripped naked for a brief and welcome wash-down.

Along came news helicopters, cameras rolling. There wasn't much to do but wave.

One of the *San Jose*'s Sea Knights arrived with breakfast: 250 English-muffin sandwiches, Snickers bars, and grape and orange soda. Ted Johnson bit into a sausage-egg-and-cheese sandwich. It was the best thing he had ever tasted.[16]

The fires were out, but the ship was still weakened and in peril. Soon after dawn, someone passed the word to start shoring up the forward bulkhead of GSK, the ship's main storeroom. On the other side of its forward bulkhead was tons of seawater in AMR 3. So far the bulkhead had held, but it had started to bow inward. Tatum helped haul shoring timbers from storage in after steering. Damage Controlman 1st Class Ward Davis and Electronics Technician 1st Class James Aston directed the work. It took seven pieces of twelve-foot four-by-four, notched to fit together like eight-foot letter "K"s. The completed shoring drew a lot of attention from shipmates, and later, damage inspectors. It was truly a textbook job.[17]

Led by Senior Chief Frost, a group of hull technicians and others gathered on the deckhouse to think about stabilizing the ship. The superstructure had cracked from main deck to roof, widening from a hairline at the main deck and widened to six-inch gaps near the 02 level. It was eerie to watch the cracks as the ship rode the light swells on the Gulf: the cracks widened and narrowed perceptibly. Clearly, the wave action was affecting the ship. Perhaps there was a way, someone mused, to tie the superstructure together.

Frost remembered the heavy-weather lifelines stashed away in the boatswain's locker. These were three-quarter-inch phosphor-bronze cables that formed the safety "railing" around the edge of the weather decks. Six lengths of the cable would be enough to rig a figure that looked like a square with an X in the middle for cross-bracing. Frost sketched a plan on yellow legal paper and presented it to Rinn. *Why not?* the captain said. *Do it.*

Under Frost's direction, Raymond and other sailors drew the cables around the 76-mm gun mount, wrapped them around the lips of the gas-turbine access ports, and through various pad eyes around the deck. Then they cinched it tight with turnbuckles. It didn't stop the flexing, but Frost and the rest swore the rigging dampened the movement.[18]

Some time later, Lt. (jg) Mike Valliere, the auxiliaries officer, had another idea for lending support to the flexing main deck: I-type shoring in the main passageway fore and aft of the cracks. Frost helped with that as well, using up the last of the steel and wooden shoring members to erect seven-foot "I"s marching down the passageway.

Later, on 15 April, the oceangoing tug *Hunter*—the same minesweeping craft that had led the *Roberts* through the Strait of Hormuz—arrived to take the wounded frigate in tow. The *Roberts* had come halfway to Dubai on its APUs, but there were still 120 miles to go. The ship would complete its trip to safety at the end of a thick steel cable.

CHAPTER THIRTEEN

Revenge

When a U.S. Navy ship approaches a foreign port, its crew customarily dons dress uniforms and arrays itself along the lifelines, a ceremonial fillip that speaks of martial discipline and diplomatic niceties and the difference between a warship and a mercantile craft hauling shopkeepers' cargo. For Rinn, the regrettable fact that the *Roberts* was approaching Dubai under tow was no excuse for making a sloppy impression. It would be, after all, the ship's first visit to the United Arab Emirates. All hands, he ordered, would report as usual in white summer uniforms.

That touched off a mad frenzy belowdecks. Plenty of sailors' whites had been lost or hopelessly soiled in the previous days' chaos; many more had been in the laundry when the ship hit the mine, and quite naturally, were still there. Eventually, enough Dixie-cup hats, rolled neckerchiefs, and white-works jumpers were found to outfit the entire crew. Everyone shaved and took a saltwater shower, and by the time the *Hunter* and the *Roberts* drew to within ten miles of the port, the sailors were out on deck.

Sparing no effort, the ship's signalmen raised the nautical pennants signifying "We are okay." Then they broke out their biggest American flag, the twenty-by-forty-foot monster they called "the Chevy-dealer model." Flying from the frigate's mast, it could be seen from horizon to hazy horizon.

The ship was headed to Dubai, an ancient port that had boomed in recent decades. The specific destination was Dubai Drydocks, the Persian Gulf's largest ship-repair facility. Oil wealth had built the facility as a hedge against fluctuating petroleum prices, and it had seen plenty of profit in patching up the maritime victims of the Iran–Iraq war.[1]

Eckelberry had visited the bustling port once before, and had found the racket almost deafening: cranes toting containers, repair crews stripping ships with pneumatic hammers, all the noises a commercial and industrial harbor can generate. But as *Hunter* towed the *Roberts* into the harbor around 3:00 PM, it dawned on him that something very strange was happening. The great port had fallen silent. Every worker on the waterfront had heard about the mining, it seemed, and had apparently put down their tools for a look at the diminutive warship that had survived the explosion. To the casual eye, the frigate looked to be in pretty good shape. The discerning viewer could see that the ship was down three feet at the stern.

Three harbor tugs nudged the warship past an Iranian tanker and up to a pier. At 4:25 PM on Saturday, 16 April, the *Roberts* came to rest. It was two days, almost to the hour, since the mine blast.[2]

DOWN IN THE WARDROOM, the officers, still in their dress whites, worried vaguely about the stability of their wired-up ship and wondered what to do next. In strode Bob Firehammer, dressed in civilian clothing. "Anyone want to hit the beach and grab a beer?" Firehammer asked. That broke the ice, and the officers scattered to change into civvies. Less than an hour later, most had their hands wrapped firmly around cold drinks at the bar at the Dubai Hilton.

The luxury hotel seemed to be one of the few places serving alcohol in the Muslim city, which had just begun to celebrate the annual Ramadan holiday. Within a few hours, the enlisted sailors had found the Hilton as well. Gary Gawor led a gang of engineers, hull technicians, and other shipmates to the hotel, rented a room, and started ordering room-service Heineken beer at an eye-popping seventy-two dollars per case. "It was the best money I ever spent, that night in the Hilton," Ted Johnson recalled fondly. "I think we even emptied the honor bar. Gawor's credit card must have melted!"[3]

But for many of their married shipmates, the arrival in Dubai had precipitated a mad dash to the pier, where a lone phone booth beckoned like a lifeline to home. About two dozen sailors' wives gathered at Perez's house in Portsmouth, Rhode Island, two towns up from Newport. They picked at brown-bag lunches and waited. At 2:00 PM, the phone rang. It was the *Roberts* sailors, who announced that they were queued up at the phone, the line stretching down the pier. Hastily, the wives arranged themselves in the same order as their husbands, forming a line along the hall to the Perez bedroom.

One by one, the sailors and their wives squeezed in a few minutes of stories and relief and love. Everyone had done their duty, the men said, but they singled out as heroes Cowan and Bent, who had pulled Perez from the oily black water. The phone call lasted two and a half hours before the last husband and wife said good-bye and hung up. Everyone in the house except Mary Perez had talked to their husbands. "The wives were so happy they were here and got to talk to them," she said. "I was happy for them."[4]

At 7:45 PM Mary finally got a call through to Alex, who had been medevaced to the Bahraini hospital. His spirits were high, she told a local reporter. "He just told me he loves me and to hang in there," she said. "The first thing [he said] was he wants to go back to the ship" and that "there is no higher honor than serving on the *Roberts*."

Cynthia Thomas talked with her husband, Randy Lee, who had been helicoptered off the ship after injuring his back moving 76-mm ammunition. "It was all so fast," he told her.[5]

For some anxious wives, children, parents, and other loved ones, the phone call from the pier was the first official word they'd gotten. Lester Chaffin's mother in West Virginia saw the damaged *Roberts* on Thursday's evening news and had worried for two days until Chaffin reached them by phone to let them know he was unhurt.[6] Other sailors had gotten word through phone trees or with telegrams. Gunner's Mate 1st Class Lawrence Lorusso had sent one such to his parents in Syracuse, New York. The delivery boy knocked on their door at 6:30 AM on Friday. The missive began, *Mom, I'm OK.*[7]

Pamela Rinn had received the news on Thursday at the family home in Charleston. She had just returned from dropping her income tax return in the mail when she heard the phone ringing through the front door. Wrestling with her dry cleaning, she managed to get the door unlocked and picked up the handset. It was someone calling from Aquilino's squadron.

Pamela spent much of the next twenty-four hours on the phone with navy officials and *Roberts* wives. They decided, among other things, that the Halfway Dinner should go on as scheduled—if no one died. The next day, she flew north from Charleston as if in a dream, walking past airport newsstands with photos of her husband's ship plastered across the front page.[8]

On Friday night Pamela Rinn joined the Newport families and gathered as planned for the dinner, a catered affair at the Officers' Club, and it had gone off as scheduled, if not exactly as anticipated. The occasion proved a good chance to get together and swap what bits of information the navy and the grapevine could provide.

Rinn finally got in touch with his wife in Newport on Saturday. Mostly, he talked of the sailors who had saved his ship. "It was close, really close," Paul told Pam. "The crew did exactly what they were supposed to do."[9]

Commodore Aquilino told Rinn that morale was holding on the home front and sent word of his medevaced sailors. Three of them, their burned faces masked with white salve and their limbs wrapped in medicated bandages, had been helicoptered to Bahrain, then flown by air force C-141 airlifters to the U.S. Army hospital in Landstuhl, Germany. Welch and Smith had turned out to be less badly burned than originally feared, although Smith's right hand would require considerable rehabilitation. Burbine, with burns over 40 percent of his body, would need plenty of treatment as well, but the sutures were holding around his eye and he was in good spirits. All three were headed to Brooks Army Hospital in Texas, one of the U.S. military's best burn-care wards.

Perez, who had suffered the crew's most grievous injuries, was still in Bahrain's Salmaniya Hospital. His upper torso was still immobilized in a body cast. A CAT scan had found fractures in his back, but had also indicated that the broken bones had stabilized.[10]

Rinn received an unexpected phone call of his own that day. His phone rang, and a voice said, "Hold for the president." *President of what?* Rinn wondered. But the voice that came on the line was instantly recognizable. "This will not go unpunished," Ronald Reagan told the *Roberts's* captain. "I'll get back to you." And with that, the president hung up. The call had lasted not more than twenty seconds, and it left Rinn just a bit stunned.[11]

But the captain's thoughts were soon back on his ship. He had a meeting scheduled on Sunday with the repair engineers at Dubai Drydocks.

He had dozens of questions, but they all boiled down to a single one: can we fix the ship here? Rinn fervently hoped so. He knew that the *Stark* had sailed home under its own power. If the *Roberts* could be patched up to do the same—or even to complete her deployment—the message to the world would be unmistakable: it's tough to knock a United States warship out of the fight. It would also prove that U.S. warships could be repaired in Gulf ports. And it might also keep Rinn in command a few weeks longer. Surely, he told himself, the navy wouldn't call him away after a moment of such triumph. When the Dubai shipwrights assured him that they could fix his ship, Rinn's spirits soared.[12]

Shortly after noon the next day, the captain laid out his case in a message addressed to Admiral Less, the Middle East Force commander, with copies sent to most of the navy's major commands. The ship had been badly damaged, Rinn began. The blast had put a twenty-foot hole in the hull. It had bent the keel into an S-shaped beam. The main engine room was still flooded to the upper catwalk; AMR 3 was inundated to its overhead I-beams. "The oil distribution box and sump, normally in lower level," he wrote, "are now lodged in overhead between gas turbines." Electrical power was shaky, and potable water was being pumped in from a hookup on the pier.

But the crew had reacted and rebounded beautifully, and had already restored many auxiliary systems. Air conditioning was keeping the computers and living spaces cool. Ford's galley gang was once again feeding the crew hot meals. The heads flushed. The showers ran cold water only, but they worked.

Now, Rinn went on, the ship needed two LM-2500 gas turbines, a new reduction gear, some auxiliary equipment, and lots of work. The Dubai engineers believed they could do the job if provided with a new propeller shaft and a few sections of HY-80 hull plate, which was not available locally. Rinn described the dry dock's chief executive as being well attuned to the "political reasons" for repairing the *Roberts* in theater.

Rinn believed the ship would be safe enough during the repairs. Besides Dubai's own port security, the *Roberts* had installed its own twenty-four-hour deck patrols. One sailor walked the deckhouse roof with an M-14 rifle, another hefted a shotgun on the main deck. The .50-caliber guns were unlimbered, loaded, and hidden discreetly under canvas.

Bottom line, Rinn declared: he wanted to restore the *Roberts* to fighting trim. "Ship is cleaned up, morale higher than ever, ship's force work underway," he wrote. "We saved her, we'll fix her and fight her again. Request max support to restore MER [main engine room]/AMR 3 ASAP . . . No higher honor!"

The decision would eventually be made back in Washington, but for now Tony Less had other things on his mind. From the White House itself, orders had filtered down to the commander of the Middle East Force, telling him to plan, not for repairs, but for revenge.

Within hours of *Roberts*'s plodding withdrawal from the minefield, wooden-hulled minesweepers and navy helicopters had begun moving in cautiously, like wary detectives arriving at the scene of a bloody shootout. They had a few clues already. The mines had been spotted in a group, which ruled out the possibility that they might have drifted far— say, down from the Farsi Island minefield, two hundred miles to the northwest, where the tanker *Bridgeton* was damaged the previous July. Floating mines that had slipped their moorings were almost always found alone. That meant someone had deliberately sowed them in the central Gulf's main shipping channel. And they had done it recently, for the mines would not long have remained undetected, or undetonated, in the busy waterway.

A helicopter pilot spotted the first mine and hovered low so that a photographer could lean out the door and snap a photo. The fat horned sphere floated on the surface, its gleaming black paint, free of marine growth, easily visible in a sea beaten white by the helicopter's rotor wash.

The EOD divers came next, blowing up a few of the mines, disarming two others. When they hauled the inert spheres aboard one of the minesweepers, they found the smoking gun they were looking for. The serial numbers matched those of the M-08s found aboard the *Iran Ajr*, the Iranian minelayer that had been caught and scuttled the previous September.

"Since the discovery of the new minefield, five mines have been identified and destroyed by international forces," a Pentagon official told reporters. "These mines were from the same series as those found on the *Iran Ajr*, leaving no doubt the mines were sown by Iran."[13]

There would be hell to pay.

IF YOU WERE going to war in the Persian Gulf, you wanted someone like Tony Less in charge. A fifty-one-year-old aviator with more than sixty-two hundred hours in jet cockpits and over a thousand carrier traps, Less had flown A-7 Corsair II attack planes on scores of bombing runs in the Vietnam War. In 1974 his leadership and cockpit skills earned him command of the newly reorganized Blue Angels, the navy's elite aerial demonstration team. More recently, Less had served on the Pentagon's joint staff and commanded the *Missouri* and *Ranger* battle groups in the Persian Gulf and the Arabian Sea.[14]

Within hours of the explosion—even before the divers had found the rest of the mines—White House officials ordered plans drawn up for military retaliation against Iran.[15] Less and his staff worked through the night to examine the options. By midday on Friday, 15 April, they had their recommendation: retaliatory strikes designed to hurt Iran's ability to mine the Gulf, bomb runs on the ports where the weapons were stored, and aerial attacks on the docks where minelayers tied up.

Less sent the recommendations off to his boss: the commander in chief of U.S. Central Command, Marine Corps Gen. George B. Crist, who oversaw U.S. military operations in and near southwest and east Asia from his headquarters in Tampa, Florida. Crist passed the package to the chairman of the Joint Chiefs of Staff, Adm. William J. Crowe, who carried them to a morning meeting in the Oval Office. President Reagan had gathered his senior advisers: Defense Secretary Frank C. Carlucci, National Security Adviser Colin L. Powell, and Secretary of State George P. Shultz. The men swiftly agreed that military action was called for. But what, exactly? There were plenty of options, thanks to the Pentagon's practice of laying plans for almost every foreseeable contingency. They ranged from a simple show of force, to Less's limited attack, to a much broader campaign.[16]

Crowe backed Less's reasoning. If there was to be retaliation, the chairman argued, it should be something that would reduce the Iranians' ability to harm U.S. forces in the Gulf.[17] The group discussed strikes on mine facilities and broadened the discussion to include an attack on Bandar Abbas, the port and missile base that covered the Hormuz strait. But Shultz argued that strikes on Iranian soil could escalate the conflict, entangling America deeper in the region's hostilities.

Eventually, the group warmed to a proposal to destroy two Iranian oil platforms in the south-central Gulf. Machinery on their steel lattices extracted natural gas from crude oil—some 150,000 barrels of oil a day, or 7 percent of the country's output.[18] They had military value as well. Revolutionary Guards had pressed the platforms into service as surveillance points, command posts, and even home ports for their raiding powerboats.

Crowe pressed for more. The admiral pointed out that U.S. forces had delivered a similar punishment—the destruction of two oilrigs—for the missile attack on the *Sea Isle City*. The damage to the *Roberts,* he argued, warranted harsher measures. He asked permission to sink an Iranian warship. After some discussion, Reagan granted the request—and added his approval to take out a third platform if no suitable man-o'-war could be located.

Having set the military in motion, the president headed for his retreat in Camp David, Maryland. Shultz flew to Augusta, Georgia, to keep a golf date. Carlucci remained in the capital to oversee military planning.[19]

Two messages were drawn up and sent out. One went to Tehran: a diplomatic protest at the mining of international waters. The other went to Crist, who passed it to Tony Less: an order to draw up plans for Operation Praying Mantis.

On Saturday, 16 April, Less summoned the heads of his combat groups to *Coronado,* which was tied up at Manama's Mina Sulman pier. The commander of Destroyer Squadron Nine and another staffer flew in from the *Enterprise* battle group, while Capt. Donald Dyer, the Redman, helicoptered in from the *Wainwright.* By 3:30 AM Sunday morning, they had a plan. Two groups of surface ships would take out the oil platforms, while a third would go gunning for one of the Iranian frigates. The *Enterprise's* fighters and bombers would join in as necessary.

Less had already summoned the ships he would need. *Roberts's* squadronmates—*Simpson, Wainwright, Jack Williams*—gathered in the southern and central Gulf, as did the *Trenton* and the destroyer USS *O'Brien* (DD 975).[20] Four more warships soon arrived from Battle Group Foxtrot, *Enterprise's* group on station in the northern Arabian Sea. The destroyer USS *Merrill* (DD 976) and guided-missile destroyer USS *Lynde McCormick* (DDG 8) made it to the Gulf first. Their squadronmates, the frigate USS *Bagley* (FF 1069) and guided-missile destroyer USS *Joseph*

Strauss (DDG 16), heading south along Africa's eastern coast to Mombasa, turned around, refueled at sea, and made twenty-five knots through the Strait of Hormuz. The *Enterprise* itself drew to within 120 nautical miles of the strait; her two remaining escorts interposed themselves between carrier and shore against the possibility that Iran might send jets or small boats their way.

The first target, the Sassan oil platform, would go to Surface Action Group (SAG) Bravo: *McCormick, Merrill,* and the *Trenton.* The attack plan reflected the lesson of the October shelling: even a thousand five-inch rounds will barely dent the steel lattice of an oil platform. The destroyers intended only to sweep the facility clear of resistance; a U.S. Marine reconnaissance team from *Trenton* would destroy it with explosive charges. SAG Bravo would then stand by for its second mission: if the hunt for an Iranian warship proved fruitless, the group would move northward and take out the platform dubbed Rakhish.

Wainwright, Bagley, and *Simpson*—SAG Charlie—were assigned to destroy Sirri-D, a platform near Sirri Island, a speck of land that supported a major oil terminal some sixty-five miles northwest of Dubai.[21] Their plan mirrored SAG Bravo's: the ships would shell the platform, and commandos from SEAL Team Two would board and destroy it.[22]

The remaining group, SAG Delta, which included *O'Brien, Joseph Strauss,* and *Jack Williams,* would go hunting for an Iranian warship. They would operate farther north, in the vicinity of the Strait of Hormuz. U.S. intelligence indicated that the best available quarry would be the *Sabalan,* a Sa'am-class ship that had acquired a bad reputation during the tanker war. Most Iranian frigate skippers were content to shoot at tankers' hulls, unleashing hellish gouts of flame but rarely sinking the double-hulled ships. The tanker crews often escaped death and even injury, escaping in lifeboats or riding their moribund ships into port behind a chartered firefighting tugboat. The victims of *Sabalan*'s attacks were rarely so fortunate. Its gunners aimed for the bridge and crew quarters. "The captain of *Sabalan* is a real fanatic," one U.S. officer told a reporter. The radio operators aboard the Gulf's commercial ships had taken to calling him "Captain Nasty."

Enterprise's Air Wing 11 would contribute four F-14A Tomcats, two A-6E Intruders, and two EA-6B Prowlers. If things got really hairy, the

Enterprise could launch a second wave of warplanes. The U.S. Air Force would lend a hand as well, furnishing KC-10 tankers for aerial refueling and AWACS planes to provide a "god's-eye view" of the battlefield.[23]

In Washington it was still Sunday evening. At 8:30 PM Reagan gathered Crowe, Carlucci, Powell, and Shultz in the family quarters of the White House to review the plans. A half hour later, five congressional leaders were ushered into the room, and the president informed them of the impending battle. Sometime after 10:00 PM—in the Gulf, it was 5:00 AM—the president signed the order to execute Operation Praying Mantis and turned in for the night.

Powell left for home. Crowe departed for the Pentagon, where he settled into its National Military Command Center to monitor the action on expansive video displays. Shortly thereafter, U.S. diplomats notified their counterparts in Britain, France, Italy, the Netherlands, and Belgium—NATO allies with naval forces in the Gulf. The governments of the Soviet Union, China, and several other Persian Gulf states, including Iraq, were informed of the plan just before the strikes began.[24]

The catalyst for all this furious activity, the *Samuel B. Roberts,* was relegated to the sidelines. Tied up to its Dubai pier, about sixty-five miles southeast of Sirri, the ship had received word that some sort of retaliatory strike was on way. Some crew members longed to take part—maybe shoot off a Harpoon missile if something came within range—but the idea of firing from a damaged ship in UAE waters was clearly out of the question. So sailors packed into the bridge and CIC and tuned the radios to the bridge-to-bridge frequencies that the various ships would be using during the operation. As spectator seats go, pierside in Dubai was not a bad place to be.[25]

And in a way, the first move of Operation Praying Mantis belonged to the wounded frigate. At dawn on 18 April, the *Roberts's* SH-60 Seahawk lifted from *Trenton's* flight deck and flew toward the Sassan platform. With Cdr. Tim Matthews at the controls, Magnum 447 buzzed off to give the platform a final visual check, and to stand by to evacuate wounded troops.

Soon afterward, the rest of SAG Bravo went into action. *Trenton* launched CH-46 helos bearing marines and armed Cobra gunships for protection. About 7:55 AM, the *Merrill's* captain broadcast warnings in English and Farsi: "You have five minutes to abandon the platform; I intend to destroy it at 0800." Some of the Iranian soldiers on its metal decks trained their ZSU antiaircraft guns at the U.S. ships—safely out of reach about five thousand yards away. Many more rushed onto two tug-boats and cast off. At 8:04, the *Merrill* opened up, silencing the ZSUs within minutes. *Lynde McCormick* briefly joined in the barrage. Both ships soon checked fire to allow a tug to evacuate the rest of the platform's besieged occupants.

The twin-rotor CH-46s swooped in about 9:25 AM, and marines slid down two-inch ropes onto the deck. Demolitions experts set fifteen hundred pounds of plastic explosive charges while intelligence specialists scoured the facility. The charges detonated around noon, sending black smoke billowing into the sky.

A hundred miles to the west, SAG Charlie had started off the same way at the Sirri platform: warnings and then an 8:00 AM bombardment. But the shells soon detonated tanks of compressed gas, turning the platform into an inferno and eliminating both need and opportunity to drop in the SEALs. An Iranian tugboat came by to pick up survivors in the water; *Wainwright*'s captain dropped some of his cruiser's lifeboats as well.[26]

Only SAG Delta was left without a target. As the sun rose high in the sky, U.S. ships and aircraft crisscrossed the Strait of Hormuz, searching for an Iranian warship. Visibility was three to five miles, not bad for April, but the waterway was packed with tankers, fishing boats, mer-chantmen, and warships. Lookouts peered through binoculars at an end-less series of hulls and masts, while radar operators in their darkened spaces studied a mass of green blips. Where was *Sabalan?* And the rest of the Iranian fleet?[27]

As it happened, the Iranian high command was a bit distracted. About an hour before the U.S. ships opened fire, Iraqi troops had begun to storm the Fao Peninsula, a strategic sliver of land between the Kuwaiti and Iranian gulf coasts. The offensive combined a northern feint, a barrage of missiles on Iranian cities, and artillery bombardments of poison gas. Com-pared to the assault on the western front, the loss of two oil platforms may not have struck Iranian commanders as a particularly urgent matter.[28]

Around 11:00 AM, Iranian forces stirred themselves. Two F-4s lifted off from their base and headed for the strait. The attack was fairly crafty. Like thieves watching a guard's flashlight beam, their ground controllers monitored the Tomcats' search radars, waited until the F-14s pointed southward—and then sent the Phantoms to engage. But they could not elude the full-circle radar sweep of the Hawkeye. When the Tomcats eagerly turned to fight, the Iranian pilots broke off and fled.[29]

Their comrades on the water had better luck, at least initially. A collection of small craft, including five Boghammars from Abu Musa, streamed into the southern Gulf, spraying machine-gun bullets and rocket-propelled grenades at ships, oilrigs, and pumping stations alike. As the American tug *Willi Tide* moved in to douse one burning rig with fire hoses, a trio of speedboats raked the tug with machine guns and sped off. "They are firing at anything and everything that moves," one civilian chopper pilot radioed as he flew into the gritty haze offshore.[30]

Around 11:30 AM, an Iranian patrol boat moved onto SAG Charlie's radarscopes. Bagley's helicopter identified it as the *Joshan,* out of the northern Gulf port of Bushehr. Built for the shah by French shipyards, the 147-foot patrol boat packed the same OTO Melara 76-mm gun as the *Roberts*. More ominously, *Joshan* also carried a Harpoon missile—the last of a dozen sold to Tehran by the United States shortly before the Iranian revolution in 1980. To U.S. forces, the Harpoon made the patrol boat the most dangerous ship in the Gulf.[31]

But *Joshan's* arrival created a quandary for Admiral Less. Reagan's battle orders authorized him to sink just one major Iranian ship. Hitting the 247-ton *Joshan* could mean passing up a chance at a *Sa'am* frigate nearly six times its displacement. Banking on U.S. intelligence guesses that the *Sa'ams* would eventually put to sea, Less decided to wait. He ordered *Wainwright* to warn the *Joshan* off. The cruiser promptly issued four VHF radio calls, but the patrol boat pressed on. The *Joshan* closed to less than fifteen nautical miles, well within Harpoon range and not far beyond the reach of 76-mm shells. Suddenly, the patrol boat was not a target but a threat, and there were different rules for that. *Wainwright* asked Less for permission to open fire, and the admiral swiftly gave it.

Wainwright's next radio call to *Joshan* echoed the warnings given to the oil platforms three hours earlier: "Stop your engines and abandon ship; I intend to sink you." It hearkened to the earliest days of the U.S. Navy, when sailing captains delivered such ultimatums by megaphone. *Joshan's* skipper replied in the most violent way he could. In a plume of white smoke, his Harpoon blasted from its launcher and headed toward *Wainwright,* by then about thirteen miles away. The U.S. ships turned their bows toward *Joshan,* fired off clouds of radar-deceiving metallic chaff, and attempted to jam the incoming missile. The Iranian weapon flew close aboard the *Wainwright*'s starboard side and zoomed away, taking *Joshan*'s hopes with it.

Simpson and *Wainwright* returned fire immediately, launching a total of five Standard missiles in less than five minutes. All five found their marks, setting *Joshan* afire. After a Harpoon from *Bagley* missed the blazing wreck, the *Simpson* and *Wainwright* finished off the Iranian ship with gunfire. It had been history's first missile duel between surface warships.

As smoke and fire belched from the *Joshan,* an Iranian F-4 streaked in from Bandar Abbas—perhaps the tardy air component of a would-be coordinated attack. *Wainwright* chased the fighter off with a pair of SM-2s, sending it back to base with minor tail damage.

To the east, Iran's smaller boats continued to wreak havoc in the Mubarek oilfield. Around 1:15 PM, Iranian gunboats set fire to the *York Marine,* a British-flagged oil tanker that was serving as a floating storage tank. Fifteen minutes later, a handful of Boghammars began firing guns and grenades at the *Scan Bay,* a Panamanian-registered jack-up barge with fifteen American workers aboard.

Scan Bay radioed for help, but again, engagement rules tied Less's hands. Throughout Earnest Will, U.S. forces in the Gulf had refrained from aiding foreign ships under fire, and today's rules allowed no exception. But Less felt he had to do something to help the victims of the Iranian rampage sparked by the destruction of the oil platforms. He appealed to Crist, who sent his request to the Pentagon, which forwarded it to the White House. Monday's dawn had not yet broken in Washington, but Reagan responded within minutes: go after the Boghammars.

Moments later, two A-6 Intruders departed their holding patterns over the Strait of Hormuz and streaked southwest, guided by the air controller aboard *Jack Williams.* Nimble as the Boghammars were, they could not elude a deadly rain of one-pound Rockeye submunitions from the Intruders. One boat soon went to the bottom, and the rest fled for the safety of nearby Abu Musa, beaching themselves in their haste.[32]

Reagan's quick decision was momentous. Tactically, it helped put an end to the day's small-boat operations. More broadly, it marked the beginning of a Gulf policy shift that permitted U.S. forces to protect third-party shipping. And it demonstrated how modern communications could allow commanders at every level to weigh in on battles from half a world away, a development that delighted some and worried others.[33]

Iran finally committed a frigate to the battle around 3:00 PM, when one of the *Sa'ams* weighed anchor near Bandar Abbas and headed for the Gulf. Less radioed SAG Delta, "The *Sahand* is in your vicinity. Take him."[34]

The *Enterprise* launched another A-6, which spotted the frigate heading southwest past Larak Island at twenty-five knots. The frigate showed up clearly through the A-6's infrared camera, but the rules of engagement, designed to prevent mistakes in the crowded Gulf waters, required the aviators to put eyeballs on their targets before an attack.

So the Intruder headed in low and fast—then jinked to avoid the anti-aircraft shells and infrared missiles that poured up from the Iranian frigate. The high-speed run positively identified the watercraft as the *Roberts*'s old playmate. The A-6 popped flares to confuse the heat seekers and wheeled around to counterattack. In quick succession, the attack plane fired off a Harpoon, launched two Skipper rocket bombs, and dropped a laser-guided bomb. The attack left *Sahand* dead in the water, her blazing deck a beacon for the next wave of U.S. planes.[35]

The rest of the strike group—six A-7 Corsairs and another A-6—was soon pounding the motionless frigate with Harpoons, Skippers, Walleyes, and bombs. Twenty miles away, *Joseph Strauss* unleashed a Harpoon, which leveled off, trailed white smoke over the horizon, and plowed into the *Sahand*. The Iranian ship's magazines blew up with a violence that buffeted the U.S. destroyer. Afire from stem to stern, the frigate sank some hours later.[36]

Around 5:00 PM, *Strauss* picked up a new set of signals. It was the *Sabalan*. When the morning's attacks began, the frigate had run for cover, hunkering down between two merchant ships off Bandar Abbas. Shielded from air and sea attack, the warship could have sat out the day's action. But at some point the Iranian skipper, or his superiors, had decided to join the battle. At long last, Captain Nasty had come out to fight.

The Americans were ready. *Strauss's* air traffic controllers sent one of the Intruders hurtling toward Larak Island. The A-6 crew drew a bead on the frigate with a forward-looking infrared camera and dropped down for the mandatory low-level pass. *Sabalan* responded with antiaircraft fire, and the attack plane withdrew to a higher altitude before coming in for their attack. Dodging three heat-seeking missiles, an A-6 dropped a laser-guided bomb down the ship's smokestack. It exploded in the engine room and broke the *Sabalan's* keel.[37]

Another group of planes was inbound from *Enterprise* when Crowe, monitoring the battle in the Pentagon's command center, called off the attack. "We've shed enough blood today," he told Carlucci. Iranian tugs eventually retrieved the damaged *Sabalan* as U.S. ships looked on.[38]

The day's final tally: the U.S. Navy had sunk one Iranian frigate, one patrol boat, and three Boghammars; eliminated two oil platforms-cum-radar picket stations; and put another frigate out of action. No fleet had lost such a large fraction of its fighting force in a single battle since Leyte Gulf in 1944.

The only U.S. casualties came long after the warships had secured from general quarters. Two marine aviators died when their AH-1T Sea Cobra gunship, flying reconnaissance from the *Wainwright,* crashed some fifteen miles southwest of Abu Musa.[39]

Throughout the day, the men aboard the *Roberts*—and ship captains and shipping executives around the Gulf—listened intently to the bursts of radio chatter. The frigate's crowded spaces were largely silent—until cheers erupted with each report of damage done to Iranian ships. *Payback,* thought Chuck Dumas.[40] It was the best medicine his crew could get, Gunner Reinert decided.[41]

The next day, the *Roberts* crew learned about their air detachment's role through a message from Matthews on the *Trenton.* The aviator wrote that the *Roberts's* helicopter had flown several sorties during the day to provide extra eyes in the sky and search-and-rescue capability. "The crew is exhausted," Matthews wrote, "but morale is high. . . . We have very strong desires to return to our own ship." He signed off: "No higher honor."[42]

Soon after the battle, *Trenton* pulled into Dubai and tied up next to the *Roberts.* The two crews used a pierside crane to transfer the frigate's missiles and torpedoes to the amphibious ship, as required by both the shipyard and the UAE government before the ship could head into dry dock. Some *Roberts* crew members also took advantage of the *Trenton's* undamaged living spaces to grab their first hot showers in a week. Reinert paid a visit to the chiefs' mess and was rewarded with a videotape of the battle. Back on the *Roberts,* they popped the tape into the VCR— and promptly dubbed it the voyage's best movie call. The sailors loved the part where one of the U.S. captains warned the Iranians aboard the Sassan oil platform to abandon ship because he intended to destroy it. For Reinert, it didn't get any better than that.[43]

AMERICANS WHO PICKED up their morning papers on 22 April may have read about Tennessee senator Al Gore's withdrawal from his pursuit of the Democratic presidential nomination, leaving Michael Dukakis as the front-runner to battle George H. W. Bush in the upcoming November election. The *New York Times* reported the removal of a hard-line Politburo rival to Mikhail Gorbachev, whose perestroika was unfettering the Soviet government's first cautious public debates. But the front pages of the *Times,* the *Washington Post,* and scores of other newspapers carried stories of the mining and the damage control effort that saved the *Roberts.*

The stories had emerged from a Thursday afternoon press conference held at the Pentagon by a pair of three-star admirals. One was Vice Adm. Henry Mustin, the deputy chief of naval operations for plans, policy, and operations. Two years and two weeks previously, he had stood on a podium in Maine and welcomed the *Roberts* to commissioned service. The other was Vice Adm. William Rowden, the head of Naval Sea System Command (NAVSEA) and the navy's top shipbuilder.

Rowden began the press conference by gesturing to a large model of a *Perry*-class frigate, explaining to the Pentagon press corps just how the mine had maimed the ship. The explosion had broken the keel and sent a thousand tons of water into her machinery spaces, and yet the *Roberts* had held up well under the tremendous stress. But the real heroes of the story were not the main deck or the onboard firefighting equipment, Rowden said. "Had she been left to her own devices, she likely would have sunk," the admiral said. "The real thing that separates losing this ship from saving this ship was the performance of the crew."

As the flag officers described the effort, the reporters added it up. "So, simultaneously, they were backing out of a mine field, controlling flooding, putting out a fire, moving magazines, and repairing the ship?" one asked.

"And telling people in Washington what had happened," Mustin said, drawing laughs.

Another journalist wanted to know about the prospects for fixing the *Roberts*. "Now, I don't know from ships, but I know from cars, and when you get a chassis that's sort of bent, I mean, it'll still work, but it never works as well as it did when it was new," the reporter said. "You might as well sell it."

"We don't intend to sell it," said Mustin, to more laughs, and Rowden assured the group that the contemplated repairs were well within the possible.

"We can't speak highly enough of those young fellows who brought us back a ship," Mustin finished up. "We don't think it could have been done better by anybody, and we think we're the finest navy in the world, and we think a lot of other people understand that now."[44]

The event was a public relations coup. The press accounts followed the admirals' lead, and the *Roberts* sailors were praised as heroes on America's front pages.

Aboard the *Roberts* in Dubai, a trickle of congratulatory notes soon became a flood. Dozens of letters flowed in from military officers, politicians, and well-wishers around the globe. "I was totally amazed at your calm, coherent reports under terrible conditions," wrote the commanding officer of the USS *Fearless* (MSO 442), a U.S. minesweeper that had destroyed two mines a few months earlier in the Gulf. "Having witnessed the awesome destructive power of two M-08s which we found in the Farsi MDA [mine danger area], I hope I could maintain my composure under similar condition."[45]

The chief of naval operations, Adm. Carlisle Trost, applauded "a magnificent performance by all hands" and quoted Chester Nimitz, the great Pacific Fleet admiral of World War II: "Everyone admires a ship that can't be licked."[46] General Crist noted the low number of injuries, which he said stemmed "not from good fortune but from solid leadership, dedication, and hard work—before the fact."[47]

More than one hundred sailors in the engineering department aboard the aircraft carrier USS *Carl Vinson* signed a note of support and mailed it off to the *Roberts*. The piece of paper, which had become quite grubby as it passed from sailor to sailor, was dated 16 April and read: "On behalf of the Engineering department on the Battlestar, I would like to express our feelings of solidarity to the men of your Engineering department and to the entire crew of the *Samuel B. Roberts*. We think of the Navy Hymn and Naval History, and we know that only a few of our countrymen fully understand what we do and why we do it."[48]

For his part, Rinn sent praise to his squadronmates. "Just like the team player on the injured reserve list, SBR listened, prayed, and cheered for our teammates who were doing the job 18 Apr," he wrote. "From all angles, your performance was superb. Thanks for a great surface Navy day."[49]

The nationally syndicated columnist James Kilpatrick wrote in May about some high-level attention being given the ship. "President Reagan watched a movie the other night," wrote Kilpatrick, whose son was a senior chief petty officer on *Roberts*'s sister ship *Nicholas*.

> Nothing new in that, but this movie was enough to move a man to tears. It was a brief film prepared by the Navy on the saving of the *Sammy B*. The story is more than a month old, but it will bear retelling for years to come. . . .
>
> By all the rules of naval warfare, the wounded frigate should have sunk, but the *Sammy B*. was a ship not meant to follow ordinary rules. Over the next five hours, before the peril of sinking passed, the crew wrote a story of heroism and ingenuity. They literally bound the frigate together with steel wire. They kept the ship alive to fight again.[50]

For Rinn, the apogee came when a phone call from the White House was patched into the *Roberts*'s communications circuits. A voice came over the wire, immediately familiar from televised speeches. It was Ronald Reagan, calling with praise for captain and crew. The president also offered a hearty "Bravo Zulu," although the old army veteran confessed that he wasn't entirely sure what that meant. (It was navy-speak for "good job.") Rinn rode the high for days.[51] A month later, Reagan praised the *Roberts* in his national radio address for Armed Forces Day.[52]

TWO WEEKS AFTER the battle, Admiral Crowe arrived to spend five days in high-level meetings with Admiral Less, General Crist, and political and military leaders in Bahrain and the UAE. Crowe also intended to visit the fleet, hand out awards for Operations Earnest Will and Praying Mantis, and chat with the officers and crew about life in the Gulf.

Crowe paid his visit to the *Roberts,* by then perched high and dry in Dubai's number two repair facility, on the afternoon of 3 May. Barely a week had passed since Rinn had signed off on several dozen award recommendations, but a chain of navy yeomen from Bahrain to Washington had hustled the paperwork along.

The crew turned out in dress whites for the medal ceremony on the dry-dock wall. Under canvas canopies, the sailors sweated in their summer uniforms: short-sleeved shirts and creased pants for the chiefs and officers; long-sleeved sweaters, Dixie-cup hats, and rolled black neckerchiefs for the enlisted men.

Crowe made a few remarks, and then the citations were read. First came Rinn, who received the Legion of Merit with Combat V. A five-armed star with white enameling, it was the navy's seventh-highest decoration. The citation read, in part: "By his superb leadership and untiring efforts, he extricated his ship from the mine field, led his crew in extinguishing the fires, and kept the severely damaged ship from breaking apart and sinking."[53] "I wish I could have broken it up and given a piece to every member of my crew," Rinn later wrote.

The trio who rescued Alex Perez received the Bronze Star with Combat V: Bent, Cowen, and Copeland. Seven others received the same award for their leadership in the damage control effort: Eckelberry, Frost, Rassler, Valliere, Van Hook, and Walker.

For their damage control efforts the Navy Commendation Medal was awarded to Dumas, Firehammer, Ford, Frank, Fridley, Gawor, Gutcher, Kingery, Lewellyn, Nicholson, Hull Technician 2nd Class Timothy Regan, Sobnosky, and Whitley. Lambert, the corpsman, also received the Commendation Medal for his work.

Two shipmates received Purple Hearts from Crowe: Dejno and Gibson. In Texas later that day, Atlantic Surface Fleet commander Vice Adm. Joseph Donnell pinned the same on Burbine, Perez, Smith, and Welch.

Every sailor aboard *Roberts* received the Combat Action Ribbon, which recognizes satisfactory performance while under enemy fire. It was the first time in twenty years that an entire ship had been granted the decoration.[54] The crew was also awarded the Navy Unit Commendation, whose citation read, in part: "By their heroic efforts, the crew restored electrical power and firemain pressure, controlled the flooding, extinguished the fires, and effected temporary repairs which saved their severely damaged ship. By their conspicuous display of professionalism, determination, teamwork, and loyal devotion to duty, the officers and enlisted personnel of USS *SAMUEL B. ROBERTS* (FFG 58) reflected great credit upon themselves and upheld the highest traditions of the United States Naval Service."[55]

Finally, Crowe hauled out a Battle E flag and handed it to Rinn.

All told, thirty-one *Roberts* sailors received medals that day, and another dozen or so would eventually get various individual decorations. Mike Tilley and Rick Raymond received the Commendation Medal with Combat V, for example, while Lester Chaffin received the Navy Achievement Medal.[56] But others who received only the Combat Action Ribbon and Navy Unit Commendation felt slighted; it rankled some for years.

Afterward, Crowe asked to see the ship—from the outside. So Rinn called for boots and coveralls, and the pair descended to the dry dock floor, moving slowly to accommodate the admiral's limp. The gash in the ship's side shook Crowe, a former submariner.

"Son, you were really close," the admiral told Rinn. "I don't think anybody in the States knows how close this was. You really did a great job. What would you like to do in the navy?"

Rinn picked that moment to make a joke. "This is a pretty darn risky business," he replied. "I thought I'd go back to the States and buy a Burger King and live happily ever after."

Crowe didn't smile.

Many years later, Rinn was still shaking his head. "Here's a guy who's offering me the world. You know, literally: 'I'd like to be the CNO's EA [executive assistant]'—done. I'm sure that anything I said at that moment, he would have made happen."[57]

But there was little time for might-have-beens. Rinn had just a few weeks left in his command, and he would spend them tending to his wounded ship.

CHAPTER FOURTEEN

Return and Repair

Two days after the explosion, a few members of the navy's damage inspection team touched down at Dubai International Airport—those who had been granted funds for a commercial airline ticket. The rest straggled into town a week later aboard a military transport. They had flown halfway around the world to figure out just how badly the *Roberts* was damaged. Their recommendations would help determine whether Rinn would get his wish.[1]

The group included three engineers from Naval Sea Systems Command, a handful of experts from the Atlantic Surface Fleet, an officer from the Navy Safety Center, and one man who knew FFG-58 as well as anyone: Lt. Eric Sorensen. The former damage control assistant had rotated off the ship as scheduled in late 1987, but he hadn't gone far. The navy had assigned him to the Naval Training Center in Newport, less than a mile away from the *Roberts*'s home pier. Sorensen ran the school's pocket fleet of yard patrol craft, the hundred-foot vessels that gave many junior officers their first taste of shiphandling.

When word of the mining swept across campus, Sorenson ran to Surface Group Four headquarters, where he found a pack of officers glued to CNN. As images of the *Roberts* flashed on the television, Sorensen knew he had to go see his ship. The lieutenant rang up a captain he knew at NAVSEA and begged for a spot on the inspection team. The senior officer was noncommittal. Sorensen called back two days later, gripping a message that had arrived unexpectedly on 17 April. "We saved our ship after hitting a mine in no small part because of your relentless training and insistence on SBR's damage control readiness," Paul Rinn had written to Sorensen. "Your shipmates thank you for giving us the edge in the battle between life and death." The NAVSEA captain relented, but extracted a promise that Sorensen would teach a lessons-learned course at the Newport school. It was a bargain swiftly struck.

A week later, Sorensen walked into the Dubai shipyard. He found the *Roberts* at pierside and strode up the brow. The ship was still in the water, and at first glance, it didn't look too bad. But when a chief petty officer rushed up and threw his arms around him, the surprised lieutenant began to grasp the enormity of the experience. The chief thanked the former damage control assistant, told him how glad he was to be alive, and thanked him again. Sorensen blinked back tears. He had never been prouder.[2]

A week after the battle, *Roberts* was towed into Dubai Drydocks's number two, a gargantuan repair facility built to hold the world's largest supertankers. Just five years old, its concrete holding tank stretched one-third of a mile into the harbor. The great sea gate that sealed its end was wider than the length of a football field.

The dockworkers had drained the giant basin, built a double row of concrete blocks to cradle the frigate's hull, and flooded it again to allow the warship to enter. The blocks were stacked to meet the curves of the ship's hull plates and capped with soft wood to ease the transformation from buoyant hull to earthbound deadweight. Their construction had been guided by Rassler, the damage control assistant, and Johnson, the hull technician, who had unearthed a basic dry-docking plan from the ship's technical library and modified it to fit the battered hull. The men had attempted to calculate the stern sag by subtracting the current waterline from the nominal one, but guesses only went so far. The frigate's stern was coddled in flotation bladders, but floats and wooden cushions notwithstanding, there was going to be some damage when the ship's forty-one-hundred-ton weight came to rest.

The *Roberts* crew watched from its walls as the sea gate sealed out the harbor. Pumps began to hum. With more than one hundred million gallons of saltwater to drain, there was plenty of time to worry about what would happen when the ship touched down. Finally, the hull settled with a groan onto the blocks. The water receded, and gradually the hole appeared, looking like a punched-in mouth filled with broken teeth. Through the maw, the sailors could see a twisted, broken mass of pipes and grates and conduits and machinery, all covered with scorched and blasted lagging.

Ted Johnson found the sight comical; in the confines of the huge dock the *Roberts* looked like a toy boat marooned in a bathtub. Others, like Eckelberry, found reassurance in the ship's escape from saltwater; it meant they were finally safe. But the sight wrenched Reinert and others looking on from the starboard side. For the first time, they could see the huge hole in the hull. *How close the ship had come to splitting right in two,* the chief thought.[3]

Puddles of seawater still dampened the dry-dock floor as Sorensen and the rest of the inspectors began to take measurements. First, they noted that the *Roberts* seemed to have endured the docking with only minor injury. Two small sections of hull had buckled: the keel near the bow's sonar dome, and the skeg—the plates that surrounded the propeller shaft. Next, they cataloged the damage done by the explosion. They found that the main deck was bent one degree around frames 270 to 280.

But they were heartened to find that the hull had not twisted as well. Repairs were hardly going to be simple, but deformation in three dimensions would have complicated things immensely.[4] Everyone expressed their admiration for the ship's sturdiness, especially the welds. Rinn thought back to those long Maine nights he had spent talking to the Bath welders.

Within a few days, Sorensen and the team transmitted a draft report back to the United States. To Rinn's delight, the report concluded that the Dubai facility could fix the ship well enough to sail back to Newport.[5]

In Washington a constellation of flag officers gathered to weigh the options. There were several concerns: it would be a nightmare to ship certain parts, like the engine shaft, to Dubai, and then there was the issue of doing such an expensive repair in a foreign port. "It was done by committee," said Capt. Charles A. Vinroot, one of the NAVSEA officers who would oversee the repair effort. "I was in a room with half a dozen admirals, and all I know is, I had a decision when I went out, but I'm not sure who made it."[6]

Their decision put Rinn's hopes to death. "It appears impractical to make interim repairs that would be necessary to steam the ship home under her own power," navy officials told reporters in Washington on 29 April.[7] And yet, the *Roberts* would not wallow back to North America at the end of a towline. It may have been thin consolation for Rinn, but his ship would make the trip aboard one of the world's most unusual vessels, borne home like a wounded champion.

Navy officials had already picked a U.S. shipyard to repair the *Roberts*. Bill Haggett had scarcely given them a choice. The Bath Iron Works president had phoned NAVSEA within hours of the explosion, vowing to do whatever it took to restore the frigate to fighting trim. In any case, BIW was the logical choice, given the yard's intimate familiarity with the frigate, its reputation for repair and refit jobs, and its proximity to the sailors' Rhode Island homes. Navy officials awarded the job to BIW without competition, price to be negotiated later.[8]

The decision meant less work in Dubai, but the ship needed plenty of attention before its journey. One week after Sorensen and his team departed in early May, a second group arrived to start planning the permanent repairs in Bath. They stayed until the end of the month, measuring, testing, envisioning. Meanwhile, the hull had to be strengthened for towing out to deep water. The damaged gas turbines and other equipment had to be pulled out, boxed up, and shipped back to the United States. The interior had to be turned back into a clean, safe place for the crew members who would ride her home. Much of the effort to prep the damaged ship for its journey fell to the Dubai Drydock workers, and it began in earnest the day after Crowe's medal ceremony.

Surrounded by scaffolding, connected to the dock's high wall by catenaries of hose and cable, the *Roberts* resembled a trauma patient in intensive care. Like surgeons excising damaged tissue, the Dubai yard workers began with incisions. They peeled crumpled and wrinkled plates from the hull and cut out the twisted crosspieces that supported them. They removed a thirty-square-foot section around the hull breach and then twenty-foot-wide strips up the sides, slicing into undamaged plating in order to ensure a good patch. The resulting hole took the shape of a fat cross, wrapped around the bottom of the ship.

They debrided the wound, descending to pull battered, waterlogged equipment from the chaos of the damaged compartments. From AMR 3 they withdrew generators, evaporators, and high-pressure air flasks; from the main engine room they removed the great reduction gear and tons of equipment-turned-scrap metal. They pulled the gas turbines from their mangled mounts, lowering them gently to the dry dock's oil-spattered floor with chains and thick cables. The broad bronze blades of the screw came off the hub with bolts. Over the course of two days, the long propeller shaft was withdrawn from its sheath. Once empty, the damaged spaces were stripped of insulation and scrubbed down.

Filipino workers armed with welding torches cut away the HY-80 steel that held the main reduction gear in the ship. Ted Johnson stood watch as fire marshal on the *Roberts* deck, sweating and arguing with the yard men about which was harder to take: the Gulf heat or the Wisconsin cold.[9]

The *Roberts* crew had work to do as well. The ship's electricians disconnected damaged motors, switchboards, and controllers, hauling box after box of waterlogged components up and out of the ship. Prying open the cases of brass and painted metal, the sailors spread them under the beating Gulf sun to dry on the dock wall. Bent, Chaffin, and the others rewound motors and made additional repairs themselves; they sent more complicated work to the shipyard's repair shops. Chaffin often came away from such visits dumbfounded at the casual violations of safety doctrine; it was hardly uncommon to find one worker hosing down a floor while another's powerful electrical arc welder sizzled just a few feet away. Other sailors restored the air-conditioning units, patched up the ship's fire mains, and repaired the shattered serving tables on the mess deck.

But for much of the crew there was little work to do after putting the ship's living quarters back in good order. The sailors mustered each morning at 7:00 AM on the flight deck, where the temperature was often already ninety degrees. Most days, liberty would begin at 9:00 AM, and a stream of sailors would issue across the brow and into the sweltering heat. They explored Dubai's markets and other sights during the day and sampled the city's limited nightlife after the sun went down. Municipal regulations against public drunkenness were strict, and the *Roberts* sailors were generally careful to stay within their bounds. Still, Chaffin, who often volunteered for shore patrol duty—it beat standing watches aboard ship—retrieved more than one inebriated shipmate from the local police station.

Still, many *Roberts* sailors might have gone half mad with boredom if not for the expatriate community, who welcomed them as heroes and took them under their wings. Led by the American and British employees of foreign oil companies, the expats and their families fed and feted the crew, inviting them home for dinner and showing them around the small country. Employees of Conoco opened their firm's compound to the crew, who received passes to the swimming pool and the local beach club. Chaffin fondly remembered the weekly all-you-can-eat buffet, with its barbequed shrimp, octopus, squid, and every kind of seafood imaginable. The duffers in the group were treated to greens fees at the golf course just outside the city. If you ignored the sandy brown landscape in the background, it was "just like any championship course here in the States, complete with water holes," Reinert marveled. The weather was uniformly great, if you hated overcast days and loved heat. Jim Muehlberg, the electronics technician, didn't see a cloud for two months.[10]

On 10 May the crew gathered on the flight deck for a short ceremony. One week shy of a year since the *Stark* attack, the *Roberts* observed a moment of silence for those who died in the event. Rinn had sent a message to the commander of Mayport Naval Station, where the *Stark* crew awaited the repair of their own ship. Days later and half a world away, the Mayport commander read Rinn's words to the sailors, families, and dignitaries gathered for a somber memorial ceremony.

> Much attention has been paid to the material side of what *Samuel B. Roberts* learned from the USS *Stark* affair. However, the most important things are often overlooked. *Stark* was an excellent frigate operated by a superb crew; we knew and respected them, many were our friends. When disaster struck, on May 17, 1987, those men performed in a manner second to none in saving their badly crippled ship. By their actions, they sent us a message: "Never quit, trust in one another, and most importantly, believe in yourself." They taught us the essence of bravery, professionalism, and persistence. By their sacrifice, they alerted us to the sudden danger of the Persian Gulf and gave us an example to follow. Their loss is without a doubt the predominant factor that is responsible for our survival.[11]

BY 7 JUNE local machine shops had completed the temporary hull modules that would close the hole in the hull and strengthen the battered *Roberts* for its journey home. The modules included new freshwater distillers, high-pressure air flasks, and other bits of equipment the ship would need during its Atlantic transit. They also included something the originals did not: ballast.

The removal of the gas turbines and reduction gear had lightened the ship by many tons, raising its center of gravity and reducing its resistance to capsizing. Ballast had to be found, and it was, in the form of an Arabian resource even more plentiful than oil: sand. More than two hundred tons were packed into hundreds of woven plastic flour bags, which were tucked in place of the missing gas turbines.

Over a week's time, the giant patches were bolted and welded into place. In another week, the dry-dock workers finished what the navy's intrepid hull technicians had tried to do the night after the explosion: weld plates over the cracks in the *Roberts*'s deckhouse.

The crew repainted the ship from stem to stern, and on 15 June the great dry dock was flooded once again and the *Roberts* towed out to a nearby pier. As the frigate floated free of its concrete cell, its vast battle flag fluttered from its mast.[12]

There was but one task left for Dubai Drydocks: prepping the vessel that would carry the frigate home. The 558-foot *Mighty Servant 2* was an unusual ship for an unusual job. Bow on, its white-painted pilothouse and blue-ringed funnels looked normal enough for a twenty-nine-thousand-ton cargo ship. But the resemblance ended there. Its abbreviated superstructure gave way to a vast rusty platform that rode barely above the wave tops. The great slab of a cargo deck measured 450 by 120 feet, room enough to play a regulation game of soccer plus a few tennis matches. Even stranger, the *Mighty Servant* was designed to sink, at least partway. Ballast tanks allowed the ship to submerge its deck so that its outsized cargoes could be floated into place. When the tanks were once again pumped dry, the ship would rise up to shoulder its load. Its Dutch owners, the Wijsmuller shipping and salvage line, called the *Mighty Servant* a semi-submersible heavy-lift ship; they leased it to haul jack-up oilrigs across oceans. At just half the deadweight of a typical oilrig, the forty-one-hundred-ton *Roberts* would hardly strain the *Servant*'s back.[13]

The decision to use the *Mighty Servant* had occasioned some debate between Atlantic Fleet officials, who wanted to tow the frigate home, and NAVSEA Chief Rowden, who favored the heavy-lift option. "We had

a squabble, and we prevailed because I told the CNO that we had to cer-
tify the ship ready for tow, and I could not in good conscience do that,"
Rowden said. "So we won."

Rowden had his reasons. At a cost of roughly $1.4 million, the ride was
more expensive than a tow, but the eighty-one-hundred-mile transit to
Newport would take just one month, about half as long. Moreover, the
frigate was so weakened that heavy weather could represent a real threat.
"At six knots, you can't outrun a storm," NAVSEA's Vinroot said.

Besides, Rowden was curious about *Mighty Servant 2* and its sister
ship, *MS1*. How long would it take them to evacuate a damaged ship from
a war zone? Might they help ferry the navy's diminutive minesweepers
around the globe? "We sure are breaking new ground with this one,"
Vinroot said.[14]

When *Mighty Servant 2* anchored in Dubai Harbor, the dry dock sent
workers out to weld a cradle to its deck. Triangles of I-beams and steel
posts the color of red clay would hold the *Roberts* upright during its
transit. After weeks in dock number two, the yard's engineers knew the
frigate's dimensions to the quarter inch; there would be no repeat of
the damage done in the first dry-docking. But there was a complication:
the hull of the *Roberts* was to rest on the *Servant's* deck, but the frigate's
chin-mounted sonar, fin stabilizers, and rudder protruded several feet
below its keel. The Dubai engineers pondered the situation and, eventually, simply cut several rectangular holes in the *Servant's* deck plates.
The repair bill wasn't going to add much to the already high fare.[15]

For Paul Rinn the weeks passed busily enough. He oversaw the
repairs and wrote up a few more shipmates for medals. But the days
had a bittersweet edge. In sixteen years as a naval officer, he had bent his
body, mind, and heart toward command at sea. The past half decade—
ever since he received his command star in 1983—had been made up
of long days and often sleepless nights filled with thoughts of little but
the *Roberts*. Now his command was drawing to a close. His request to
see his ship home had been turned down—he'd already overstayed the
customary command tour, even for a commissioning officer.

Some moments were more bitter than sweet. When a naval ship or aircraft incurs major damage, the service holds a formal investigation. Called
the JAGMAN after the document that guides it—the Judge Advocate

General's Manual—it was quite separate from repair surveys like the one Sorensen had helped conduct. Many careers had been ended by JAGMAN investigations.

As the senior navy officer in the region, Adm. Tony Less appointed the investigating officer for the *Roberts* incident, a captain who was the commodore of one of the Gulf destroyer squadrons. Less took pains to reassure Rinn. "This investigation is being initiated at my behest and the sole intention is to document what was done right, wrong and what can be done better," Less wrote. "Your actions or those of your crew are not the subject of the investigation except to provide lessons learned. The lessons we discover will obviously help all of our ships in this volatile area."[16]

But Rinn disliked the investigating officer from the moment he arrived on the last day of May. The way Rinn remembered it, the officer walked on board and shortly thereafter declared his intention to prove that the *Roberts* should have been able to withdraw unscathed from the mine-field. Rinn's annoyance grew as the weeklong inquest progressed; for one thing, he did not recall being interviewed for the record. Rinn finally wrote a note to Aquilino to complain.

Still, every day was a reminder of how lucky he'd been. As the change of command drew near, Aquilino sent Rinn a pat on the back: "With the eyes of the world upon you, you handled the greatest of adversity and avoided certain disaster. You have set the standard for CNSG-4 and the fleet."[17]

But no farewell gesture topped the one from Mike Tilley, a wiseacre to the last. The engineman had once joked to his captain that a window in the ship's hull would greatly ease the hours spent at general quarters. Now he took up an official memo form, typed out a message, and headed up to the captain's stateroom. Screwing up his courage, Tilley slipped it into the suggestion box. It read:

Date: 8 June 88
From: EN3 Tilley
To: CO
Sub: Concerning my suggestion back in Jan. 88 for a porthole in the U-shape passageway. THANK YOU! You have exceeded all of my expectations for such a project. Again THANK YOU![18]

Rinn laughed. "Tilley, I'll never forget you," he said.

In the late afternoon heat of 20 June, the crew of the *Roberts* assembled on the flight deck, turned out in their crisp whites. Rinn pinned silver cutlasses on several enlisted sailors who had used their slack time to wrap up their surface warfare qualifications. He told his crew how proud he was of them and said they should always remember what they had done together. It was the last time Rinn ever saw his crew assembled. Within a day or two, he would turn his ship over to his successor.

"It was very solemn," recalled fireman Alan Sepelyak. "You're saying good-bye to someone who helped you save your life, and putting your life in the hands of someone you don't know. As hard as [Captain Rinn] was on us, that was how hard it was to say good-bye. He disciplined, yelled at you, patted you on the back, kicked you in the ass. After all that, you just didn't want to see someone take his place."[19]

Soon, most of the *Roberts* sailors changed into civilian clothes, hefted their sea bags, and filed down the brow. Leaving behind a skeleton crew of about forty, they crammed onto blue-and-white shuttle buses and headed for Dubai International Airport. In the terminal lounge there was an unexplained delay. Eckelberry, in charge, started to worry. "I had 130 guys in civvies, carrying their white uniforms in hanging bags, most without passports, and no Plan B," he said.

The XO lifted a phone at an unattended podium and mashed buttons until he got the operations supervisor in the Dubai tower, who told him the crew of the chartered L-1011 was trying to find parts for their broken gyrocompass.

Just about then, the digital sign over the concourse doorway rolled from "Special" to "Iran Air flight." Scores of Iran-bound travelers began filling up the lounge. The American officer smelled a potentially ugly situation.

"I grabbed a terminal guy that was wearing a blazer and carrying a radio and explained who I was and who my men were and how mixing them with these or any other Iranian passengers was really a bad idea and could he help?" Eckelberry said. "His eyes got pretty big, but he understood and took action right away. The sign rolled over to 'Charter' and he came back and announced to the Iranians that there had been a gate shift and with his helpers, got all the Iranians moved.

"I never thought that any of our crew had any grudge against Iranians, but I didn't want any hassles for any reason."

The crew cleaned out the Dubai duty-free shop, and an hour later the plane was ready. As everyone was buckling in, a flight attendant asked Eckelberry to come to the cockpit. The pilot introduced his flight engineer, who had fixed the gyrocompass—and who happened to be Iranian. Eckelberry asked whether he was flying with them. The aviators laughed, and the flight engineer pulled out a U.S. passport. The naval officer thanked them and headed back to his seat.

The celebration began as the dusty Dubai landscape vanished from the windows. The crew emptied the bar carts long before the plane landed for fuel in London. But everyone sobered up on the trip across the Atlantic, and two hours from Newport, everyone shaved and changed into whites. When the pilot announced their arrival in U.S. airspace, the cabin filled with cheers.

The captain also had a message for Eckelberry: more than just family and friends would meet the crew. The Providence tower was reporting a major welcoming party being planned—admirals, VIPs, fire trucks. Someone was even setting up a small stage. The surprised XO set about composing some remarks on a cocktail napkin.

The light was fading from the Rhode Island sky when the L-1011 touched down at T. F. Green State Airport across the bay from Newport. The hullabaloo began immediately. A pair of fire trucks escorted the plane to a hangar where more than 350 wives, girlfriends, kids, and other relatives waited behind a painted line. Behind them, a phalanx of reporters and cameramen were getting it on all on tape.

The passenger door opened; the hubbub of the crowd wafted in along with the smell of jet fuel. The commander of the Atlantic Surface Fleet strode in, Vice Admiral Donnell, the big bear of a man who had described the *Roberts*'s mining to the Washington press. "We had no idea why this giant admiral wanted to see us," Eckelberry said. "It must have shown on my face, because Vice Admiral Donnell started laughing." The admiral offered a few words of welcome and then stood aside as the crew pounded down the ladder to the cheers of hundreds.

A somewhat stunned Eckelberry was greeted on the tarmac by Commodore Aquilino—at least for a few seconds. Then Mrs. Eckelberry blasted past him and wrapped her husband in a hug. A photo of the moment played across the front of the next morning's *Providence Journal*.[20]

Dodging flowers and balloons and hand-painted signs, the sailors dashed into the arms of their loved ones. Lester Chaffin hugged his mother and grandmother amid the frenzy, and broke into tears. He was hardly alone. "It was so exciting, we were all crying like babies. It was good to be home on American soil. It smelled so good," he said.[21]

Glenn Palmer was mobbed by his daughters, Rachel and Rebecca, but he tenderly reached for his wife, Kathy, who held the son, Phillip, he'd never seen. Palmer played it cool with the reporters who asked him about coming home. "We were sent to do a job, and we did it," the CSO said. "And it's very good to be home." Kathy Palmer was not so reserved. Though she had held up well through the mining and the immediate aftermath, the waiting had become worse after the ship was laid up in Dubai. "I coped very well until May," she said. "And then I just felt the frustration of not knowing what was going to happen. The demands got more than I almost could handle."[22]

Even those without family exulted at the prospect of a month of leave. "It's great to be back! I'm going to a Cubs game," one sailor shouted.

The commander of the Atlantic Fleet dubbed the *Roberts* crew national heroes. "The ship would have sunk had it not been for the crew, there's no question about that," Donnell told the crowd.[23]

Paul Rinn relinquished command of his frigate several days later and flew home to Charleston. No crowds awaited him. Onlookers may have wondered why the tall man in naval whites was especially enthusiastic in his greetings to his wife and children.

BACK IN DUBAI, it took a few more days to ready the *Roberts* for departure. In the meantime, readers of the daily London *Guardian* received this report:

> An American navy frigate damaged by an Iranian mine in the Gulf two months ago is a write-off and will have to be scrapped, according to naval sources in the area. The US authorities are attempting to cover up the costly loss in case it reopens questions about Washington's large naval presence in the Gulf . . . The

frigate is beyond repair, but is being kept in dock to prevent the full extent of the damage being revealed . . . In the words of one naval observer, the USS *Samuel B. Roberts* "crumpled like cardboard" when it hit the mine.[24]

Iran's official Islamic Republic News Agency reprinted the article with glee. Pentagon spokesman Cdr. Mark Baker retorted, "The USS *Samuel B. Roberts* is going to Bath Iron Works to be repaired, period."

High winds and heavy swells delayed the frigate's departure from Dubai for two days. The seas were still at three feet on 25 June, but the *Mighty Servant*'s meter was running. The tugboat *Tornado* pulled taut a thick cable, eased the *Roberts* from the pier, and headed west. The rendezvous was set for deep water near the island of Abu Nu'ayr, some sixty miles from Dubai. It was as remote a spot as could be found along the busy UAE coast; nevertheless, Admiral Less sent a pair of frigates to enforce a five-mile off-limits zone. The tow cable parted a dozen miles from the rendezvous, and *Roberts* completed the trip the same way it had crept out of the minefield: ambling along on auxiliary thrusters at three knots.[25]

The crew of the *Mighty Servant* opened their ballast valves. The stern dipped as the ballast tanks filled, and water crossed the ochre deck like a rising tide. When only the superstructure remained above water, *Tornado* pushed *Roberts* into position. Sailors on the frigate tossed lines to the *Servant*'s crew, who nudged the frigate into the correct place.

When frigate and heavy-lift ship were properly aligned in three dimensions, the *Servant*'s pumps emptied the ballast tanks and the cargo ship began to rise. Navy divers and the *Servant*'s closed-circuit cameras watched as hull met steel crib. They moved slowly, deliberately as the hull approached its cradle of posts. The margin for error was measured in inches. Hull mated with cradle, and the cargo deck kept rising. As it resurfaced, the *Roberts*'s keel rose to the grand altitude of six feet above sea level. The docking had taken twelve hours.[26]

The trip home began on 1 July, which was eleven weeks to the day after the mine explosion. With its precious cargo securely aboard, *Mighty Servant* weighed anchor before dawn. Its departure time was part of a ruse; navy officials had hinted that the ships would run the strait under cover of darkness. As the mated ships approached the Strait of Hormuz, a salute boomed from the five-inch guns of the guided missile cruiser USS *Vincennes* (CG 49). The navy had rushed the high-tech Aegis warship to the Gulf to escort the *Roberts* through the strait.[27] Still, the skeleton crew of the frigate, now under the command of Cdr. John Townes III, was taking no chances. The forty officers and enlisted men stood guard on deck, gripping rifles, shotguns, and pistols, for the entire way through the strait. For many, it was the worst transit yet.

The same applied to the Suez passage. "Do you know how long it takes to go through the Suez Canal when you are holding a 12-gauge shotgun?" Ted Johnson wrote later. "Forever, man."[28]

Their course for Newport was the mirror image of the one that brought them here, an eternity of six months ago. To pass the time, the men aboard the *Roberts* did maintenance, studied for advancement exams, and worked out. Van Hook took to daily laps around the *Roberts* on the cargo deck of the *Servant*. As a running track, it beat the frigate's tiny flight deck, hands down.

The ships entered Narragansett Bay on schedule on the afternoon of 30 July. Sailboats, motor yachts, Boston Whalers, and every manner of watercraft known to New England came out for a look. Navy ships presently shooed them away so that the *Roberts* could free itself from the *Mighty Servant*'s embrace.

The following day began with fog that lifted only enough to become clouds. *Roberts* pulled into the naval station under her own power—the auxiliary propulsion units yet again—and tied up to Newport Naval Complex's Pier Two. The arrival ceremony was joyous, if not quite the spectacle of the T. F. Green airport homecoming a month earlier. A navy band played "Anchors Aweigh" as the ship was pushed to the pier. Their shipmates stood in ranks on the tarmac. A small crowd of friends and family jammed onto the pier between a long low building and the bay. Each wife wore a rose.[29]

IN LATE SEPTEMBER the *Roberts* made its way up to Maine. It was a two-day trip at the end of a towline drawn by the USS *Hoist* (ARS-40), a low-slung, fifteen-hundred-ton salvage ship launched in the waning months of World War II.[30]

Their destination was not the city of Bath; those facilities were crowded with half-built *Ticonderoga* cruisers and modules for the new USS *Arleigh Burke* destroyer to be laid down three months hence. Instead, they headed for Portland, an hour south by car. During World War II, BIW had opened two yards in Maine's largest city, an hour's drive south of Bath. The yards had built 274 wartime transports, including one-tenth of the famous *Liberty* ships. But the southern facilities had not survived the postwar slump, and BIW shut them down.

After nearly four decades, shipbuilding had returned to Portland when the iron works, buoyed by the *Perry* program, decided to expand. BIW had opened a repair-and-refit facility there in 1983, built on abandoned rail sidings next to the long state pier. You could look down upon it from the city's Fort Allen Park, which held a cannon from the battleship USS *Maine,* blown up in Havana, and a mast from the cruiser USS *Portland,* part of the surrender of Truk. Crews replaced the rotting pilings by the railhead, erected two gantry cranes and a bridge crane, and poured concrete for an 800-foot finger pier. Meanwhile, work began on the project's centerpiece, an immense floating dock that had been rusting away a thousand miles to the south. Designated AFDB-3, it was an 850-foot-long, 83-foot-deep behemoth commissioned at the end of World War II to repair battleships. The nine-section dock was built in four states and saw a few years of duty as far away as Guam before ending its naval career in the James River mothball fleet near Norfolk. Maine took possession of the dry dock for one dollar—at eighty-one thousand tons, it was the largest object ever given away as U.S. government surplus—but the $23.5 million refurbishment consumed half of the yard's construction budget. Each section's buoyancy chambers had more than a hundred hand-cranked valves, a wartime profligacy of manpower no peacetime yard could afford. Over a year's time each section was towed to Boston, overhauled and fitted with remote-controlled valves, and brought up to Portland. Completed in October 1983, the hulking dock broke free of its moorings during a winter storm with its first hoist, a destroyer, up on blocks inside.[31]

The yard was already busy when the *Hoist* and *Roberts* arrived on 25 September. A U.S. Coast Guard cutter was being refitted, and two frigates were being readied for sale to Pakistan.[32] But the city was eager to welcome the wounded warship to town. A small flotilla of pleasure craft gathered under the mid-afternoon sun as the *Hoist* and *Roberts* entered Casco Bay. A municipal fireboat, its fire cannons shooting watery arcs in salute, met the duo as they rounded Portland Head Lighthouse. A crowd of some two hundred sailors, BIW workers, and curious onlookers watched from shore as the frigate was unhitched from its tow and nudged by a pair of harbor tugs to its mooring alongside the great floating dock.

Haggett held a press conference that afternoon to describe the repair plan. The concept could be simply stated: cut out a big chunk of the ship, build a replacement, and weld it all back together. But this belied the actual complexity of one of the most difficult repair jobs an American shipyard had ever attempted. The *Stark* had been repaired with modular techniques at Ingalls Shipyard for $90 million—most of which went to replace the CIC and its combat systems—but its keel had not been broken, and the module was lowered onto the damaged ship from above.[33]

The *Roberts* repair would require BIW to shoehorn the replacement sections into the bottom of a completed frigate. The job had to be done with great precision—in some places, less than one two-hundredths of an inch. A misaligned hull section could slow the ship, reduce its gas mileage, and even make it noisier in the water—all of which would make *Roberts* a poorer warship and a better target for prowling submarines.

That such a repair was possible at all was due in large part to the ship's modular construction. BIW had delivered its twenty-fourth and final *Perry* frigate about a year previously, bringing to a close one of the century-old yard's finest chapters. But it still had the plans for each of the thirty-six massive chunks that made up each frigate, and the tapes that guided the cutting machines that shaped their steel plates, and workers who could all but turn them out in their sleep.

But the blast had mangled two of the modules, which forced a difficult choice: should they be replaced individually or with one giant piece? After much discussion, BIW engineers decided that a single chunk would be easier to work with. But that module would be a monster: 310 tons of gas turbines, generators, bulkheads, stringers, hull plates, and all the pipes, wires, and gear that make up the interior of a warship. It would be, by far, the largest single chunk of a ship the yard had ever handled.

Work had already started, Haggett told the assembled reporters. The semiautomated modular construction had allowed the Bath workers to jump right in. The tapes that drove the automated cutters had been broken out of storage, and fabrication had begun in BIW's Hardings plant in early June, within a week of the contract award. The pieces would be assembled in Bath and then barged south to Portland.

Haggett said the *Roberts* repair would be a "much more challenging job" than BIW's World War II repairs. It would be "an engineering experiment in a sense," but a "workable" task, he said. Ultimately, he estimated, it would involve up to five hundred workers—about 5 percent of BIW's workforce—and would likely cost about $96 million, split roughly evenly between parts and labor. The job would be done around the end of 1989.

Winn Price, a BIW program manager who would run the repair effort, told reporters that the ambitious schedule reflected "an intense amount of pride in this ship, and an intense desire to get her back to sea."[34]

THE DAY AFTER the press conference, the frigate USS *Vandegrift* (FFG 48) arrived in Kuwaiti waters in company with the supertanker *Townsend*. It was the sixty-seventh escort mission of the year, the eighty-ninth of Operation Earnest Will—and the last.

Thanks in part to the mining of the *Roberts* and its violent aftermath, Iran and Iraq had agreed to a cease-fire in August, and on 26 September 1988 the White House ended convoy operations in the Persian Gulf. Since July 1987, U.S. Navy warships had escorted 252 vessels through the Gulf. None except the *Bridgeton* was damaged by enemy action while under way.[35]

THE *ROBERTS* ENTERED Portland's dry dock once again on 6 October. Support blocks had been built parallel to the dry dock's keel, but about thirty feet off center, leaving room for the replacement module to be placed next to the ship. Computing the proper settings for the ballast tanks was a relatively straightforward matter for a dry dock that had been built to handle several ships at once. And unlike the Dubai dockmasters, BIW's engineers had gotten the chance to measure the hull's deformed contours. They shaped the blocks to allow for the one-degree bend in the main deck, and consequently, the *Roberts* settled down without further injury.

When inspections had confirmed that the frigate was safely ensconced, the first order of business was getting rid of the sand ballast that had come over from Saudi Arabia. A pair of holes was cut in the temporary engine room patches. But when local environmental authorities got a look at the grayish-white sandbags with the Arabic script, everything came to a quick halt. Just what had been the purpose of those bags? Concerns grew when someone managed to translate the word "flour" on the plastic webbing. Sealed samples of the sand were flown to the U.S. Department of Agriculture in Washington. Bill Forster, who ran the department's quarantine section, worried that the bags might contain khapra beetles, among the world's most voracious consumers of seeds and grain. But an inspection showed the bags and their contents to be free of insects, fungi, and disease, and workers resumed clearing the engine rooms of the sand, slitting open the bags and sucking them clean with vacuum hoses. The job took a week.[36]

The next step was more ticklish: removing the one-degree bend in the ship. Careful measurements had shown the stern to be down precisely thirty inches. Bath engineers had determined that it could be raised, and the ship returned to its normal configuration, by a phalanx of jacks pressing up—carefully, carefully!—on the aft section of the hull. "It's not a usual operation for a shipyard," said Dave Ward, who coordinated the jacking effort for BIW.

Preparations began by welding stools to the hull. These small platforms—five pairs of them—would give the jacks something to press against and would distribute the force to the ribs inside the hull plates. This would allow the jacks to lift the hull without punching holes in it. Each jacking stool was attached along a frame, spanning three longitudinal stringers. There were also nine more cribbing stools, which would help bear the burden of the hull.

Next, Ward's team removed the blocks aft of frame 280, replacing them one by one with towers of steel and concrete, one for each stool. Each tower was topped with four slim wedges of oak laid flat, then sledge-hammered into position to assure a tight fit against the stool.

Each of the ten jacking towers sported a pair of orange-painted aluminum cylinders. About double the size of a Quaker Oats canister, these jacks would lift one hundred tons when energized by a 10,000-psi pump.

Common practice called for jacks to be pressed to no more than three-quarters of their rated strength, so this setup provided fifteen hundred tons of lifting power for a thousand-ton job.[37]

Before the jacking rig went under the ship, BIW workers assembled it ashore and tested it to capacity. They also brought in extra pumps to ensure that once the jacking started, nothing would slow it down. A surveyor's transit was set up in the temporary engine room, its barrel trained directly down the tube that would hold the propeller shaft—or rather, trained along the line that should go straight down the tube. As the jacking proceeded, this transit would tell Ward and his team when they had the ship back in its original shape. Finally, Ward's workers sliced open the superstructure from roof to main deck. The thin V-shaped gap at frame 280 widened from the width of a saw blade at the main deck to about five inches at the roof. This would allow the superstructure's aft end to rotate one degree as the stern came up. They made a second vertical cut in the hull at frame 277, slicing through plating, stiffener, pipes, and wires, for the same reason. The cuts were offset and stiffeners added to make sure the main deck unbent, and did not further distort, at frame 280. This rotation was no minor matter, for it made the operation much trickier than a simple vertical lift. The stool at frame 286, for example, would rise only two inches during the jacking, but would move aft about twice as much.

The jacking began early one wintry morning. Workers with hardhats and walkie-talkies stationed themselves all along the jacking stations. Pumps hummed as the four aft jacks were pressed to about half their capacity. Next, the six forward jacks received hydraulic charges. All but imperceptibly, the hull that towered about the workers' heads began to move. Men with sledgehammers pounded the oaken marrying wedges toward each other, taking up the slack, keeping the jacks firmly pressed against the stools. Ward had his team continue jacking until one of the stations could accept a four-inch oak plank. The marrying wedges were loosened, the board was inserted, and the jacking began anew. From time to time the jacks were pressurized in alternate sequences as required by the tilting or rotation of the hull. Over time, layers of four-inch planks were replaced by foot-thick timbers, and still the work went on, centimeter by centimeter, all ten jacking crews working to keep their station working in unison with the others.

The sun rose above the islands in Casco Bay and traveled across the sky as the painstaking process went on, and the light was dying behind the waterfront warehouses when the transit finally indicated success. It had taken twelve hours to undo a bend that a mine had caused in microseconds.

The following morning, Ward and his crew rechecked the alignment. Custom wedges were cut and installed on the cribbing towers, and the jacks were depressurized and released.

In the following weeks, the temporary hull module built by Dubai Drydocks was cut from the frigate and lowered to the pontoon deck—the dock's "floor." The skeg, damaged in the post-blast docking, was replaced in prefabricated sections. Nearly thirteen hundred square feet of warped steel plating was removed from the superstructure and several longitudinal frames repaired; new plating was welded back on.

In Bath, workers wrapped up the structural part of the replacement module. The 160-ton assembly of framing, stringers, and hull plates, looking rather like a bathtub squared off on both ends, was rolled out of the long main assembly building, across the concrete apron, and into the paint shack, where it was sandblasted clean and freshly painted. So far, the module contained little of the machinery it was built to carry. The reason: the Japanese-designed level-luffing crane could handle no more than 200 tons. Even the Bath engineers weren't sure just how heavy the replacement module would be when completed, but they were guessing 350 tons.

So the candy-striped crane lifted the incomplete structure onto a 200-by-56-foot barge brought up the Kennebec River for the purpose and then added two gas turbines, a reduction gear, and the other large chunks of machinery. The large components were secured for the trip down to Portland, but final adjustment would wait until the module had been welded into the ship. High winds and November seas delayed the departure for two days; the barge finally left on its forty-mile trip down the river and the coast.[38]

But there remained a quandary: how would this heavy module—it had ultimately weighed in at 315 tons—get from barge to floating dock? BIW dockmasters considered ballasting the barge until its deck was level with the pontoon deck and dragging the module across the gap. They also mulled sinking the dry dock to let the barge come aboard and then lowering the module to the pontoon deck with jacks. Both options were eventually deemed too risky. Instead, BIW sent all the way to Virginia for a floating crane called the Chesapeake 1000, a herculean piece of equipment named for its ability to hoist a thousand-ton load. It arrived on its own barge and was so tall it required FAA approval for use near Portland's airport. BIW bought one-hundred-ton wire ropes for the lift and rigged them from the Chesapeake's hook through pairs of sixty-ton chainfalls to four points on the module.[39]

The lift operator pulled a lever, and the module rose slowly off its barge. BIW workers adjusted the chainfalls so that the module hung level in the air, sixteen feet above the calm harbor waters. A tug nudged the crane's barge alongside the dry dock so that its long boom extended over the dock's six-story wall, the heavy module dangling over the pontoon deck. The dry-dock wall prevented the crane operator from seeing his load, so a lift coordinator walked along the wall, relaying instructions via walkie-talkie.

The tug pushed the barge some 240 feet along the dry dock, until the module was next to the clean-cut hole in the *Roberts*. Three rails had been set on the pontoon deck, perpendicular to the frigate's centerline. Working blind, with only the radio instructions to guide him, the crane operator lowered the module to within one inch of the rails. BIW workers adjusted its position with cables and ratchet come-alongs and lowered it the thumb's width to the rails. When they measured their work, they found that the 315-ton chunk of ship was within a quarter inch of the ideal position.

The final leg of the module's journey—shoving the module into its hole and jacking it up into position—was a sufficiently complex endeavor that BIW sought outside help. The company hired Atlantic Industrial Contractors of Richmond, Virginia, who had set up the system of rails and jacks that now supported the module. In a single daytime shift, Atlantic workers used the jacks to move the module on graphite-coated rails, easing it sixteen feet horizontally until it was directly under the ship.

The final lift resembled the stern-jacking operation that had unbent the ship. Over the course of a day, BIW workers used eight one-hundred-ton jacks to lift the module—and the skidding rails and jacks—straight up, pounding in oaken wedges and piling up boards until the steel form fit snugly in its void.

The final adjustments were measured in hundredths of an inch. The path of the propeller shaft had to be straight—really straight. BIW workers had already fixed a fingernail-thin dent in the shaft caused by the explosion. (It would have been preferable to simply replace the shaft, but no extras had been manufactured for the *Perry* class.) A laser transit was trained up the shaft line, and with infinitesimal adjustment, the module was aligned for the final time. Welders wielded their tools, and the shattered ship was whole again.

Measurements showed that the placement of the forty-five-foot, 315-ton module deviated from the ideal by just one-sixth of an inch laterally and one-eighth of an inch vertically. Even this tiny deviation required some machining of the stern tube, which had shifted about an eighth of an inch to port and a quarter of an inch up. Parts to fit the tube were taken from an *Arleigh Burke* destroyer under construction at Bath, then modified to suit the *Roberts*. By 9 March the shaft was back in place, its bronze blades remounted on their swivels. Three weeks later, under a sliver of midnight moon, the vast dry dock filled once again with water. As dawn and high tide arrived in Portland together, the frigate floated free. At an afternoon press conference, the *Roberts's* captain, Cdr. John Townes, took reporters aboard his ship and challenged them to find the seams. They could not.[40]

Still ahead was the reattaching of wires, cables, pipes, vents, and the rest of the mechanics that transport fluids, air, and electrical current around the ship. The difference between the module installation and the rest was "the difference between setting a bone and brain surgery," Price said. "We're taking the next five months to do the nervous system."

The workers laid more than eleven miles of cable to connect the combat systems, and twice as much to hook up the lights, heating, cooling, and the rest. It was grinding work—each of the hundreds of connections in each cable was tested twice—and it went on all summer long and into autumn.

But progress was steady. The new gas turbines were spun up for the first time in early August. The crew moved back aboard in mid-September. The engineers tested the equipment in October. And on a damp, chilly

Monday morning—16 October 1989—a crowd gathered on the Portland docks to bid the ship adieu. After thirteen months, the $89.5 million job was done, three weeks ahead of schedule and $3.5 million under budget.

The *Roberts* was moored pierside. Its crew stood in ranks on the flight deck. Hundreds of workers crowded onto the pier in hardhats, flannel shirts, down vests, jean jackets, and safety glasses. A clutch of VIPs sat in chairs and made brief speeches. There were three congressmen, the NAVSEA deputy for surface combatants, the Bath SupShip, an assistant secretary of the navy, BIW President Duane Fitzgerald, and of course, Bill Haggett.

In a short speech, Haggett declared that the technologically advanced repairs would have been impossible just a few years earlier. "We have proven that, by employing innovative methods, a severely damaged ship, which might have been scrapped only five years ago, can be returned to superb operating condition," he said.

The navy's head shipbuilder added his praise. "Restoration of the ship required engineering skills and shipbuilding expertise not previously seen or experienced," said Rear Adm. Robert Reimann, NAVSEA's deputy head for surface ships. "Many of the techniques used, such as pre-construction of the main engine room assembly, had never before been utilized in a battle damage situation."[41]

James Mackie, the chief union steward in Portland, put it this way: "We did something that nobody has ever done before in shipbuilding," and he was right.[42]

THE FRIGATE DEPARTED on 23 October. After a stop to pick up training weapons at Earle, New Jersey, the ship came home to Newport on a bright fall day. Dozens of cheering friends and family members packed the freshly painted Pier Two, waving balloons and pushing strollers. The *Roberts* was home, until duty called again.

Epilogue

The mine explosion that nearly sank the USS *Samuel B. Roberts* on 14 April 1988 sent ripples through the Gulf, the U.S. Navy, and the world. The American retaliation did more than destroy half of the ayatollah's naval striking force; it shattered the calcified state of war between Iran and Iraq. Khomeini, who did not start the eight-year conflict but had prolonged it, took Operation Praying Mantis as a sign that further fighting was useless, that Washington would not allow Iran to win. Subsequent events further eroded his resolve. Iraqi troops, likely fortified with U.S. intelligence, seized the strategic Fao Peninsula. The Saudi government, emboldened by the U.S. naval action, severed diplomatic relations with Iran. "The whole situation in the gulf changed tremendously in April," a Bahraini official said the following month. "The Americans went farther, in the clashes on the 18th, than anyone expected they would and showed clearly, for the first time, that they were really serious about the security of the gulf."[1] The final straw came on 3 July, when the U.S. cruiser *Vincennes,* which had rushed to the Gulf to protect the wounded *Roberts,* accidentally downed an Iranian airliner near the Strait of Hormuz. The ayatollah, who believed the attack was a deliberate provocation by a newly aggressive United States, allowed his diplomats to be ushered to a United Nations bargaining table. In mid-July, before the *Roberts* had even reached Newport, Iraq and Iran agreed to a cease-fire.[2]

The ripples widened. The Praying Mantis operations "illustrated the front edge of what would become a new philosophy about the role that the United States would play in the world," wrote Craig L. Symonds, a Naval Academy history professor.[3] In the decade and a half that followed, the nation would emerge as a world policeman—sometimes reluctant, sometimes otherwise.

When Saddam Hussein invaded another of his neighbors—Kuwait—in August 1990, the Bush administration did not hesitate to send thousands of troops, scores of ships, and hundreds of warplanes to the Gulf. Among the many ships sent to support Operations Desert Shield and Desert Storm was the newly repaired *Samuel B. Roberts,* which returned to war as part of the USS *Kennedy* battle group in the Red Sea and eastern Mediterranean.

OPERATION PRAYING MANTIS was a watershed battle in naval warfare as well. It was the first clash between groups of warships since World War II, and it featured the first missile duel between surface forces. Moreover, it was the first test of a new way of war that depended as much on electronic networks as it did on ordnance. "It offered only the first glimpse of the stunning technological revolution, already underway, that would over the next decade and a half make the United States not merely a 'superpower,' not merely the greatest power on earth, but the greatest military power the world had ever seen," the academy professor wrote.[4]

But the mining of the *Roberts* also showed the limits of that power. The frigate had warded off warships and warplanes only to fall victim to a far more primitive weapon. A military empowered by and enamored of technology had demonstrated its inability to grapple with low-tech warfare.

The near-sinking of the *Roberts* did not persuade the naval service to take mines seriously. "The Navy was little better prepared in 1990 to deal with sea mines than it had been in 1987," the service's own historians wrote.[5] Two more U.S. warships were damaged by underwater weapons during Desert Storm. One string knocked out the amphibious assault ship USS *Tripoli* (LPH 10), whose repair bill came to $5 million.[6] Another damaged the guided missile cruiser USS *Princeton* (CG 59), a billion-dollar ship commanded by Capt. Ted Hontz—the man who had advised Rinn to take Eric Sorensen as damage control assistant. "None of us got much training in mine warfare," Hontz said later. "My officers and I had gotten what little there was at the various surface warfare schools over the years, but there was no specific training prescribed simply because we were going somewhere that was known to be mined."[7]

The *Roberts* attack demonstrated that a low-tech enemy could inflict dramatic damage, the kind that got on television and influenced public perceptions. To Middle East scholar Anthony Cordesman, it foretold the future of conflict. Far overmatched in conventional military and political power, the enemies of the United States would henceforth use unconventional means to strike. "Any force which is not tailored to respond to all known low level threats from a given country is poorly planned and improperly equipped," Cordesman wrote.[8]

In October 2000, suicide bombers piloted a small boat up to the guided missile destroyer USS *Cole* (DDG 67), moored in the Yemeni harbor of Aden. They blew themselves up, killing seventeen *Cole* sailors and opening the engine room to the sea. The crew's response harkened straight back to the *Roberts: Cole's* sailors fought fire and flood to save their ship, and the destroyer was eventually hauled back to the United States aboard the heavy-lift ship *Blue Marlin*.[9]

But the problem of low-tech weapons would only grow worse. In the years that followed the 2003 invasion of Iraq, hundred of U.S. troops died in the blasts of homemade bombs.

IN OCTOBER 1988 the Naval Sea Systems Command released its final report on the mining of the *Roberts*. The report concluded, first of all, that the U.S. Navy provided far too little damage control gear to its warships. It noted that the *Roberts* crew had run out of hose fittings and other vital equipment despite all the extras accumulated in predeployment scavenging. The navy needed to do better, the report said, echoing earlier criticism from Eric Sorensen, the *Stark* investigators, and the navy's own deputy undersecretary for survivability. "This reaffirms a *Stark* finding," it noted dryly.

The report also concluded that a mine could have done even more damage to the frigate than it did. For one thing, the turbine exhaust plenum provided a ready-made pressure valve for the gas bubble. If the hull had been pierced in a space without a ready vent, the explosive force might have wrecked even more internal spaces. The ship was also fortunate that the seas were fairly calm during its transit to Dubai; larger waves would have increased the strain on the main deck, perhaps to the breaking point.

Above all, the report praised the crew of the *Samuel B. Roberts* for saving their ship. "The intensive training and repetitive drills provided the baseline knowledge that allowed common sense, quick thinking, and innovation to successfully combat the catastrophic situation."[10] The NAVSEA authors did say that the effort to wire the ship together with lifeline cables probably hadn't made much difference, but no one blamed the crew for trying.

In the wake of the *Roberts* mining, the navy modified its ships, equipment, and procedures. More gate valves were retrofitted to fire mains, emergency tag-out procedures were developed, and sterile sheets were added to the repair lockers. The report found that preparations taken between spotting the mines and the explosion undoubtedly saved lives. The engineers' order to come up from the bilges in a minefield was enshrined in navy regulations: "In a mine or torpedo threat situation, all personnel not required for the continued operation of the ship shall be moved as high in the ship as practical. Prior to a known torpedo hit or mine strike, personnel shall be warned to brace for shock."[11] And the next edition of the basic training manual led off its damage control chapter with a quote from Paul Rinn: "The events of 14–15 April 1988 have proven that solid damage control, good training, and sound leadership based on experience can save a ship that is on fire and sinking, to fight another day."

Years later, William Rowden, the former head of Naval Sea Systems Command, was still awed by the damage control effort aboard *Roberts* and amazed that the ship had stayed afloat. "When you reflect back on it, it was a tougher task than the *Cole,* or the *Princeton,* or the *Stark.* She went to five thousand tons [total displacement]; she was on her way to the bottom, and those guys kept her together, and kept her afloat. I don't take anything away from *Stark,* but she was hit in the berthing space. The point was that it was a different set of casualties on the *Roberts;* they tended to put the ship to the bottom."[12]

MANY OF THE officers and enlisted sailors who saved the *Roberts* went on to success in the navy. Executive Officer John Eckelberry was promoted to captain and commanded two warships. Combat Systems Officer Glenn Palmer retired as a commander after planning operations for an amphibious squadron and helping to test a new version of the Tomahawk missile launcher. Chief Engineer Gordan Van Hook received command of the U.S. Navy's most fabled destroyer squadron: DesRon 23, the "Little Beavers" that were led in World War II by future three-time CNO Arleigh Burke.

Eric Sorensen spoke out against a skipper he found abusive and was transferred off his ship with a bad performance review. The former *Roberts* damage control assistant went to Nova Scotia as a NATO liaison officer and was forced out of the navy after fifteen years' service. He started a consulting business and wrote a well-received book about powerboats.

Many of the *Roberts's* enlisted sailors made chief petty officer: the injured Mark Dejno, Chuck Dumas, Serge Kingery, Kim Sandle, and more. Quartermaster Dan Nicholson was named 1995 Atlantic Fleet Sailor of the Year and later became command chief of the USS *Constitution,* the navy's oldest ship.

Chief Cook Kevin Ford was honored for his role in the damage control effort of 14 April 1988 with his induction sixteen years later into the Surface Navy Association's hall of fame. Gunner Tom Reinert became a fleet instructor in Little Creek, Virginia, and retired in 1991. Alex Perez, horribly burned in the main engine room, remained in the hospital for about six months, returned to active duty, and retired in 1993.

Dave Walker, the gas turbine chief, became a chief warrant officer and an instructor at Surface Warfare Officers' School before retiring from the service. After U.S. forces overthrew Saddam Hussein in 2003, Walker found work in Iraq, first teaching army soldiers about riverine warfare and then running gas-turbine-powered power-generation plants.

Others left the navy after their hitches were up. Several dozen settled in and near Maine—Joe Baker and Mike Tilley among them—and commemorated 14 April with an annual Mine Blast party.

Many carried the psychological effects of the mining for years, including insomnia and sensitivity to loud noises. Lester Chaffin, who deployed a second time to the Persian Gulf aboard another frigate, began experiencing anxiety attacks as his ship approached the Gulf. His skipper sent him back home from Bahrain. The electrician moved to West Virginia and became an independent repair contractor.

Many former *Roberts* sailors spoke of their time aboard the ship as the best of their service. John Preston, who left the navy and rose to chief petty officer in the U.S. Coast Guard, called his *Roberts* shipmates "the greatest crew I ever sailed with." Engineman Alan Sepelyak said it turned a boy into a man.

But some are still rankled by what they say was an unfair distribution of medals after the mining. More than a decade later, Rinn still regretted that he didn't get decorations for more of the crew—especially those who sustained injuries—and he worked for several years to correct that. "Absolutely my fault," he later said. "Probably twenty-five to thirty guys more should have gotten Purple Hearts." He said that others had no doubt deserved medals as well, but that no one had come forward in the wake of the mining to bear witness to them. "I thought once about asking for a Navy Achievement Medal for everyone, but when was that ever done? Never. The *Indianapolis?* At Leyte Gulf? No."

After Rinn turned over command of his frigate in summer 1988, he was appointed the navy's head of ship survivability. It was a post he accepted with some irony. "Up until I hit the mine in the *Samuel B. Roberts,* I'd probably shot as many missiles as anybody else in the navy . . . I wasn't the damage control guy; I just stressed it on the ship. I'd say I was a big-time warfighter. Now, ship blows up, guy saves ship, all of a sudden you're the guru, and you can't escape it." He was promoted to captain, selected early for major command, tapped as the assistant to the navy's surface warfare chief, and sent back to sea in 1994 in one of the surface navy's most prominent jobs: captain of an Aegis guided missile cruiser, the USS *Leyte Gulf* (CG 55). His second command tour brought a successful deployment to the Persian Gulf and the prestigious John Paul Jones Leadership Award from the U.S. Navy League. He followed that with an assignment as special assistant to two chiefs of naval operations.

A vanishingly small proportion of captains are selected to become admirals: 1 or 2 percent a year. But when Rinn's name went to the flag selection board, he was optimistic. He had a strong record, and he figured it would be hard for the navy to say "no" to a captain who'd saved his ship and gotten on the nation's front pages for it.

The first time Rinn came up for promotion to admiral, the flag officers' board rejected him. The board met in secret, per navy custom, and destroyed its notes afterward. There is no official record of the reason for his rejection. Rinn waited a year, was passed over by a second board, and retired, disappointed, in 1997. "I'll always feel bad that it didn't happen, because I think I could have made a difference," he said.

But he was proud of his naval service and his two commands at sea, and time along with a senior executive position with a respected consulting firm near Washington, DC—eased the sting. In 2003 he spoke to a packed hall of midshipmen as part of a prestigious lecture series at the U.S. Naval Academy. Moreover, Rinn kept the ear of top navy leaders, who came to him from time to time for his opinion. "If I were a flag officer, I wouldn't be living where I'm living, I wouldn't be as well off, my family wouldn't have seen me, I'd probably look older," he said in 2005. "Life is funny. Be careful what you ask for; you may get it."[13]

FIVE U.S. WARSHIPS have been lost through hostile action since World War II—all in the Korean War, all to naval mines. Since then, none has come closer to sinking than the *Roberts* did in 1988.

In the years since the mining, the *Roberts* burnished its reputation as an outstanding ship. It won six awards in a row for crew reenlistments and was a perennial contender for its squadron's Battle E. The frigate served well in Operations Desert Shield and Storm. It set records for Caribbean Sea drug seizures. Two of its commanding officers went on to become admirals.

In September 2005 the *Roberts* was transferred to the Navy Reserve, where it was slated to carry on much as it had for a decade, performing counterdrug operations and participating in international naval exercises. Its retirement was foreseen, but not for many years. Decommissioning was planned for 2018.

FOR THE U.S. NAVY, the story of the third USS *Samuel B. Roberts* became a touchstone tale of courage and competence under fire. Nearly two decades after the mining, sailors still learned about Ford and Fridley at boot camp. Midshipmen debated Rinn's decisions at the U.S. Naval Academy. Officers studied the ship's damage control effort at department-head school in Newport. For a crew of brave sailors, there is no higher honor.

Ship's Muster

This unofficial list of the men aboard the USS *Samuel B. Roberts* (FFG 58) on 14 April 1988 is based in large part upon the official muster of 23 March 1988, as provided by the Naval Personnel Command, with revisions to names and rates where credible sources provided reason.

OFFICERS

CDR Paul X. Rinn
LCDR John R. Eckelberry
LCDR Glenn P. Palmer
LT Robert L. Firehammer
LT Bradley G. Gutcher
LT David A. Llewellyn
LT Gordan E. Van Hook
LT Goeff L. Walborn
LTJG Robert Chambers
LTJG John D. Sims
LTJG Michael L. Valliere
ENS Steven Giannone
ENS Michael Infranco
ENS Robert H. Miessau Jr.
ENS Robert B. Sobnosky
ENS Kenneth J. Rassler

ENLISTED

BMCS George E. Frost
BM1 Richard L. Fridley
BM1 Warren F. Whitman
BM2 William B. Buttery
BM2 Darrel Hyche
BM2 Kim T. Sandle
BM3 Eric W. Cross
BM3 Joel Echevarria
BM3 Doug Medland
BM3 Jim Owens
BM3 Patrick Sawyer
BM3 Eduardo Segovia
SN Bobby F. Gibson
DC1 Ward Davis
DK2 B. Robinson
DKSN Rufus Siler
DSC James Norman
DS3 David Matthews
EMC Robert C. Bent
EM1 Lester Chaffin
EM1 James Seward
EM1 James E. Whitley
EM2 Edwin B. Copeland
EM2 John Kolynitis
EMFA Jeffrey Oster
ENC George A. Cowan
EN1 Charles Kunesh

EN1 Joseph Reineke
EN1 Ronald Starks
EN1 Mark T. Dejno
EN3 Robert Bunn
EN3 William Dodson
EN3 Darryl A. Heath
EN3 Jeffrey Kelley
ENFN Dean Simmons
ENFN Mike Tilley
FN Joe Baker
FN Robert King
FN Marvin Moore
FN Alan Sepelyak
ET1 James Aston
ET1 Alden Weiss
ET2 Lawrence Deem
ET2 James Muehlberg
ET2 Shawn Scully
ET3 Joseph LaJudice
ET3 Benjamin J. Ledo
ET3 Will McCarthy
EW2 Fernando Cruz
EW2 Ronald Easton
EW3 Dave Laycock
EWSN David Robinson
FA Anthony Dizillo
FA Bobby Isaacs
FCC Mark Guay
FCC Alan G. Jochem
FCC Dale A. Lynch
FC1 Dana W. Loney
FC1 Matt Shannon
FC2 M. Krzyminski
FC2 John Preston
FC2 Randall Winchester
FC3 David Jacobs

FC3 Jack T. Paprocki
SN Robby Ramkumar
FN Chris Seward
FR James A. Ford
FR P. Hernandez
FR L. Williams
GMCS Thomas Reinert
GMG2 J. McClintock
GMG2 Derek Whidden
GMG3 Robert Lewis
GMG3 Edward Rivera
GMG3 Javier Velez
GMM1 Lawrence F. Lorusso
GMM2 Robert Clark
GMM3 Randy Lee Thomas
GSEC Alex Perez
GSE1 Michael C. Wallingford
GSE2 David Claus
GSE2 Malcolm Grazier
GSE2 Thomas Wagner
GSE2 Larry A. Welch
GSE3 Craig Poulos
GSMC David J. Walker
GSM2 Valen Hemmer
GSM2 Thomas Holcomb
GSM2 Randy A. Tatum
GSM3 David J. Burbine
GSM3 Michael Raines
GSMFA Michael Horta
GSMFN Wayne J. Smith
HM1 James E. Lambert
HN Kenneth Jones
HT1 Gary W. Gawor
HT2 Ted Johnson
HT2 Timothy Regan
HT3 Lonny Louwers

HTFN Christopher Pond
IC1 Donald Shankweiler
IC2 Michael Flynn
IC2 Robert Nares
MA1 Stanley Bauman
MR2 William Brad Aiken
MSC Kevin Ford
MS1 Anton Doctor
MS1 Joseph Fortin
MS2 Steven Fout
MS2 Scott W. Frank
MS2 Scot Joseph
MSSA Luciano DeFeo
MSSA Vernon Gowler
MSSA Angelo Ortiz
MSSN R. Puricelli
OSC Phil Voorhes
OS1 Scott Beals
OS1 Kenneth Dalton
OS1 Thomas Gavin
OS1 Mark A. Rajotte
OS1 Carlos Salinas
OS2 David Jackson
OS2 Kevin Keeler
OS2 Thomas Mowry
OS2 Richard Raymond
OS2 John Smetak
OS3 Stephen Kimball
OS3 Craig McGivney
OS3 Jeffrey McKee
OS3 David Mikos
OS3 Gregory Tanner
OSSA Navin Helms
OSSN Andrew Flood
PC2 Hermann Timm
PN1 Eric Blair

PNSN Charles Morin
QMCS Robert L. Grafing
QM2 Randall W. Graves
QM2 Daniel J. Nicholson
QM3 Mike O'Connor
RMC John Williams
RM1 Daniel Clancy
SK2 Ronald Kelley
SK2 John Ruppert
SK3 William Stephens
SM1 Charles R. Dumas
SM1 Serge E. Kingery
SM2 Mike Roberts
SMSN Billy Moore
SN Jose Burgos
SN Christensen
SN Charles Gatewood
SN Richard Klemme
SN Norbert Rios
SN Nelson Riviera
SN Julia Walker
SR David Fountain
SR M. Franchitti
SR James A. Frey
SR Rod Hernandez
SR James Horn
SR S. McKeon
SR Brian Perkins
SR Schlotzhauer
SR D. Stutzke
SR Salvad Zamont
STGC John D. Carr
STG1 John Bailey
STG1 Joseph D. Boyd
STG1 Daniel Whaley
STG2 George Liggins

STG2 George Tarley
STG3 Arthur DiRocco Jr.
STG3 Kenneth Lenox
STG3 David Pieratt
STGSN Ularislao Cordova III
STGSN Thomas Wolf
TM1 Alan L. Van Reese
TMSN Steven David
YN1 Paul D. Hass
YN3 B. Landgraff
YN3 Don Walton

HSL-44 DETACHMENT 5

LCDR Tim Matthews
LCDR Dan Smith
LT Steve Blaisdell

LT John Funk
LT Craig Miller
AD2 Gurule
AE1 Sim Samuels
AE3 Mark Filley
AE3 Robert Schill
AMH1 Blunt
AMH2 Crandall
AT2 Russell
AW2 Wesley Deti
AW2 Gerry Robertson
AW3 Robert Schill
AXC Jim Lee
AX2 Billy Ross
AZ2 Sanders

NOTES

CHAPTER 1

1. PH1 Chuck Mussi, "To See the Dawn," *All Hands,* August 1988.

CHAPTER 2

1. At Marist, Paul Rinn displayed a rough-and-tumble attitude in a student newspaper article about intramural basketball: "One should not really try to classify the type of defenses used by the various teams, for more often than not, they appear to border on the hand-to-hand-combat-type zone. However, the important thing to remember is that the larger the bumps and sprains are now, the better the memories will be later." (Rinn, "Hoops for Goofs," *The Circle,* 16 December 1965.)

2. The *Sarsfield* tour also gave Rinn his first taste of international crisis. In 1971, the destroyer was sent to the north Indian Ocean. The Pakistani military was battling Bengali separatists, while India, beset by refugees, was preparing to send its own troops to settle the situation. "We didn't have standoff weapons on that ship," Rinn said. "If someone threw a cruise missile at us or if there were a gun battle, there was no doubt in my mind that we were going to get hit."

3. Interview, Paul Rinn with author, 30 November 2004.

4. Rinn, as quoted in *Hudson Valley* magazine, December 1990.

5. Cdr. Alan W. Swinger, "FFG 7 Class Pre-Commissioning," *U.S. Naval Institute Proceedings* (hereafter, *Proceedings),* January 1982.

6. Letter, Rinn to Capt. John P. Doolittle, 24 January 1985.

7. Interview, Rinn.

8. Interview, Chuck Dumas with author, 28 January 2002.

9. Interview, Rinn.

10. Roberts's first sea tours were aboard the battleship USS *California* (BB 44) and the troop transport USS *Heywood* (AP 12). *Heywood* is listed, incorrectly, in most official FFG 58–related publications as AD 12. *Bellatrix* was initially designated AK 20 and reclassified AKA 3 in 1943. See, for example, "U.S. Navy Ships—USS *Bellatrix* (AK-20, later AKA-3), 1942–1963," Department of the Navy, Navy Historical Center, http://www.history.navy.mil/photos/sh-usn/usnsh-b/ak20.htm. FFG 58's 1984 launch booklet misstates the original designation as AKA 20. (Launch booklet, FFG 58, Database, "Changes in Ships' Status, v. 3.4, 22 May 2005," compiled by Christopher P. Cavas.)

11. Lt. Col. Frank O. Hough, Maj. Verle E. Ludwig, and Henry I. Shaw Jr., *Pearl Harbor to Guadalcanal: History of U.S. Marine Corps Operations in World War II,* vol. 1, p. 314 (Historical Branch, G-3 Division, Headquarters, U.S. Marine Corps, 1958).

12. This is the way official navy documents tell the story, but there is a footnote, or perhaps an asterisk, to add. The coast guard also honors one of

its own who died valiantly in the Matanikau withdrawal, and its scholars tell the tale a bit differently. According to coast guard battle reports, the navy coxswain was accompanied that day by a coast guard petty officer, Raymond J. Evans. The signalman reported that the boats carried their marines to shore, dropped them off, and withdrew, confirming the navy version. But Evans maintained that when the rest of the boats headed back to base, he and Roberts stuck around, intending to evacuate any troops wounded early on. "Due to our inexperience, we did not anticipate fire from the beach and allowed our boat to lay too close in," Evans recalled in a 1999 interview with coast guard historians. A sudden burst of machine-gun bullets caught Roberts in the head and neck. Evans threw the throttle to the stops and raced back to Lunga Point, but the navy coxswain was beyond help. When the marines' mayday call arrived, Evans headed back to the landing zone in a boat with Douglas Munro, a close friend and fellow signalman. According to coast guard historians, Munro led the rescue mission, steered his boat between the enemy and the landing craft, and was killed by a single bullet while helping to tow a grounded landing craft off the beach. In 1942 the War Department approved the coast guard's request to award Munro the Medal of Honor. He remains the only guardsman to receive the country's highest military decoration. Whichever version is true—coast guard or navy—the fact remains that Roberts risked his life to aid U.S. Marines, and gave it in service of his country. (Robert M. Browning Jr., "Douglas Munro at Guadalcanal," U.S. Coast Guard Web site, http://www.uscg.mil/hq/g-cp/history/Munro.html, September 1999.)

13. Roberts's Navy Cross was awarded on 10 February 1943. The citation read, in part: "Roberts, although he knew that his boat was to be maneuvered into an exposed position for the purpose of drawing enemy fire away from the other boats being used to rescue the trapped Marines, courageously volunteered as a member of the crew. The lightly armed boat was made a target for the enemy fire during the entire evacuation and Roberts was wounded just as the operation was completed. His gallant action, taken without regard for his own safety, contributed directly to the highly successful rescue, and was in keeping with the highest traditions of the Naval Service." This was somewhat shortened from an earlier draft, which read, "For extraordinary heroism as member of the crew of a Higgins boat assisting in the rescue of a group of Marines surrounded by enemy Japanese forces on a beachhead on Guadalcanal, Solomon Islands, on September 27, 1942. Although he knew that his boat was to be used for the purpose of drawing enemy fire away from other craft evacuating the trapped Marines, Roberts, with utter disregard for his own personal safety, volunteered as a member of the crew. With his lightly armed boat sta-

tioned in an exposed position, he gallantly remained at his post until, at the close of the operations, he was wounded by enemy fire. By his great personal valor and fearless devotion to duty he contributed directly to the success of his mission, saving the lives of many who might otherwise have perished."

14. J. Henry Doscher Jr., *Little Wolf at Leyte* (Austin, TX: Eakin Press, 1996), 2.
15. Samuel E. Morison, *Sailor Historian* (New York: Houghton Mifflin, 1977), 210.
16. Rear Adm. Robert W. Copeland, with Jack E. O'Neill, *The Spirit of the Sammy-B.,* unpublished manuscript, ca. 1952.
17. Among the U.S. sailors who helped win the battle of Surigao Strait was young Elmo Zumwalt, a target evaluator aboard the destroyer *Robinson* and future chief of naval operations. (Lt. Cdr. Thomas J. Cutler, *The Battle of Leyte Gulf: 23–26 October 1944* [New York: HarperCollins, 1994], 205.)
18. Robert Jon Cox, *The Battle Off Samar: Taffy III at Leyte Gulf* (Groton, CT: Ivy Alba Press, 2003), 60.
19. Copeland, *Spirit of the Sammy-B,* ch. 5. The eminent naval historian Samuel Eliot Morison concluded: "The Battle off Samar, thus unexpectedly joined at 0648, was the most remarkable of the Pacific war, since the tactics had to be improvised." (Morison, *Sailor Historian,* 212.)
20. The *Roberts's* propeller shafts were rated for 420 revolutions per minute (rpm), the boilers for 440 pounds of pressure per square inch (psi). "As soon as we fire our fish," Copeland told his engineer, "I will ring up flank speed, and I want you to hook on everything you've got. Don't worry about your reduction gears or your boilers or anything, because there's all hell being thrown at us up here, and we are just fortunate we haven't been hit yet, so don't worry about it." The engineer shut the safety valves. The steam pressure rose to 670 psi, producing 477 shaft rpm and propelling the ship to 28.5 knots. It is likely that no *Butler*-class ship ever went faster (Copeland, *Spirit of the Sammy-B,* ch. 6). Four decades later, FFG 58 would set a speed record for its own *Perry* class.
21. Details of the Battle of Leyte Gulf are drawn from Cutler, *Battle of Leyte Gulf;* Doescher, *Little Wolf at Leyte;* Robert W. Love Jr., *History of the U.S. Navy* (Harrisburg, PA: Stackpole Books, 1992); and Jack Sweetman, *American Naval History: An Illustrated Chronology of the U.S. Navy and Marine Corps, 1775–Present,* 3rd ed. (Annapolis, MD: Naval Institute Press, 2002).
22. See Andrew C. Toppan, "Dictionary of American Naval Fighting Ships," "DD-823," *Haze Gray & Underway: Naval History and Photography,* http://www.hazegray.org/danfs/destroy/dd823txt.htm, 1994–2003.
23. Norman Polmar, *The Death of the USS* Thresher (Guilford, CT: Lyons Press, 2001), 63.
24. L. A. Olsson, "History of Ships Named *Samuel B. Roberts,*" Naval History Division, Office of the Chief of Naval Operations, ca. 1971.

25. Letter, Mark Unhjem to Rinn, 23 February 1988. This letter, which was actually sent after the 14 April 1988 mining, is dated improperly.

26. Letter, Robert J. Cressman to Rinn, 1 February 1984.

CHAPTER 3

1. Ralph Linwood Snow, *Bath Iron Works: The First Hundred Years* (Bath, ME: Maine Maritime Museum, 1987), 13.

2. The young scion of wealthy merchants, Hyde had marched off to war at the head of an infantry company and returned to Maine a twenty-four-year-old brigadier general. Hyde's valor at Antietam—three horses were killed under him as he charged toward Stonewall Jackson's headquarters—was recognized in 1896 with the Medal of Honor.

3. The gunboats, USS *Machias* and USS *Castine,* would one day sail around the world with Teddy Roosevelt's Great White Fleet. ("List of Ships: The Hulls of Bath Iron Works," BIW promotional booklet, 2002.)

4. Snow, *Bath Iron Works,* 317, 386. Eight of the eighty-two destroyers produced during World War II were lost in combat. ("A Legacy of Pride . . . A Future of Promise: The First Hundred Years of Bath Iron Works," BIW promotional booklet, 1984.)

5. Toppan, "Dictionary of American Naval Fighting Ships," "DD 724."

6. Snow, *Bath Iron Works,* 422.

7. For example: "A 'Bath-built ship' holds a near-legendary status among the U.S. Navy's engineering personnel, testimony to this builder's commitment to quality that quite literally spans decades," wrote Randall D. Bennett and Crystal D. Sloan in "Repeating Design Errors, or 'Where's the History?'", a paper presented at the 2003 symposium of the International Council on Systems Engineering.

8. Interview, William Haggett with author, 5 August 2002.

9. Snow, *Bath Iron Works,* 485.

10. After retiring from the navy, Sonenshein served a two-year term on the National Advisory Committee on Oceans and Atmosphere, which stirred up controversy in 1985 with a report suggesting that U.S. shipyards be allowed to go out of business rather than be propped up by government subsidy. (Michael Isikoff and Howard Kurtz, "Shipbuilders on the Skids," *Washington Post,* 17 July 1985.)

11. Snow, *Bath Iron Works,* 496.

12. Adm. Elmo R. Zumwalt Jr. (Ret.), *On Watch* (New York: Quadrangle/New York Times Book Co., 1976), 72. *See also* Jan S. Breemer, *U.S. Naval Developments* (Annapolis, MD: Nautical and Aviation Publishing, 1983), 7: "The Navy has been inclined to buy the best of everything. Generally speaking . . . the Navy has put its money into the high-capability ships, on the prem-

ise that a few well-coordinated, highly capable ships will out-perform a larger number of less expensive ones."

13. Between 1968 and 1977, the number of navy surface combatants fell from 304 to 182. (Naval Historical Center, Ships History Branch, "U.S. Navy Active Ship Force Levels, 1917–Present," http://www.history.navy.mil/branches/org9-4.htm, 2 March 2003.)

14. Naval Sea Systems Command (hereafter, NAVSEA), "Building Patrol Frigates for the United States Navy," pamphlet, 1974.

15. Predicted costs were calculated in projected 1973 dollars, the budget year in which the first ship would be purchased. (Norman Friedman, *U.S. Destroyers: An Illustrated Design History* (Annapolis, MD: Naval Institute Press, 1982), 378, 381.)

16. Ibid., 384.

17. High-tensile steel has a yield strength of 45 kilograms per square inch; medium steel, 33; and HY-80, 80. (NAVSEA, draft report, NAVSEA Damage Assessment Team, 27 April 1988.)

18. NAVSEA, "Building Patrol Frigates."

19. Price's planners also reasoned that the DX and plenty of other ships already carried the new SQS-53, so the smaller SQS-56 ought to suffice for the new frigate. Among the other equipment postponed or simply deleted from the plan: stabilizing fins; the RAST, a kind of giant winch to help helicopter pilots land on the ship's tiny flight deck in bad weather; the SLQ-32 Nixie noise-maker, which trailed behind the ship to confuse enemy subs and torpedoes; the Naval Tactical Data System networking system, which allowed a navy battle group to fuse sensor data into a single electronic picture of the area; and the Mk 36 Super RBOC, a fan of deck-mounted tubes that fired flares and strips of aluminum to distract incoming missiles. The flight decks of the early *Perrys* were built long enough for the original LAMPS helicopters, the SH-2 Seasprites, but three feet too short for their LAMPS-3 successors, the larger SH-60 Sea Hawks, which began to appear in 1985. (NAVSEA, final report, "Survivability Review Group Report on USS *Samuel B. Roberts* [FFG 58] Damage Analysis," October 1988, p. 2–1, p. 7–39; Bernard Prézelin, and A. D. Baker III, *The Naval Institute Guide to Combat Fleets of the World 1990–1991* [Annapolis, MD: Naval Institute Press, 1990], 805–6; Norman Polmar, *The Naval Institute Guide to Ships and Aircraft of the U.S. Fleet,* 14th ed. [Annapolis, MD: Naval Institute Press, 1987]; Friedman, *U.S. Destroyers;* etc.)

20. Friedman, *U.S. Destroyers,* 383.

21. The new frigate's propulsion system would be functionally half of Bath's four-turbine, two-shaft design for the DX—which the navy had forced Litton to use instead of the Mississippi yard's own proposal. (Snow, *Bath Iron Works,* 512–13.)

22. Friedman, *U.S. Destroyers,* 383. After this meeting, only two major changes were introduced to the PF 109 design. In November, Zumwalt decided that the frigates ought to carry two helicopters. This forced designers to push the landing pad back from just aft of amidships to the stern of the ship, and to double the size of the hangar. It also meant that the air intakes and exhaust for the gas turbines would funnel straight up between the two indoor helo parking spots, instead of wrapping around a single bay. And in April 1972, a fourth ship's service diesel generator was added to the machinery complement.

23. A smaller design award went to the West Coast Todd Shipyards, part of the navy's attempt to ensure that more than one yard could build the new ships. (Snow, *Bath Iron Works,* 510.)

24. Interviews with the author, Erik Hansen, Ed Moll, and Bill Blakelott, 6 August 2002.

25. Snow, *Bath Iron Works,* 514.

26. George Wilson, "Destroyer Built On Time, Under Budget," *Washington Post,* 5 December 1978.

27. Ibid.

28. The rare exceptions were mostly ships that introduced major design changes to the class, like the stern step added to accommodate the larger Seahawk, or LAMPS-3, helicopter.

29. Bath Iron Works called the nascent ship Hull 394, noting its place in the yard's "List of Ships."

30. Interview, William Haggett with author, 5 August 2002.

31. Lt. Cdr. Bruce R. Linder, "FFG 7s: Square Pegs?" *Proceedings,* June 1983. Several other developments seemed to reduce the importance of the navy's purpose-built escort ship. The surface fleet eagerly anticipated the arrival of the long-range Tomahawk missile, which the FFG launcher could not handle. At the same time, it came to seem far-fetched that a Soviet invasion might be blunted with materiel convoyed in from the U.S. mainland.

32. Capt. Alan W. Swinger, Letter to the editor, *Proceedings,* August 1984.

33. Rinn, Letter to the editor, *Proceedings,* May 1984.

34. Launch booklet, FFG 58; "Changes in Ships' Status."

35. The congressmen were Sen. George Mitchell (D) and Rep. John McKernan Jr. (R). Platform List, 8 December 1984.

36. Launch booklet, FFG 58.

CHAPTER 4

1. The title of a December 1988 *Proceedings* article says it all: "Damage Control: Adopting an Unwanted Stepchild." The author, Cdr. Joseph W. Glass, notes that the damage control assistant (DCA) was typically a junior officer with less than two years' experience. The program for the August 1988

graduation of DCA school shows one lieutenant and one lieutenant commander among the other twenty-nine ensigns and lieutenants junior grade.

2. Interview, Eric Sorensen with author, 29 November 2003.

3. Ibid.

4. At the time, Rinn was chief of staff of Destroyer Squadron 36, the Charleston, South Carolina–based group to which *Briscoe* belonged. But he held orders to command *Roberts* and was already putting together his precommissioning team.

5. The damage control training team was usually made up of hull technicians and damage controllers, along with other senior enlisted members.

6. Interview, Rinn; interview, Sorensen.

7. Pierside at home, the list of watertight fittings was relatively small. Once under way, however, the rules got more restrictive, and when the crew went to general quarters—what Hollywood movies generally call "battle stations"—they would button up just about everything they could.

8. Fire hose fittings included male-to-male, female-to-female, reducing couplings (to join hoses of different widths), wye couplings (a Y-shaped device to divide the water flowing from one hose into two or three others), and Siamese coupling (the reverse of a wye). A crew fighting a serious fire could produce some truly Byzantine arrangements. To rig just one eductor, you located a pair of fireplugs and attached two 1 1/2-inch hoses. The hoses attached with male-male adapters to a Siamese coupling, from which a single 2 1/2-inch hose connected to the eductor inlet with another male-male coupler. A 4-inch hose ran from the eductor to a jettison fitting in the hull, where it was connected by a final male-male coupler.

9. Sprinklers were fitted, for example, in the helicopter hangars, machinery rooms, and six of the ship's seven magazines. Lt. Eric Sorensen, USS *Samuel B. Roberts Damage Control Booklet* ([unpublished], Bath, ME: 1985), 47.

10. Jeffrey L. Levinson, and Randy L. Edwards, *Missile Inbound: The Attack on the* Stark *in the Persian Gulf* (Annapolis, MD: Naval Institute Press, 1997), 30.

11. Sorensen, *Damage Control Handbook*, 56.

12. Interview, Sorensen.

13. NAVSEA, final report, October 1988, 6–37. The full list: access man, AFFF station operator, boundary man, chemical-biological-radiological internal/external survey team member, chemical-biological-radiological on-station monitor, closure detail member, conflagration station operator, crash and salvage crewman/rescueman, crash and salvage scene leader, desmoking team member, dewatering team member, electronic/electrical firefighter, fire extinguishing agency supply man, firefighting team member, investigator, isolation detail member, material decontamination team member, messenger, personnel decontamination team member, pipe patching team member, plotter, plugging team member, plugman, post-fire gas-free test assistant,

repair party electrician, repair party leader, sounding team member, sound-powered telephone talker, and stretcher bearer.

14. Sorensen, *Damage Control Handbook,* v–vi; "A Crew Saves Their Ship to Fight Again," *Ships Safety Bulletin,* Naval Safety Center, June 1988.
15. E-mail, Tom Reinert to author, 24 February 2002.

CHAPTER 5

1. Preston, John. "The Gulf Story." Unpublished memoir, ca. 1989.
2. Familygram, FFG 58 to crew families, ca. December 1985.
3. Document, "Samuel B. Roberts, FFG 58," 11 November 1984.
4. E-mail, Reinert to author, 24 February 2002.
5. The new contract froze wages, created new bonuses, cut medical benefits, boosted life insurance, and created a two-tier wage scale that brought new employees up to parity after three years. (Kim Clark, "BIW Shipbuilders OK Contract," *Portland Press Herald,* 8 October 1985.)
6. Message, Commander, Fleet Training Center, Norfolk to Commander, Naval Surface Group 4, "Outstanding Performance of USS *Samuel B. Roberts* (FFG 58) Precommissioning Assignment," 27 February 1986.
7. BIW delivered *Kauffman* on 13 February 1987, wrapping up a twelve-year *Perry* program that delivered two dozen frigates a total of four hundred weeks early and more than $200 million under budget. BIW had executed the frigate program while building ships to six other designs, performing naval repair work, and handling bits of other industrial production as well. (Snow, *Bath Iron Works,* 541.)
8. Interview, Robert C. Bent with author, 16 June 2004.
9. Interview, Gordan Van Hook with author, 7 March 2004.
10. E-mail, Reinert to author, 24 February 2002.
11. E-mail, Richard Raymond to author, 2 December 2003.
12. Letter, Rear Adm. John D. Bulkeley to Vice Adm. Joseph Metcalf III, 19 February 1986.
13. Material Inspection and Receiving Report (FFG 58), 1 April 1988.
14. Program, FFG 58 commissioning ceremony, 12 April 1986.
15. E-mail, Mike Roberts to author, 7 February 2002.
16. Many of Rinn's invitees who couldn't make it had sent congratulatory notes; the letters had been pouring in for weeks from old friends, colleagues, and service dignitaries. Navy Secretary John Lehman and CNO Adm. James Watkins sent their regards, as did the president of Rinn's alma mater and the governors of Connecticut, Maine, and Rhode Island.
17. Message, USS *Samuel B. Roberts* to Chief, Navy Information, "Samuel B. Roberts FFG 58 Commissioning Principal Speaker," 19 December 1985.
18. Oddly, there were men named Copeland, Carr, and two Robertses among the plank owners of FFG 58, just as there had been aboard DE 413.

19. Command History, USS *Samuel B. Roberts* (FFG 58), 1986.

20. Paul Downing and Tux Turkel, "Hero First to Board New Ship," *Portland Press-Herald,* 13 April 1986.

21. Lt. Jim Dryer, "Roberts Comes Home with Honors," *Newport Navalog,* 28 November 1986.

22. Interview, Dumas.

23. Swinger, "Getting a Handle on FFG 7 Shiphandling," *Proceedings,* August 1982.

24. Rinn served aboard *Blakely* under Cdr. E. H. Wainwright Jr.

25. Interview, Rinn.

26. Ibid.

27. Interview, Preston with author, 2 February 2002; Preston, "The Gulf Story," 18.

28. Dryer, "Roberts Comes Home with Honors."

29. E-mail, Roberts to author, 7 February 2002.

30. Message, Commander, Naval Surface Group 4 to FFG 58, "OPPE Performance," 1645Z 31 July 1986.

31. Visual message, *Stark* to *Roberts* (FFG 58), 1632Z 24 July 1986.

32. Message, Commander, Naval Surface Group 4 to Commander, Naval Surface Forces, Atlantic, "Battenburg Cup Award Nomination," 0400Z 25 April 1988.

33. Message, Commander, Naval Surface Forces, Atlantic, to FFG 58, "Final Contract Trials," 1256Z 10 November 1986.

34. This long-scheduled yard period—a post-shakedown availability, the navy called it—featured some light repairs to the ship and its equipment. There was also the new SQR-19 sonar array to be installed. Towed behind the ship, riding beneath the water's surface, isolated from the hull's vibrations, the underwater ears would sharpen the sonarmen's ability to find and track submarines.

35. Command History, USS *Samuel B. Roberts* (FFG 58), 1986.

CHAPTER 6

1. Dilip Hiro, *The Longest War: The Iran-Iraq Military Conflict* (London: Paladin, 1990), 2.

2. Capt. Thomas M. Daly, "The Enduring Gulf War," *Proceedings,* May 1985.

3. The fighters were part of French arms sales that totaled $5.1 billion in 1980–1985. (Levinson and Edwards, *Missile Inbound,* 7.)

4. Daly, "Enduring Gulf War."

5. Ronald O'Rourke, "The Tanker War," *Proceedings,* May 1989.

6. Hiro, *Longest War,* 186.

7. Baghdad apologized immediately for the attack, which Iraqi officials called accidental, and eventually paid $27.3 million in restitution to the families of the dead sailors. But some Reagan administration officials could never shake

the suspicion that the attack had been one more deliberate attempt to draw more U.S. forces into the Gulf. (Elaine Sciolino, *The Outlaw State* (New York: John Wiley, 1991).

8. It was not two weeks after Iraqi missiles killed more than thirty U.S. sailors aboard *Stark* that assistant defense secretary Richard Armitage said, "We can't stand to see Iraq defeated." (Hiro, *Longest War,* 186.)

9. Michael Vlahos, "The Stark Report," *U.S. Naval Institute Proceedings,* May 1988.

10. *Roberts* had emerged from the Portland yards in April; hard work by sailors and BIW employees had kept things on schedule through a winter of blizzards. (Letter, W. A. Rehder to Commander, Naval Surface Group 4, 30 April 1987.)

11. Interview, Rinn, 30 November 2004.

12. Letter, Vice Adm. W. F. McCauley to Rinn, 22 June 1987.

13. "Missile Inbound, Starboard Side," *Surface Warfare,* November–December 1987, 7.

14. Message, Commander, Fleet Training Group Guantanamo Bay Cuba to Commander, Naval Surface Forces, Atlantic, "End of Training Report," 1212Z 24 July 1987. "The *Samuel B. Roberts* Has Come a Long Way," *Newport Navalog,* 21 August 1987.

15. Message, FFG 58 to Commander, Naval Surface Group 4, "Personnel Transfer," 1930Z 11 July 1987; "Mass Conflagration Training: Battling the Big Blaze," *Surface Warfare,* November–December 1987.

16. "USS Roberts Achieves Highest Level of Readiness and Excellence in Two Years," *Newport Navalog,* 31 July 1987.

17. Message, Commander, Fleet Training Group Guantanamo Bay Cuba, 1212Z 24 July 1987; Message, Commander, Fleet Training Group Guantanamo Bay Cuba to Rinn, "Unclas Personal for Capt Rinn from Commo Johnson," 1842Z 3 May 1988.

18. Richard Pyle, "U.S. Flags Go Up on Reflagged Kuwaiti Tanker," Associated Press (hereafter, AP), 21 July 1987.

19. Robin Wright, *In the Name of God: The Khomeini Decade* (New York: Touchstone, 1989), 251.

20. Interview, Capt. Frank C. Seitz Jr. by Paul Stillwell, published in "SS *Bridgeton:* The First Convoy," *Proceedings,* May 1988.

21. Anthony Cordesman, *The Iran-Iraq War* (London: Mansell, 1988), 62; Gregory K. Hartmann, with Scott C. Truver, *Weapons That Wait* (Annapolis, MD: Naval Institute Press, 1991), 256.

22. Hartmann and Truver, *Weapons That Wait,* 237.

23. The list of ships damaged by enemy attack since World War II is not long, considering the dozens of operations and thousands of deployments ranging over more than half a century. USS *Liberty* (AGTR 5), USS *Higbee* (DD 806), and the *Stark* were hit in aerial attacks, and USS *Cole* (DDG 67) by suicide bombers in a small boat. But the other fourteen were hit by mines. (Albert J.

Tucker, Office of Naval Research, "Opportunities and Challenges in Ship Systems & Control and ONR," briefing presented at the IEEE Conference on Decision & Control, 4 December 2001.)

24. Frank Elliot, "The Navy in 1987," *Proceedings,* May 1988.
25. Interview, Seitz; "Iran Mines Still in Gulf Near Kuwaiti Oil Station," *Philadelphia Inquirer,* 16 July 1987.
26. Richard Pyle, "Navy Learns Many Lessons in Gulf's 'Do-It-Yourself War,'" AP, 26 October 1988.
27. The missile was later identified as one of the Stinger heat seekers supplied by the CIA to the Afghan mujahideen. (David B. Crist, "Joint Special Operations in Support of Earnest Will," *Joint Forces Quarterly,* Autumn–Winter 2001–2002.)
28. Frank Colucci, "Special Ops," *Popular Mechanics,* January 1999.
29. Ronald O'Rourke, "Gulf Ops," *Proceedings,* May 1989; "Kuwaiti Call for Help Led to U.S. Role in Gulf," *Los Angeles Times,* 4 July 1988. With ninety-one attacks on merchants by Iran and eighty-eight by Iraq, 1987 would end as the most violent year of the war. (Hiro, *Longest War,* 191; Cordesman, *Iran-Iraq War,* 17.)
30. "Remember All Who Served," *Providence Journal,* 12 November 1987; Linda Borg, "Newport-Based Frigates Heading for Mediterranean, Maybe Gulf," *Providence Journal,* 13 November 1987.
31. E-mail, Reinert.
32. Interview, Joe Baker with author, 30 March 2004.
33. Interview, Preston.
34. Letter, Commander, Naval Surface Forces, Atlantic, Vice Admiral McCauley to Rinn, 18 November 1987.
35. "USS *Samuel B. Roberts* FFG 58 Ammunition Expended 1987."
36. Interview, Robert Sobnosky with author, 28 March 2004.
37. Lt. Cdr. David D. Bruhn, with Capt. (Ret.) Steven C. Saulnier and Lt. Cdr. James L. Whittington, *Ready to Answer All Bells: A Blueprint for Successful Naval Engineering* (Annapolis, MD: Naval Institute Press, 1997), 103–5.
38. Interview, Kevin Ford with author, 29 March 2004.
39. NAVSEA, final report, 6–12, 46.
40. Message, Commander, Naval Surface Forces, Atlantic, to all subordinate ships and commands, "FFG 7 Major DC Lessons Learned," 0110Z 19 July 1987.
41. Levinson and Edwards, *Missile Inbound,* 30.
42. Message, FFG 58 to U.S. Defense Attaché Office, Cairo, "Suez Canal Transit Report," 1517Z 24 January 1988 (Declassified 2 February 1989.)
43. Frieda Squires, photo caption, "On the Line," *Providence Journal*-Bulletin, 15 April 1988.
44. D. Morgan McVicar, "A Familiar, But Still Painful, Goodby," *Providence Journal,* 12 January 1988.
45. E-mail, Christopher Pond to author, 18 January 2004.

46. Message, Commander, Naval Surface Group 4, to Rinn, "Departure on Deployment," 2212Z 11 January 1988.

CHAPTER 7

1. Message, Commander, Destroyer Squadron 22, to FFG 58, "Tone," 1500Z 2 September 1987.
2. Interview, Rinn.
3. Interview, Raymond.
4. Iran had completed a midget sub at its Bandar Abbas shipyard in 1987, but it had failed operating tests (Prézelin and Baker, *Guide to Combat Fleets,* 256).
5. E-mail, Pond.
6. Command History, USS *Samuel B. Roberts* (FFG 58), 1988.
7. Familygram, FFG 58 to crew families, March 1988.
8. The skipper of the first *Samuel B. Roberts* had described his own ship's encounter with a typhoon on the way to Leyte. "The seas were so rough and the ship pounded so badly that for the first two or three hours many of the crew were afraid the ship would sink," Lt. Cdr. Robert Copeland wrote in his memoirs. "For the next sixteen to eighteen hours many of them were so sick that they were afraid she wouldn't sink."
9. Interview, Baker.
10. Interview, Preston.
11. Videotape, Kevin Ford, January–February 1988.
12. Interview, Ford.
13. Visual message, *Simpson* to *Roberts* (FFG 58), 4 February 1988.
14. Interview, Mike Tilley with author, 5 August 2002.
15. The shipments of antiaircraft missiles, spare parts, and other materiel were engineered by White House operative Lt. Col. Oliver North to raise money for Nicaraguan rebels. When news of the 1986 shipments broke, White House officials publicly played down their military significance. But at least one Middle East expert in the administration believed differently: "The Iranians bought critical radar and landing gear components that at times . . . enabled Iran to double the number of sorties flown by its McDonnell Douglas F-4 aircraft against Iraq," the official told the *New York Times.* (Paul Mann and James K. Gordon, "Iran Secures Operational Gains from U.S.-Backed Military Aid," *Aviation Week & Space Technology,* 17 November 1986.) Dilip Hiro reckoned that the covert flow of parts had doubled the number of operational Iranian F-14s to twenty-four. (Hiro, *Longest War,* 168.)
16. The downed planes were French-built Mirage F1s. ("Iran Claims Three Iraqi Planes Downed, U.S. Navy Turnover," AP, 9 February 1988.)
17. Baghdad radio later claimed a successful attack on "two large maritime targets" in the southeast Gulf. (Richard Pyle, "U.S. Warship Warns Off Iraqi Jet Threatening Convoy," AP, 13 February 1988.) In part to fool the U.S.-built

Mavericks' optical seekers, which were programmed to pick out contrasting patterns, U.S. warships headed to the Gulf painted out the high-contrast black lines of their hull numbers.

18. Message, FFG 58 to CTU 801.9.1, "Tovr Completion," 1720Z 11 February 1988 (Declassified 15 March 1988). The U.S. Navy had purchased more than eight thousand Stingers to provide close-range antiair protection, but they were standard equipment aboard few warships. Instead, itinerant missile teams came aboard when a ship arrived in the Gulf region, staying behind when it departed. Many of the missile shooters were "nonrates," junior sailors who had been through Stinger training but little else. Their reward for a year of itinerant missile duty was a slot in a training program that would qualify them as an engineman, electrician, or one of the navy's other job specialties. One member of the *Roberts*'s Stinger team was reportedly a "single-digit midget"—that is, had fewer than ten days left in his Gulf tour—when the *Roberts* hit the mine. (E-mail, Tom Mowry to author, 20 January 2004; Polmar, *Naval Guide to Ships and Aircraft of the U.S. Fleet,* 16th ed., 457; Norman Friedman, *Naval Institute Guide to World Naval Weapons Systems* (Annapolis, MD: Naval Institute Press, 1989), 243.)

19. The gun magazine was protected by 3/4-inch aluminum alloy, the combat information center by 5/8-inch steel plates. Several vital electronics and command spaces were wrapped in a 3/4-inch Kevlar blanket. (Friedman, *U.S. Destroyers,* 384.)

20. Message, Capt. Donald A. Dyer to Task Unit 801.9.1, "Transit Competition," 1012Z 10 February 1988; interview, Glenn Palmer with author, 4 January 2004; interview, Rinn.

21. Richard Pyle, "Two Speedboats Approach U.S. Convoy in Strait of Hormuz," AP, 10 June 1988.

22. Letter, Rinn to Greg Rinn, 23 February 1988; interview, Preston.

23. "Iraq Claims Ship Attack; Convoy Sails," AP via *Journal of Commerce,* 17 February 1988.

24. Interview, Rinn.

25. Letter, Rinn to Greg Rinn, 23 February 1988.

26. Interview, Preston.

27. Letter, Rinn to Greg Rinn, 23 February 1988.

28. Transcript, U.S. House Armed Service Committee's Defense Policy Panel hearing into the USS *Vincennes'* attack on the Iranian airliner, 21 July 1992.

29. Interview, Raymond.

30. Plan of the Day, 17 February 1988.

CHAPTER 8

1. Letter, Rinn to Greg Rinn, 23 February 1988.

2. Interview, Anthony A. Less with author, 29 October 2002.

3. Prézelin and Baker, *Guide to Combat Fleets,* 257. Vosper called the *Sa'am* the Mark V.

4. Michael A. Palmer, *On Course to Desert Storm: The United States Navy and the Persian Gulf* (Washington, DC: Naval Historical Center, 1992), 392.

5. Letter, Rinn to Greg Rinn, 23 February 1988.

6. Hiro, *Longest War,* 15.

7. Crist, "Joint Special Operations." Also Cordesman, *Iran-Iraq War,* 41: "Iran had conducted some 88 ship attacks in 1987, and 72 percent of these occurred in the shipping routes between the UAE and Abu Musa. All Iranian ship attacks from November 1987 to April 1988 were conducted in the southern Gulf, and nearly 50 percent were conducted at night."

8. Letter, Rinn to Greg Rinn, 23 February 1988.

9. Interview, Dave Walker with author, 30 March 2004.

10. Admiral Less sent praise for the *Roberts*'s work—and a word of caution against being too provocative.

11. Letter, Rinn to Greg Rinn, ca. 13 March 1988.

12. USS *Samuel B. Roberts* Deck Log, 3 March 1988; interview, Rinn; letter, Rinn to Greg Rinn, ca. 13 March 1988.

13. Richard Pyle, "U.S. Navy Frigate Fires at Suspected Speedboats," AP, 6 March 1988.

14. Interview, Rinn.

15. Letter, Rinn to Greg Rinn, ca. 13 March 1988. Misdated as 5 March.

16. Interview, Tilley.

17. The Night Stalkers were formed in 1981 as the 160th Aviation Battalion, renamed the 160th Aviation Group (Airborne) in 1986, and again renamed the 160th Special Operations Aviation Regiment (Airborne) in 1990.

18. Squires, "Price of Protection."

19. E-mail, Mike Roberts.

20. Bruhn, Saulnier, and Whittington, *Ready to Answer All Bells,* 115.

21. Aboard the *Roberts* there were fifteen officers and five surface-warfare watch stations: officer of the deck, junior officer of the deck, tactical action officer, CIC watch officer, and engineering officer of the watch. But neither the captain nor the executive officer stood watches, and the supply officer and disbursing officer took turns in the flight control tower. That left eleven officers to handle the five stations. Early in the deployment, Rinn had tried two-section watches—four hours on, and four off—and found his officers exhausted. So the captain switched to three-section duty—four on, eight off—and relied on chief petty officers to fill in the deck and engineering watches. (E-mail, Glenn Palmer.)

22. Squires, "Price of Protection."

23. Letter, Rinn to Greg Rinn, ca. 13 March 1988. Misdated as 5 March.

24. Interview, Glenn Palmer.

25. Interview, Rinn.

26. E-mail, Palmer.

27. Interview, Palmer; interview, Rinn.

28. Interview, John Eckelberry with author, 26 October 2002.

29. Interview, James Muehlberg with author, 21 January 2002.

30. Squires, "Price of Protection."

31. Ibid.

32. Randy Tatum and Ted Johnson, letter to *Wisner News Chronicle,* 14 April 1988.

33. Squires, "Price of Protection."

34. Interview, Rinn.

35. Familygram, March 1988.

36. Preston, "Gulf Story."

37. Alan Cowell, "54 Feared Dead on Two Oil Tankers in Iraqi Attack on Iran Terminal," *New York Times,* 22 March 1988; "Attack on Iran Ships May Have Killed 51," *Los Angeles Times,* 22 March 1988; Richard Pyle, "Officials Say U.S. Crews Alert in Gulf," AP, 22 March 1988.

38. Richard Pyle, "Frigate Shadows Landing Craft," AP, 24 March 1988.

39. USS *Samuel B. Roberts* Deck Log, 24 March 1988; Mona Ziade, "Iraq Concedes Losing Land, Fires Missiles into Tehran," AP, 26 March 1988.

40. Supertanker skippers tended to worry more about aerial and naval attack than mines, and when unencumbered by minesweepers, they tended to put the throttles to their pegs. With power plants built to move hundreds of thousands of tons, the supertankers could get up to twenty-five knots on the unloaded west-to-east run. Bringing them to a stop could take miles and more than half an hour. (Letter, Rinn to DE 413 Survivors' Association, 10 March 1988, reprinted in the organization's 20 April 1988 newsletter.)

41. Interview, Rinn.

42. Pyle, "Officials Say U.S. Crews Alert in Gulf."

43. Interview, Rinn.

44. USS *Samuel B. Roberts* Deck Log, 28 March 1988.

45. Interview, Rinn.

46. Message, FFG 58 to USS *Exploit,* "Battle 'E,'" 0640Z 13 April 1988.

47. E-mail, John R. Eckelberry to author, 12 December 2002.

48. Message, Commander, Naval Surface Group 4 to Commander, Naval Surface Forces, Atlantic, "Battle Efficiency Competitive Cycle 01 Oct 86–31 Mar 86 Award Nominees," 0400Z 1 April 1988.

49. Message, Commander, Naval Surface Group 4 to Rinn, "Humpday Congratulations," 1930Z 8 April 1988.

50. E-mail, Eckelberry.

51. PH1 Frank Gregory, "Surviving a Mine," *Surface Warfare,* May–June 1999.

CHAPTER 9

1. Mussi, "To See the Dawn."
2. E-mail, Reinert.
3. Interview, Rinn.
4. E-mail, Roberts.
5. Interview, Lester Chaffin with author, 8 February 2004.
6. E-mail, Pond.
7. Gregory, "Surviving a Mine."
8. Preston, "Gulf Story."
9. Interview, Walker.
10. Interview, Bent.
11. Interview, Walker; interview, Bent; NAVSEA, final report, 2–1.
12. Interview, Walker.
13. E-mail, Baker; GSE2 Randy A. Tatum, Written recollections for the NAVSEA investigators, ca. 16 April 1988.
14. Interview, David Burbine with author, 24 March 2004.
15. Interview, Van Hook.
16. John Sullivan, "*Roberts* Sails Back to Newport," *Providence Journal*-Bulletin, 28 October 1989.
17. NAVSEA, final report, 6–49.
18. Interview, Rinn.
19. Friedman, *Guide to World Naval Weapons Systems,* 450.
20. If the *Roberts*'s rendezvous with the tanker had been an hour or two earlier, the frigate might have floated right over the mine without setting it off. Tides in the central Gulf ran about eight feet, and extreme low tide was just forty-five minutes away. (Tide information calculated with *Mr. Tides* software by August Hahn.)
21. NAVSEA, final report.
22. Ibid.
23. Speech, Rinn to Fleet Damage Control Symposium, 26 April 1989, as reported in Rinn, "If You're Not Prepared, It's Already Too Late," *Surface Warfare,* March–April 1990, 8.
24. Interview, Rinn.
25. E-mail, Roberts.
26. E-mail, Johnson.
27. E-mail, Raymond.
28. E-mail, Pond.
29. Interview, Walker.
30. George C. Wilson and Molly Moore, "Reagan, Aides Weigh Response to Damaging of Ship in Gulf; Evidence Indicates Iran Placed Mines Found in Area," *Washington Post,* 16 April 1988.
31. NAVSEA, final report, 3–4.

32. Interview, Rinn.

33. Interview, Bent.

34. Interviews, Tilley, Walker; recollections, Tatum; NAVSEA, final report.

CHAPTER 10

1. NAVSEA, final report, 3–3, 7–18, 7–36. After the fire was out, the chilled-water system was brought back online.

2. Interview, Walker.

3. NAVSEA, final report.

4. Interview, Bent.

5. But Palmer kept many of the other CIC consoles shut down to preserve electrical power and reduce waste heat in the absence of air conditioning. ET1 James Muehlberg and other electronics technicians rigged fans to keep the circuits from overheating. (NAVSEA, final report; interview, Palmer; interview, Muehlberg.)

6. YN1(SW) Paul D. Hass, the ship's yeoman, kept track of the damage control effort for the bridge watch. (Letter, Hass to Pamela Rinn, 30 April 1988.)

7. Interview, Rinn.

8. Interview, Less.

9. Speech, Chief of Naval Operations Adm. Carlisle Trost to U.S. Naval Institute's Annual Meeting, Newport, RI, 21 April 1988.

10. E-mail, Raymond.

11. Interview, Ford.

12. E-mail, Raymond.

13. Interview, Ford.

14. NAVSEA, final report, 3–4.

15. NAVSEA, final report, 6–47.

CHAPTER 11

1. NAVSEA, final report, 3–4.

2. E-mail, Reinert.

3. Rinn, "If You're Not Prepared"; The Ordnance Shop, "Historical Mishaps," http://www.ordnance.org/mishaps.htm, 21 August 2004.

4. NAVSEA, final report, 6–16.

5. Interview, Rinn.

6. Conversation as reported in *All Hands,* August 1988. Rinn confirms this account. Less, however, said in a 2003 interview that he did not recall the exact words, but "I hope I didn't ask about abandoning ship."

7. Mussi, "To See the Dawn."

8. Interview, Tilley.

9. Interview, Rinn.

10. NAVSEA, final report.

11. NAVSEA, draft report.

12. Interview, Rinn.

13. Afterward, Rinn wondered whether there was a better alternative. The NAVSEA final report, 6–47, suggested using the wardroom, as is prescribed aboard U.S. Navy submarines.

14. Interview, Eckelberry.

15. Gutcher would later spend a dozen hours in the helicopter control shack, helping to guide the various aircraft that touched down on the flight deck, bringing aid and evacuating wounded shipmates. The shack protruded from the hangar, about fifty feet aft of the exhaust stack fire. (E-mail, Gutcher to author, 22 April 2004; interview, Rinn.)

16. E-mail, Bill Dodson to author, 22 April 2004.

17. Interview, Rinn.

CHAPTER 12

1. E-mail, Chaffin.

2. NAVSEA, final report, 6–25.

3. E-mail, Pond.

4. E-mail, Ted Johnson to author, 7 January 2004.

5. Interview, Rinn.

6. Mussi, "To See the Dawn."

7. Letter, Joseph Boyd to DE 413 survivor Vince Goodrich, as reprinted in the 20 May 1988 Survivors' Association newsletter.

8. Mussi, "To See the Dawn."

9. Interview, Rinn.

10. Unbeknownst to Van Hook, GSE2 Randy Tatum and HT3 Ted Johnson had tried attacking the plenum fire through a scuttle next to the paint locker, but their handheld extinguishers had proven inadequate for the task. (E-mail, Johnson; recollections, Tatum.)

11. Interview, Van Hook.

12. NAVSEA, final report, 5–2.

13. Rudyard Kipling, *Destroyers at Jutland* (Garden City, NY: Doubleday, Page & Company, 1916).

14. Interview, Eckelberry.

15. E-mail, Roberts.

16. E-mail, Johnson.

17. NAVSEA, final report, 6–47.

18. E-mail, Raymond.

CHAPTER 13

1. The war benefited Dubai with more than repair jobs. The turmoil in the Persian Gulf drove much maritime cargo to the city, which was closer to

the Strait of Hormuz than any Saudi port. And trade with Iran grew and grew, topping $1 billion in 1987. (Hiro, *Longest War,* 237.)

2. Tyler Marshall, "Commercial Traffic Resumes Following U.S.–Iranian Clashes," *Los Angeles Times,* 23 April 1988.

3. E-mail, Johnson.

4. "*Roberts* Crew Members Make First Phone Calls Home since Accident," AP, 17 April 1988.

5. Mary Cronin, "Frigate *Roberts'* Surprise Wives," *Newport Daily News,* 18 April 1988.

6. E-mail, Chaffin.

7. Don Cazentre, "Sailor's Family Hears Good News from Gulf," *Syracuse Post-Standard,* 17 April 1988.

8. Interview, Pamela Rinn with author, 30 July 2005.

9. "*Roberts* Crew Members Make First Phone Calls."

10. Message, Commander, Naval Surface Group 4 to Rinn, "Various," 1730Z 16 April 1988. When the four passed through Washington, DC, they were met by a delegation led by an admiral. (Message, Commander, Naval Personnel Command, to Rinn, "Personal for Capt. Rinn," 2256Z 25 April 1988.)

11. Interview, Rinn.

12. Ibid.

13. Transcript, *MacNeil/Lehrer NewsHour,* 18 April 1988.

14. Michael A. Palmer, "Operation Praying Mantis," in *Great American Naval Battles,* edited by Jack Sweetman (Annapolis, MD: Naval Institute Press, 1998), 384.

15. Planning details are drawn from Palmer, "Operation Praying Mantis"; Palmer, *On Course to Desert Storm;* "Nine Hours That Sank Iran's Navy," *Times* (London), 24 April 1988; William J. Crowe, with David Chanoff, *The Line of Fire* (New York: Simon and Schuster, 1993); and Wilson and Moore, "Reagan, Aides Weigh Response."

16. Wilson and Moore, "Reagan, Aides Weigh Response."

17. Crowe, *Line of Fire,* 201.

18. Iran's daily output in the late 1980s was about 2 million barrels in 1986, 2.2 million in 1987, 2.1 in 1988, and 2.7 in 1989. (United States Energy Information Administration, "Iran," one of the U.S. Energy Department's country briefs, http://www.iet.com/Projects/HPKB/Web-mirror/EIA_CABS/iran.html, April 1997.)

19. Melissa Healy and John M. Broder, "Had to Act Quickly on Mining, Officials Say; Decision to Retaliate Was Made after Firm Evidence That U.S. Warship Had Been Target," *Los Angeles Times,* 18 April 1988.

20. Capt. J. B. Perkins III, "Operation Praying Mantis: The Surface View," *Proceedings,* May 1989.

21. Sirri pumped about 180,000 barrels a day. Palmer, "Operation Praying Mantis," 389.

22. SECNAV Instruction 1650.1G, 7 January 2002.

23. Capt. Bud Langston and Lt. Cdr. Don Bringle, "Operation Praying Mantis," *Proceedings,* May 1989, 54.

24. James Gerstenzang, "U.S. Sinks or Damages Six Iran Ships in Persian Gulf Clashes; Tehran Strikes Back after Oil Rig Shillings," *Los Angeles Times,* 19 April 1988; Healy and Broder, "Had to Act Quickly on Mining."

25. E-mail, Reinert to author, 24 February 2002.

26. Perkins, "Operation Praying Mantis," 69; Richard Pyle, "Missing Helicopter on Night Mission after U.S.–Iran Battle Ended," AP, 20 April 1988.

27. Langston and Bringle, "Operation Praying Mantis," 56; Perkins, "Operation Praying Mantis," 70; Richard Pyle, "Warship's Crew Had Much to Cheer About," AP, 20 April 1988.

28. Palmer, "Operation Praying Mantis," 392; Richard Pyle, "Navy Analyses One-Day Missile War with Iran," AP, 22 April 1988.

29. Langston and Bringle, "Operation Praying Mantis," 56.

30. "The Day in Detail: What Happened Where," *Washington Post,* 19 April 1988; "U.S. Sinks or Cripples 6 Iranian Ships in Gulf Battles," *Washington Post,* 19 April 1988; Patrick E. Tyler, "Iran Hits Back with Attack on Arab-Owned Oil Complex," *Washington Post,* 19 April 1988.

31. Friedman, *Guide to World Naval Weapons Systems,* 95.

32. "How to Waste a Navy," *The Economist,* 23 April 1988; Gerstenzang, "U.S. Sinks or Damages Six Iran Ships"; Palmer, "Operation Praying Mantis," 392–93; Langston and Bringle, "Operation Praying Mantis," 57; Pyle, "Warship's Crew Had Much to Cheer About."

33. O'Rourke, "The Tanker War," 47.

34. Pyle, "Missing Helicopter on Night Mission."

35. The Skipper II was a thousand-pound bomb mated to the engine from a Shrike missile, allowing an aviator to attack a ship from a safer, more distant position. Brendan M. Greeley Jr., "U.S. Sinks Iranian Frigate in Persian Gulf Action," *Aviation Week & Space Technology,* 25 April 1988.

36. Langston and Bringle, "Operation Praying Mantis," 59; Richard Pyle, "U.S. Officers Satisfied with Action against Iran," AP, 20 April 1988.

37. "U.S. Forces Preplanned Attack on Iranian Frigate," AP, 21 April 1988.

38. Crowe, *Line of Fire,* 202; Palmer, "Operation Praying Mantis," 395.

39. The Sea Cobra was part of Marine Light Attack Helicopter Squadron (HMLA)-167, based at Marine Corps Air Station New River, North Carolina, and was assigned to Marine Air-Ground Task Force 2-88 aboard *Trenton.* The bodies of its aircrew, Capt. Stephen C. Leslie, 30, of New Bern, North Carolina, and Capt. Kenneth W. Hill, 33, of Thomasville, North Carolina, were recovered by navy divers in May; the wreckage raised later that month showed no sign of battle damage, though the aircraft could have crashed while trying to evade Iranian fire. (Richard Pyle, "Navy Reverses Decision, Will Recover

Helicopter Wreckage," AP, 20 May 1988; Richard Pyle, "Navy Analyses One-Day Missile War with Iran," AP, 22 April 1988; Palmer, "Operation Praying Mantis," 399; Greeley, "U.S. Sinks Iranian Frigate.")

40. Interview, Dumas.
41. E-mail, Reinert.
42. Message, HSL 44 Det 5 to HSL 44, "LAMPS Matters," 1035Z 19 April 1988.
43. E-mail, Reinert.
44. Transcript, Pentagon press conference by NAVSEA chief Vice Adm. William Rowden and DCNO for plans, policy, and operations Vice Adm. Henry Mustin, 21 April 1988.
45. Message, USS *Fearless* to Rinn, "Lessons to Live By," 1805Z 17 April 1988.
46. Message, CNO to Rinn, "Well Done," 2226Z 19 April 1988.
47. Message, USCINCCENT to Rinn, "Well Done," 1730Z 17 April 1988.
48. Letter from USS *Carl Vinson* Engineering Department to crew of USS *Samuel B. Roberts,* 16 April 1988, courtesy of Gordan Van Hook.
49. Message, Rinn to *Wainwright, Simpson,* and *Jack Williams,* "Professional Performance," 1840Z 20 April 1988.
50. James J. Kilpatrick, "The Navy Saves a Ship," *St. Petersburg Times,* 20 May 1988.
51. Letter, Rinn to DE 413 Survivors' Association, 2 May 1988.
52. Radio address, Ronald Reagan, 21 May 1988.
53. Citation, Legion of Merit.
54. Secretary of the Navy Instruction 1650.1g.
55. Citation, Navy Unit Citation.
56. E-mail, Chaffin; interview, Tilley.
57. Crowe didn't forget. Some time later, the admiral, now retired and serving on a corporate board, met Rinn's brother Greg at a company function. "Hi, Admiral Crowe. I believe you know my brother. My name is Greg Rinn. My brother Paul was the CO of the *Samuel Roberts.*" "Oh, yeah, the Burger King guy," Crowe said. (Interview, Rinn.)

CHAPTER 14

1. Some members of the NAVSEA team flew commercial airlines and arrived in the UAE two days after the mining; others took military transport and straggled in a week later. They produced a draft report on 27 April. The team's final report took note of the delays and mechanical problems on the way over and dryly recommended that future teams fly commercially. (NAVSEA, draft report.)
2. Interview, Sorensen.
3. E-mail, Johnson; interview, Eckelberry; Alan Flippen, "Crew of Ship That Hit Iranian Mine Returns," AP, 21 June 1988; e-mail, Reinert.
4. James R. Landau, and Stephen J. Lardie, "Repair of Damage to the Guided Missile Frigate USS *Samuel B. Roberts* (FFG 58)," a paper presented at the

annual meeting of the Society of Naval Architects and Marine Engineers in New York in 1989.

5. NAVSEA, draft report.

6. Colin Sargent, "Legend of the Roberts," *Portland Monthly,* November 1988.

7. "Frigate to Be Repaired at Maine Shipyard," AP, 29 April 1988.

8. Interview, Haggett.

9. E-mail, Johnson.

10. E-mail, Roberts; e-mail, Reinert; e-mail, Chaffin; interview, Muelhberg, 21 January 2001.

11. Message, FFG 58 to NAVSTA Mayport, "Remembrance," 0700Z 10 May 1988.

12. Landau and Lardie, "Repair of Damage"; message, FFG 58 to JCS Washington DC, et al., "Samuel B. Roberts Underway," 15 June 1988 (Declassified 31 July 1988); message, FFG 58 to CANCOMDESRON ONE, "No Higher Honor," 15 June 1988 (Declassified 31 July 1988).

13. Richard Pyle, "Mine-Damaged U.S. Frigate Leaves for Home," AP, 1 July 1988. There was one ship in the U.S. fleet that could have handled the task, but the *American Cormorant* was tied up in the Indian Ocean, laden with supplies, as part of the navy's prepositioning fleet. ("MSC Contracts for Roberts Lift," *Sealift,* July 1988.)

14. Interview, Vice Adm. William H. Rowden (Ret.) with author 16 December 2004; Sargent, "Legend of the Roberts."

15. Pyle, "Mine-Damaged U.S. Frigate Leaves for Home"; "Dutch Boat to Bring in Damaged Frigate," *Portland Press Herald,* 7 June 1988.

16. Message, Commander, Joint Task Force Middle East, Less to Rinn, "Investigation," 23 May 1988. "I know you will welcome Commodore Kaiser in Samuel B. Roberts style."

17. Message, Commander, Naval Surface Group 4 to FFG 58, "Change of Command," 17 June 1988.

18. Memo, EN3 Mike Tilley to Rinn, 8 June 1988.

19. Interview, Alan Sepelyak with author, 25 February 2004.

20. E-mail, Eckelberry.

21. E-mail, Chaffin.

22. "Roberts' Crew Is Home," United Press International, 21 June 1988.

23. Flippen, "Crew of Ship That Hit Iranian Mine Returns."

24. George Williams, "Costly Blow to US Navy," *Guardian* (London), 23 June 1988.

25. Richard Pyle, "Mine-Damaged Frigate Towed Out for Loading aboard Cargo Ship," AP, 25 June 1988; "Frigate Loaded aboard Dutch Cargo Ship," AP, 27 July 1988.

26. Dockwise Heavy Transport Shipping Web site, http://www.dockwise.com/?sid=47&project=48, 4 August 2003.

27. Pyle, "Mine-Damaged U.S. Frigate Leaves for Home."

28. E-mails, Ted Johnson.

29. "Roberts Welcomed Home to Newport," AP, 1 August 1988. In 1999, the *Mighty Servant 2* collided with an uncharted granite pinnacle near the Indonesian island of Singkep. The heavy-lift ship rolled onto its side and was lost, along with five mariners and the offshore production facility it was carrying from Singapore. (http://www.tertiary.net/sinking/, 22 February 2003; "Maritime Casualties 1999 and Before," Cargo Letter Web site, http://216.239.37.104/search?q=cache:9YT4BexkkGMJ:www.cargolaw.com/presentations_casualties_a.html+site:cargolaw.com+%22mighty+servant%22&hl=en&ie=UTF-8, 22 February 2004.)

30. Command History, USS *Samuel B. Roberts* (FFG 58), 1988; "Spectators Greet the USS Roberts," *Brunswick (Maine) Times Record,* 26 September 1988; Polmar, *Guide to Ships and Aircraft,* 16th ed., 247.

31. NavSource Online: Service Ship Photo Archive, "AFDB-3 ex ABSD-3 Sections, A through I," http://www.navsource.org/archives/09/6703.htm; "BIW Dry Dock Proves Biggest GSA Giveaway," *Portland Press Herald,* 11 January 1982; "BIW Hoping to Make Up for Lost Time," *Portland Press Herald,* 16 June 1982; "New Landmark Takes Shape," *Portland Press Herald,* 13 August 1982; "BIW Dry Dock Set in Place," *Portland Press Herald,* 10 October 1983; "BIW to Investigate Why Dry Dock Broke Free," *Portland Press Herald,* 4 April 1984.

32. Polmar, *Guide to Ships and Aircraft,* 143.

33. Friedman, *Guide to World Naval Weapons Systems,* vii.

34. "Gulf Frigate in Portland for Repairs," *Portland Press Herald,* 26 September 1988.

35. The *Townsend* had been part of the *Roberts*'s first convoy escort mission in February. ("On Board the Last U.S. Gulf Convoy," *Christian Science Monitor,* 28 September 1988.) The total included 177 ship transits by reflagged tankers, 57 by MSC ships, 14 by other U.S.-flagged ships, and 4 by foreign flag ships. (Cordesman, *Iran-Iraq War,* 68.)

36. Command History, USS *Samuel B. Roberts* (FFG 58), 1988; Sargent, "Legend of the Roberts."

37. "Hydraulic Rams Align Damaged Frigate for Repair," *Hydraulics & Pneumatics,* February 1989. See also SPX Power Team Web site: http://66.201.84.143/fullcat.php; Landau and Lardie, "Repair of Damage."

38. Command History, USS *Samuel B. Roberts* (FFG 58), 1988.

39. "Modern War Ship Crippled by Mine Begins Recovery," *Portland Press Herald,* 28 December 1988; Landau and Lardie, "Repair of Damage."

40. Command History, USS *Samuel B. Roberts* (FFG 58), 1989; Landau and Lardie, "Repair of Damage"; "*Samuel B. Roberts* Repairs Complete," *Times Record.*

41. "USS *Roberts* Damaged in Sea Trials," United Press International, 23 October 1989; Photo, "*Roberts* Sails Out," *Portland Press Herald,* 24 October 1989;

"Workers Send Roberts Back to Sea," *Brunswick (Maine) Times Record,* 17 October 1989; BIW press release, 24 October 1989; "Battle-Damaged Frigate Is Back in the Water," AP, 13 April 1989.

42. Bath Iron Works was sold in 1995 to defense giant General Dynamics. Its new owner bankrolled the first major improvements to the shipyard in two decades. The sloping building ways were abandoned for a level concrete apron. When half-complete ships were ready for launch, they rolled on sturdy tracks into a dry dock, which lowered the hulls gently into the Kennebec River. In 2004 Bath failed to win the big surface-ship job of the new century: the design contract for the navy's next-generation DD(X) destroyer. Many observers believe the yard's future is in doubt. BIW's long history gives reason to believe otherwise.

EPILOGUE

1. Michael Ross, "Role in Gulf Bolsters U.S. Credibility, Ties to Arabs," *Los Angeles Times,* 15 May 1988.

2. Javier Perez De Cuellar, *Pilgrimage for Peace* (New York: Palgrave, 1997), 169–70. Despite the cease-fire, Iran and Iraq never formally ended the war.

3. Craig L. Symonds, *Decision at Sea: Five Naval Battles That Shaped American History* (New York: Oxford University Press), 317.

4. Ibid., 320.

5. Edward J. Marolda, "The United States Navy and the Persian Gulf," Naval Historical Center Web site, http://www.history.navy.mil/wars/dstorm/sword-shield.htm.

6. Lt. Cdr. C. A. Donohoe, "Mines: Will They Sink the U.S. Navy?" Marine Corps University Command and Staff College paper, 1999.

7. Gregory, "Surviving a Mine."

8. Cordesman, *Iran-Iraq War,* 63.

9. The *Providence Journal* called the heavy-lift operation "unprecedented." It fell to Scot Joseph, who had been one of Kevin Ford's cooks aboard the *Roberts,* to set the record straight. "Has it been that long that the *Journal* forgets one of Rhode Island's own naval high points? It was only 12 years ago," Joseph wrote the newspaper. (Letter, Scot Joseph to *Providence Journal,* 19 November 2000.)

10. NAVSEA, final report, es-5.

11. NAVSEA, final report, 6–19.

12. Interview, Rowden.

13. Interview, Rinn.

BIBLIOGRAPHY AND SOURCES

BOOKS

Bearden, Bill, and Bill Wedertz. *The Bluejackets' Manual,* 20th ed. Annapolis, MD: Naval Institute Press, 1978.

Bissell, Allen M., E. James Oertel, and Donald J. Livingston. *Shipboard Damage Control.* Annapolis, MD: Naval Institute Press, 1976.

Breemer, Jan S. *U.S. Naval Developments.* Annapolis, MD: Nautical and Aviation Publishing, 1983.

Bruhn, Lt. Cdr. David D., with Capt. (Ret.) Steven C. Saulnier and Lt. Cdr. James L. Whittington. *Ready to Answer All Bells: A Blueprint for Successful Naval Engineering.* Annapolis, MD: Naval Institute Press, 1997.

Cooper, Tom, and Farzad Bishop. *Iran-Iraq War in the Air, 1980–1988.* Atglen, PA: Schiffer Publishing, 2000.

Copeland, Rear Adm. (Ret.) Robert W., with Jack O'Neill. *"The Spirit of the Sammy-B,"* [unpublished], ca. 1952. Available at http://www.de413.org.

Cordesman, Anthony. *The Iran-Iraq War.* London: Mansell, 1988.

Cox, Robert Jon. *The Battle Off Samar: Taffy III at Leyte Gulf,* 3rd ed. Groton, CT: Ivy Alba Press, 2003.

Crowe, Adm. William J. Jr., with David Chanoff. *The Line of Fire.* New York: Simon and Schuster, 1993.

Cutler, Lt. Cdr. Thomas J. (Ret.) *The Battle of Leyte Gulf: 23–26 October 1944.* New York: HarperCollins, 1994.

De Cuellar, Javier Perez. *Pilgrimage for Peace.* New York: Palgrave, 1997.

Doscher, Capt. J. Henry Jr. (Ret.) *Little Wolf at Leyte.* Austin, TX: Eakin Press, 1996.

Eskew, Garnett Laidlaw. *Cradle of Ships: A History of the Bath Iron Works.* New York: G. P. Putnam's Sons, 1958.

Frieden, David R., ed. *Principles of Naval Weapons Systems.* Annapolis, MD: Naval Institute Press, 1985.

Friedman, Norman. *Naval Institute Guide to World Naval Weapons Systems.* Annapolis, MD: Naval Institute Press, 1989.

———. *U.S. Destroyers: An Illustrated Design History.* Annapolis, MD: Naval Institute Press, 1982.

Gardner, J. Anthony. *The Iraq-Iran War: A Bibliography.* Boston: G. K. Hall, 1988.

Hartmann, Frederick H. *Naval Renaissance: The U.S. Navy in the 1980s.* Annapolis, MD: Naval Institute Press, 1990.

Hartmann, Gregory K., with Scott C. Truver. *Weapons That Wait,* updated edition. Annapolis, MD: Naval Institute Press, 1991.

Hiro, Dilip. *The Longest War: The Iran-Iraq Military Conflict.* London: Paladin, 1990.

Hornfischer, James D. *The Last Stand of the Tin Can Sailors.* New York: Bantam, 2004.

Hough, Lt. Col. Frank O., Maj. Verle E. Ludwig, and Henry I. Shaw Jr. *Pearl Harbor to Guadalcanal: History of U.S. Marine Corps Operations in World*

War II. Vol. 1. U.S. Marine Corps, Historical Branch, G-3 Division, Headquarters, 1958.

Kemp, Paul. *Convoy!: Drama in Arctic Waters*. London: Arms and Armour Press, 1993.

Kipling, Rudyard. *Destroyers at Jutland*. Garden City, NY: Doubleday, Page & Company, 1916.

Levinson, Jeffrey L., and Randy L. Edwards. *Missile Inbound: The Attack on the Stark in the Persian Gulf*. Annapolis, MD: Naval Institute Press, 1997.

Love, Robert W. Jr. *History of the U.S. Navy*. Harrisburg, PA: Stackpole Books, 1992.

Mack, Vice Adm. (Ret.) William P., and Cdr. Albert H. Konetzni Jr. *Command at Sea*, 4th ed. Annapolis, MD: Naval Institute Press, 1982.

McCarton, Matthew. *One Hundred Years of Sweeping: A Historical Review of the Efficacy of Organic-to-the-Battleforce Mine Countermeasures*. Arlington, VA: Naval Sea Systems Command, 2000.

Morison, Samuel E. *Sailor Historian*. New York: Houghton Mifflin, 1977.

Noel, Capt. John V. Jr. (Ret.), and Cdr. Frank E. Bassett. *Division Officer's Guide*, 7th ed. Annapolis, MD: Naval Institute Press, 1976.

Palmer, Michael A. *On Course to Desert Storm: The United States Navy and the Persian Gulf*. Washington, DC: Naval Historical Center, 1992.

———. "Operation Praying Mantis," in *Great American Naval Battles*, edited by Jack Sweetman. Annapolis, MD: Naval Institute Press, 1998.

Peniston, Bradley. *Around the World with the U.S. Navy*. Annapolis, MD: Naval Institute Press, 1999.

Polmar, Norman. *The Death of the USS* Thresher. Guilford, CT: Lyons Press, 2001.

———. *The Naval Institute Guide to Ships and Aircraft of the U.S. Fleet*, 14th ed. Annapolis, MD: Naval Institute Press, 1987. Also, 16th ed., 1997; 18th ed., 2004.

Prézelin, Bernard, and A. D. Baker III. *The Naval Institute Guide to Combat Fleets of the World 1990–1991*. Annapolis, MD: Naval Institute Press, 1990.

Rowe, William Hutchinson. *A Maritime History of Maine: Three Centuries of Shipbuilding and Seafaring*. New York: W. W. Norton, 1948.

Rubin, Barry. *Cauldron of Turmoil: America in the Middle East*. New York: Harcourt, Brace, and Jovanovich, 1992.

Sanders, Michael S. *The Yard: Building a Destroyer at the Bath Iron Works*. New York: HarperCollins, 1999.

Sciolino, Elaine. *The Outlaw State*. New York: John Wiley, 1991.

Snow, Ralph Linwood. *Bath Iron Works: The First Hundred Years*. Bath, ME: Maine Maritime Museum, 1987.

Sorensen, Lt. Eric. USS *Samuel B. Roberts Damage Control Booklet*. [unpublished], Bath, ME: 1985.

Sweetman, Jack. *American Naval History: An Illustrated Chronology of the U.S. Navy and Marine Corps, 1775–Present*, 3rd ed. Annapolis, MD: Naval Institute Press, 2002.

Symonds, Craig L. *Decision at Sea: Five Naval Battles That Shaped American History.* New York: Oxford University Press, 2005.

Wright, Robin. *In the Name of God: The Khomeini Decade.* New York: Touchstone, 1989.

Zumwalt, Elmo R. Jr. *On Watch.* New York: Quadrangle/New York Times Book Co., 1976.

ARTICLES: NEWSPAPERS, MAGAZINES, WEB SITES

"A Crew Saves Their Ship to Fight Again," *Ships Safety Bulletin,* Naval Safety Center, June 1988.

Anderson, Paul. "Round Holes Aplenty," *U.S. Naval Institute Proceedings,* April 1984.

"Attack on Iran Ships May Have Killed 51," *Los Angeles Times,* 22 March 1988.

"Battle-Damaged Frigate Is Back in the Water," Associated Press, 13 April 1989.

Beecher, Capt. John D. "FFG 7: The Concept and Design," *U.S. Naval Institute Proceedings,* March 1987.

Bennett, Randall D., and Crystal D. Sloan. "Repeating Design Errors, or 'Where's the History?'" Presented at the 2003 symposium of the International Council on Systems Engineering.

"BIW Dry Dock Proves Biggest GSA Giveaway," *Portland Press Herald,* 11 January 1982.

"BIW Dry Dock Set in Place," *Portland Press Herald,* 10 October 1983.

"BIW, Frigate Praised at Perry Launching," *Maine Sunday Telegram,* 26 September 1976.

"BIW Hoping to Make Up for Lost Time," *Portland Press Herald,* 16 June 1982.

"BIW to Investigate Why Dry Dock Broke Free," *Portland Press Herald,* 4 April 1984.

"BIW to Repair Ship Damaged in Gulf," *Portland Press Herald,* 30 April 1988.

Borg, Linda. "Newport-Based Frigates Heading for Mediterranean, Maybe Gulf," *Providence Journal,* 13 November 1987.

Browning, Robert M. Jr. "Douglas Munro at Guadalcanal," U.S. Coast Guard Web site, http://www.uscg.mil/hq/g-cp/history/Munro.html, September 1999.

Brumley, Bryan. "Mine-Damaged U.S. Warship En Route from Persian Gulf to Newport, R.I.," Associated Press, 1 July 1988.

Buell, Barbara, and Seth Payne. "Bath: A Tight Ship That Could Spring a Leak," *Businessweek,* 20 May 1985.

Cazentre, Don. "Sailor's Family Hears Good News from Gulf," *Syracuse Post-Standard,* 17 April 1988.

"Chronology of U.S.-Gulf Developments," Associated Press, 4 July 1988.

"City, State Aid Key to BIW Expansion," *Portland Press Herald,* 16 July 1981.

Clark, Kim. "BIW Shipbuilders OK Contract," *Portland Press Herald,* 8 October 1985.

Cole, Lt. Cdr. Bernard. "Comment," *U.S. Naval Institute Proceedings,* ca. July 1978.

Colucci, Frank. "Special Ops," *Popular Mechanics,* January 1999.

Cowell, Alan. "54 Feared Dead on 2 Oil Tankers in Iraqi Attack on Iran Terminal," *New York Times,* 22 March 1988.

Crist, David B. "Joint Special Operations in Support of Earnest Will," *Joint Forces Quarterly,* Autumn–Winter 2001–2002.

Cronin, Mary. "Frigate *Roberts'* Surprise Wives," *Newport Daily News,* 18 April 1988.

Daly, Capt. Thomas M. "The Enduring Gulf War," *U.S. Naval Institute Proceedings,* May 1985.

Dockwise, "Samuel. B. Roberts Recovery," http://www.dockwise.com/projects/marine/samuel.html, 4 August 2003.

Don Cazentre. "Sailor's Family Hears Good News from Gulf," *Syracuse Post-Standard,* 17 April 1988.

Donohoe, Lt. Cdr. C. A. "Mines: Will They Sink the U.S. Navy?" Submitted as coursework paper to Marine Corps University Command and Staff College, 1999.

Downing, Paul, and Tux Turkel. "Hero First to Board New Ship," *Portland Press Herald,* 13 April 1986.

Dryer, Lt. Jim. "Roberts Comes Home with Honors," *Newport Navalog,* 28 November 1986.

"Dutch Boat to Bring in Damaged Frigate," *Portland Press Herald,* 7 June 1988.

Elliot, Frank. "The Navy in 1987," *U.S. Naval Institute Proceedings,* May 1988.

Flippen, Alan. "Crew of Ship That Hit Iranian Mine Returns," Associated Press, 21 June 1988.

"Former BIW Head Returning to Maine," Associated Press via *Portland Press Herald,* 20 February 1997.

Friedman, Norman. "World Naval Developments," *U.S. Naval Institute Proceedings,* July 1988.

"Frigate Loaded aboard Dutch Cargo Ship," Associated Press, 27 July 1988.

"Frigate Spotted Mines before One Ripped Hull," Associated Press report in the *San Diego Union-Tribune,* 15 April 1988.

"Frigate to Be Repaired at Maine Shipyard," Associated Press, 29 April 1988.

Fyfe, CW2 Michael P. "Persian Excursion (The Graveyard Shift)," part of the Task Force 118 unit history book, as reproduced at http://www.mindspring.com/~cjenkins/TF118.htm, 1 June 2004.

Gerstenzang, James. "Tehran Strikes Back after Oil Rig Shellings," *Los Angeles Times,* 19 April 1988.

———. "U.S. Sinks or Damages 6 Iran Ships in Persian Gulf Clashes," *Los Angeles Times,* 19 April 1988.

Glass, Cdr. Joseph W. "Damage Control: Adopting an Unwanted Stepchild," *U.S. Naval Institute Proceedings,* December 1988.

Greeley, Brendan M., Jr. "U.S. Sinks Iranian Frigate in Persian Gulf Action," *Aviation Week & Space Technology,* 25 April 1988.

Gregory, PH1 Frank. "Surviving a Mine," *Surface Warfare,* May–June 1999.

"Gulf Frigate in Portland for Repairs," *Portland Press Herald,* 26 September 1988.

Harkavy, Jerry. "A Look at a Shipyard That Works," Associated Press, 11 May 1981.

"Heading for the Gulf," *Providence Journal* Bulletin, 12 January 1988.

Healy, Melissa, and John M. Broder. "Had to Act Quickly on Mining, Officials Say; Decision to Retaliate Was Made after Firm Evidence That U.S. Warship Had Been Target," *Los Angeles Times,* 18 April 1988.

Heine, Lt. (jg) Kenneth. "'This Is No Drill': Saving the 'Sammy B.'" *Surface Warfare,* July–August 1988.

Hillinger, Charles. "The Joy of Victory Prevails in Bath," *Los Angeles Times,* 5 April 1985.

"Historical Mishaps," The Ordnance Shop, http://www.ordnance.org/mishaps.htm, 21 August 2004.

Holmes, Kendall. "BIW's War of Wages," *Maine Sunday Telegram,* 21 July 1988.

Hooton, E. R. "Perking Up the Perry-Class," *Jane's Defence Systems Modernization,* 1 December 1996.

Houston, Roger W., "Death of a Division, Birth of a Concept: The Evolution of the 2nd Armored Cavalry Regiment from the 9th Infantry Division (Motorized)," http://orbat.com/site/data/vignettes/vignette14.html (2003).

"How to Waste a Navy," *The Economist,* 23 April 1988.

"Hydraulic Rams Align Damaged Frigate for Repair," *Hydraulics & Pneumatics,* February 1989.

"Iran Claims Three Iraqi Planes Downed, U.S. Navy Turnover," Associated Press, 9 February 1988.

"Iran Mines Still in Gulf near Kuwaiti Oil Station," *Philadelphia Inquirer,* 16 July 1987.

"Iraq Claims Ship Attack; Convoy Sails," Associated Press via *The Journal of Commerce,* 17 February 1988.

Isikoff, Michael, and Howard Kurtz. "Shipbuilders on the Skids," *Washington Post,* 17 July 1985.

"John Wayne Launches Perry with a Push," *Maine Sunday Telegram,* 26 September 1976.

Kidder, Rushworth M. "Building Navy Ships Faster—And for Less," *Christian Science Monitor,* 23 July 1981.

Kilpatrick, James J. "The Navy Saves a Ship," *St. Petersburg Times,* 20 May 1988.

"Kuwaiti Call for Help Led to U.S. Role in Gulf," *Los Angeles Times,* 4 July 1988.

Lamb, Gregory M. "Bath Shipyard: $1 Billion Backlog—And Growing," *Christian Science Monitor,* 9 June 1982.

Landau, James. R., and Stephen J. Lardie. "Repair of Damage to the Guided Missile Frigate USS Samuel B. Roberts (FFG 58)." Presented to the Society of Naval Architects and Marine Engineers, 1989 annual meeting.

Langston, Capt. Bud, and Lt. Cdr. Don Bringle. "Operation Praying Mantis," *U.S. Naval Institute Proceedings,* May 1989.

Linder, Lt. Cdr. Bruce R. "FFG 7s: Square Pegs?" *U.S. Naval Institute Proceedings,* June 1983.

Livezey, Emilie Tavel. "Bringing a Ship to Life," *Christian Science Monitor,* 11 December 1980.

Mann, Paul, and James K. Gordon. "Iran Secures Operational Gains from U.S.-Backed Military Aid," *Aviation Week & Space Technology,* 17 November 1986.

"Maritime Casualties 1999 and Before," Cargo Letter Web site, http://216.239.37.104/search?q=cache:9YT4BexkkGMJ:www.cargolaw.com/presentations_casualties _a.html+site:cargolaw.com+%22mighty+servant%22&hl=en&ie=UTF-8, 22 February 2004.

Marolda, Edward J. "The United States Navy and the Persian Gulf," Naval Historical Center Web site, http://www.history.navy.mil/wars/dstorm/sword-shield.htm.

Marshall, Tyler. "Commercial Traffic Resumes Following U.S.–Iranian Clashes," *Los Angeles Times,* 23 April 1988.

"Mass Conflagration Training: Battling the Big Blaze," *Surface Warfare,* November–December 1987.

McVicar, D. Morgan. "A Familiar, But Still Painful, Goodby," *Providence Journal,* 12 January 1988.

"Missile Inbound, Starboard Side," *Surface Warfare,* November–December 1987.

"Modern War Ship Crippled by Mine Begins Recovery," *Portland Press Herald,* 28 December 1988.

"MSC Contracts for Roberts Lift," *Sealift,* July 1988.

Mussi, PH1 Chuck. "'To See the Dawn,'" *All Hands,* August 1998.

Naval Historical Center, Ships History Branch. "U.S. Navy Active Ship Force Levels, 1917–Present," http://www.history.navy.mil/branches/org9-4.htm (2 March 2003).

"Navy Finds Anti-Aircraft Missiles, Rockets on Iranian Boat," Associated Press, 31 March 1988.

Navy Historical Center. "U.S. Navy Ships—USS *Bellatrix* (AK-20, later AKA-3), 1942–1963," http://www.history.navy.mil/photos/sh-usn/usnsh-b/ak20.htm.

NavSource Online: Service Ship Photo Archive. "AFDB-3 ex ABSD-3 Sections, A through I," http://www.navsource.org/archives/09/6703.htm.

"New Landmark Takes Shape," *Portland Press Herald,* 13 August 1982.

"Nine Hours That Sank Iran's Navy," *Times* (London), 24 April 1988.

Olsson, L. A. "History of Ships Named *Samuel B. Roberts,*" Naval History Division, Office of the Chief of Naval Operations, ca. 1971.

"On Board the Last U.S. Gulf Convoy," *Christian Science Monitor,* 28 September 1988.

Orchard, Lt. Curtis L. "A Threat to Which Navy?" *U.S. Naval Institute Proceedings,* April 1984.

O'Rourke, Ronald. "Gulf Ops," *U.S. Naval Institute Proceedings,* May 1989.

———. "The Tanker War," *U.S. Naval Institute Proceedings,* May 1989.

Perkins, Capt. J. B. III. "Operation Praying Mantis: The Surface View," *U.S. Naval Institute Proceedings,* May 1989.

Purcell, David. "Bath Iron Works—100 Years and Still Bidding," *Christian Science Monitor,* 24 May 1984.

Pyle, Richard. "Alarms and Tension as U.S. Awaits Possible Iranian Attacks," Associated Press, 21 April 1988.

———. "Frigate Shadows Landing Craft," Associated Press, 24 March 1988.

———. Media Pool Report from USS *Wainwright,* 0758Z 16 April 1988.

———. "Mine-Damaged Frigate Towed Out for Loading aboard Cargo Ship," Associated Press, 25 July 1988.

———. "Mine-Damaged U.S. Frigate Leaves for Home," Associated Press, 1 July 1988.

———. "Missing Helicopter on Night Mission after U.S.-Iran Battle Ended," Associated Press, 20 April 1988.

———. "Navy Analyses One-Day Missile War with Iran," Associated Press, 22 April 1988.

———. "Navy Learns Many Lessons in Gulf's 'Do-It-Yourself War,'" Associated Press, 26 October 1988.

———. "Navy Reverses Decision, Will Recover Helicopter Wreckage," Associated Press, 20 May 1988.

———. "Navy Strives to Deal with Stress of Persian Gulf Duty," Associated Press, 4 August 1988.

———. "Officials Say U.S. Crews Alert in Gulf," Associated Press, 22 March 1988.

———. "Previous Incident Raised Question about Radar Reliability," Associated Press, 6 August 1988.

———. "Two Speedboats Approach U.S. Convoy in Strait of Hormuz," Associated Press, 10 June 1988.

———. "U.S. Commander Says Iran Building New Silkworm Missile Site," Associated Press, 1 June 1988.

———. "U.S. Flags Go Up on Reflagged Kuwaiti Tanker," Associated Press, 21 July 1987.

———. "U.S. Navy Frigate Fires at Suspected Speedboats," Associated Press, 6 March 1988.

———. "U.S. Navy Gulf Command Changes, Force Cutback Completed," Associated Press, 28 February 1988.

———. "U.S. Officers Satisfied with Action against Iran," Associated Press, 20 April 1988.

———. "U.S. Warship Warns Off Iraqi Jet Threatening Convoy," Associated Press, 13 February 1988.

———. "Warship's Crew Had Much to Cheer About," Associated Press, 20 April 1988.

"Remember All Who Served," *Providence Journal,* 12 November 1987.

Rinn, Cdr. Paul X. "Hoops for Goofs," *The Circle,* 16 December 1965.

———. *Hudson Valley* magazine, December 1990.

———. "'If You're Not Prepared, It's Already Too Late,'" *Surface Warfare,* March–April 1990. Abstract available at http://www.dcfp.navy.mil/mc/museum/ROBERTS/Roberts1.htm.

———. "Letter from the Gulf," *Newport Navalog,* 1 April 1988.

———. Letter to the editor, *U.S. Naval Institute Proceedings,* May 1984.

"Roberts' Crew Is Home," United Press International, 21 June 1988.

"Roberts Crew Members Make First Phone Calls Home since Accident," Associated Press, 17 April 1988.

"*Roberts* Sails Out," photo, *Portland Press Herald,* 24 October 1989.

"Roberts Welcomed Home to Newport," Associated Press, 1 August 1988.

Ross, Michael. "Role in Gulf Bolsters U.S. Credibility, Ties to Arabs," *Los Angeles Times,* 15 May 1988.

"*Samuel B. Roberts* Repairs Complete," *Times Record.*

"San Diego-Based Cruiser Ordered to Gulf Region," *San Diego Union-Tribune,* 22 April 1988.

Sargent, Colin. "Legend of the Roberts," *Portland Monthly,* November 1988.

Seitz, Capt. Frank C. Seitz Jr. Interview by Paul Stillwell, published in "SS *Bridgeton:* The First Convoy," *Proceedings,* May 1988.

Sharp, Victoria. "Saving the Samuel B. Roberts," *Fathom,* fall 1988.

Smith, Lt. Cdr. J. Morgan. "The Original 'Sammy B,'" *All Hands,* August 1998.

"Spectators Greet the USS Roberts," *Brunswick (Maine) Times Record,* 26 September 1988.

SPX Power Team Web site. http://66.201.84.143/fullcat.php.

Squires, Freida. "The Price of Protection," photo caption, *Providence Journal-Bulletin,* 10 April 1988.

———. "On the Line," *Providence Journal,* 15 April 1988.

Stevens, David Weld. "Floating the Navy the Bath Way," *Fortune,* 5 October 1981.

Stillwell, Paul. "SS *Bridgeton:* The First Convoy," *U.S. Naval Institute Proceedings,* May 1988.

Sullivan, John. "*Roberts* Sails Back to Newport," *Providence Journal*-Bulletin, 28 October 1989.

Swinger, Capt. Alan W. Letter to the editor, *U.S. Naval Institute Proceedings,* August 1984.

———. "FFG 7 Class Pre-Commissioning," *U.S. Naval Institute Proceedings,* January 1982.

——— "Getting a Handle on FFG 7 Shiphandling," *U.S. Naval Institute Proceedings,* August 1982.

Taussig, Capt. Joseph Jr. (Ret.) "Upgrading Deckplate Safety," *U.S. Naval Institute Proceedings,* December 1988.

"The 'USS Vincennes': Public War, Secret War" (transcript), *Nightline,* 1 July 1992.

"The Day in Detail: What Happened Where," *Washington Post,* 19 April 1988.

"The Navy Heeds Shipyard Complaints," *Businessweek,* 15 March 1976.

"The Samuel B. Roberts Has Come a Long Way," *Newport Navalog,* 21 August 1987.

"The USS Perry Launched," *Maine Sunday Telegram,* 26 September 1976.

Toppan, Andrew. "Dictionary of American Naval Fighting Ships," "DD 823," "DD 724," *Haze Gray & Underway: Naval History and Photography,* http://www.hazegray.org/danfs/htm, 1994–2003.

"Tried by Fire," *Surface Warfare,* March–April 1990.

Truver, Scott C. "Tomorrow's U.S. Fleet." *U.S. Naval Institute Proceedings,* March 2001.

———. "Weapons That Wait . . . And Wait . . ," *U.S. Naval Institute Proceedings,* February 1988.

Tyler, Patrick E. "Iran Hits Back with Attack on Arab-Owned Oil Complex," *Washington Post,* 19 April 1988.

"U.S. Forces Preplanned Attack on Iranian Frigate," Associated Press, 21 April 1988.

"U.S. Navy Sinks or Cripples Six Iranian Vessels in Major Persian Gulf Battle; Two Iranian Oil Platforms Destroyed," *World News Digest,* 22 April 1988.

"U.S. Sinks or Cripples Six Iranian Ships in Gulf Battles," *Washington Post,* 19 April 1988.

"U.S. to Meet Iraqis on Close Encounters," *Chicago Tribune,* 17 February 1988.

"U.S. Trims Gulf Armada," *Los Angeles Times,* 2 November 1988.

"USS Roberts Achieves Highest Level of Readiness and Excellence in Two Years," *Newport Navalog,* 31 July 1987.

"USS *Roberts* Damaged in Sea Trials," United Press International, 23 October 1989.

Vlahos, Michael. "The Stark Report," *U.S. Naval Institute Proceedings,* May 1988.

Whiteman, John. "Repairs Near Completion," *Portsmouth Herald,* 17 February 1989.

Williams, George. "Costly Blow to US Navy," *Guardian* (London), 23 June 1988.

Wilson, George. "Destroyer Built On Time, Under Budget," *Washington Post,* 5 December 1978.

Wilson, George C., and Molly Moore. "Reagan, Aides Weigh Response to Damaging of Ship in Gulf, Evidence Indicates Iran Placed Mines Found in Area," *Washington Post,* 16 April 1988.

"Workers Send Roberts Back to Sea," *Brunswick (Maine) Times Record,* 17 October 1989.

Ziade, Mona. "Iraq Concedes Losing Land, Fires Missiles into Tehran," Associated Press, 26 March 1988.

GOVERNMENT DOCUMENTS

Biography, Commanding Officer, FFG 58, ca. 1984.

Command Histories, USS *Samuel B. Roberts* (FFG 58), 1984–2000.

Country Brief, United States Energy Information Administration, "Iran," http://www.iet.com/Projects/HPKB/Web-mirror/EIA_CABS/iran.html, April 1997.

Document, "Samuel B. Roberts, FFG 58," 11 November 1984.

Familygram, FFG 58 to crew families, ca. December 1985.

Familygram, FFG 58 to crew families, March 1988.

Launch booklet, FFG 58, 1984.

Material Inspection and Receiving Report (FFG 58), 1 April 1988.

Memo, EN3 Mike Tilley to Rinn, 8 June 1988.

Message, American Embassy, Nassau, Bahamas, to Cdr. Paul X. Rinn, "Port Visit Nassau 16–20 October 1986," 1432Z 21 October 1986.

Message, Capt. Donald A. Dyer to Task Unit 801.9.1, "Transit Competition," 1012Z 10 February 1988.

Message, Capt. Nutwell to FFG 58, "Award for HSL-44 Det 5 OIC," 0900Z 27 May 1988.

Message, CINCLANTFLT to COMNAVSURFLANT et al., "Public Affairs—USS *Samuel B. Roberts* Repair Announcement," 2246Z 29 April 1988.

Message, CJTFME to FFG 58, "Investigation," 23 May 1988.

Message, CNO to FFG 58, "Well Done," 2226Z 19 April 1988.

Message, COGDSEVEN To COMLANTAREA, "Sentencing Report for the Month of May 1987," 2047C 11 June 1987.

Message, COGDSEVEN to FFG 58, "S/V *Melanie*," 2330Z 24 September 1986.

Message, COMDESRON 22 to FFG 58, "Tone," 1500Z 2 September 1987.

Message, COMFLETRACEN Norfolk to COMNAVSURFGRU 4, "Outstanding Performance of USS Samuel B. Roberts (FFG 58) Precommissioning Assignment," 27 February 1986.

Message, COMFLETRAGRU Guantanamo Bay Cuba to COMNAVSURFGRU Four, "USS Samuel B. Roberts Weekly Sitrep 05, 13–16 July," 1352Z 17 July 1987.

Message, COMFLETRAGRU Guantanamo Bay Cuba to COMNAVSURFLANT, "End of Training Report," 1212Z 24 July 1987.

Message, COMFLETRAGRU Guantanamo Bay Cuba to FFG 58, "Unclas Personal for Capt Rinn from Commo Johnson," 1842Z 3 May 1988.

Message, COMLANTAREA to FFG 58, "Coast Guard Meritorious Unit Commendation," 0444Z 15 July 1987.

Message, COMNAVMILPERSCOM to FFG 58, "Personal for Capt. Rinn," 2256Z 25 April 1988.

Message, COMNAVSURFGRU 4 to COMNAVSURFLANT, "Battenburg Cup Award Nomination," 0400Z 25 April 1988.

Message, COMNAVSURFGRU 4 to COMNAVSURFLANT, "Battle Efficiency Competitive Cycle 01 Oct 86–31 Mar 86 Award Nominees," 0400Z 1 April 1988.

Message, COMNAVSURFGRU 4 to FFG 58, "Change of Command," 17 June 1988.

Message, COMNAVSURFGRU 4 to FFG 58, "Departure on Deployment," 2212Z 11 January 1988.

Message, COMNAVSURFGRU 4 to FFG 58, "Humpday Congratulations," 1930Z 8 April 1988.

Message, COMNAVSURFGRU 4 to FFG 58, "OPPE Performance," 1645Z 31 July 1986.

Message, COMNAVSURFGRU 4 to FFG 58, "Various," 1730Z 16 April 1988.

Message, COMNAVSURFGRU 4 to NAVSURFGRU 4, "Damage Control," 1530Z 21 July 1987.

Message, COMNAVSURFLANT to all subordinate ships and commands, "FFG 7 Major DC Lessons Learned," 0110Z 19 July 1987.

Message, COMNAVSURFLANT to FFG 58, "Final Contract Trials," 1256Z 10 November 1986.

Message, CTG 801.3 to FFG 58, "CPGE Ops," 1808Z 28 February 1988.

Message, Dyer to Task Unit 801.9.1, "Transit Competition," 1012Z 10 February 1988.

Message, FFG 58 to COMNACSURFGRU 4, "Thunderstorm Incident Sitrep 001," 0645Z 2 August 1986 (Declassified 30 Aug 1986).

Message, FFG 58 to CTG801.3, "Emotional Message Prevention," 1600Z 13 March 1988 (Declassified 11 July 1988).

Message, FFG 58 to USS *Exploit,* "Battle 'E,'" 0640Z 13 April 1988.

Message, FFG 58 to USS *Wainwright, Simpson, Jack Williams,* "Professional Performance," 1840Z 20 April 1988.

Message, HSL 44 Det 5 to HSL 44, "LAMPS Matters," 1035Z 19 April 1988.

Message, Roberts to COMFLETRAGRU Guantanamo Bay, "FFG 7 Major DC Lessons Learned," 18 July 1987.

Message, *Stark* to *Roberts,* "Battle Orders," 1530Z 14 March 1988.

Message, SWOSCOLCOM to FFG 58, "Lessons Learned," 1427Z 4 March 1988.

Message, SWOSCOLCOM to FFG 58, "Training Support," 1343Z 4 November 1986.

Message, *Trenton* to FFG 58, "Unrep Discrepancies," 1840Z 12 March 1988.

Message, USCINCCENT to FFG 58, "Well Done," 1730Z 17 April 1988.

Message, USS *Fearless* to FFG 58, "Lessons to Live By," 1805Z 17 April 1988.

Message, FFG 58 to CANCOMDESRON ONE, "No Higher Honor," 15 June 1988 (Declassified 31 July 1988).

Message, FFG 58 to CCGD 7 (Miami), "Law Enforcement—Sitrep Two—S/V Melanie (US)—Seized," 0345 24 September 1986.

Message, FFG 58 to CHINFO, "Samuel B. Roberts FFG 58 Commissioning Principal Speaker," 19 December 1985.

Message, FFG 58 to COMNAVSURFGRU 4, "Law Enforcement Ops," 0415Z 24 September 1986.

Message, FFG 58 to COMNAVSURFGRU 4, "Personnel Transfer," 1930Z 11 July 1987.

Message, FFG 58 to CTG 801.3, "Possible Patrol Area," 2100Z 26 February 1988 (Declassified 31 December 1988).

Message, FFG 58 to JCS Washington DC et al., "Samuel B. Roberts Underway," 15 June 1988 (Declassified 31 July 1988).

Message, FFG 58 to NAVCOMMU, "MSG CK 37," 1655Z 5 February 1988.

Message, FFG 58 to NAVSTA Mayport, "Remembrance," 0700Z 10 May 1988.

Message, FFG 58 to USDAO Cairo, "Suez Canal Transit Report," 1517Z 24 January 1988 (Declassified 2 February 1989).

NAVSEA. "Building Patrol Frigates for the United States Navy," pamphlet, 1974.

———. Draft report, NAVSEA Damage Assessment Team, 27 April 1988.

———. Final report, "Survivability Review Group Report on USS *Samuel B. Roberts* (FFG 58) Damage Analysis," October 1988.

Navy Cross citation, Coxswain Samuel Booker Roberts, 10 February 1943.

Plan of the Day, 17 February 1988.

Program, FFG 58 commissioning ceremony, 12 April 1986.

Report, "Liquified Natural Gas (LNG) Import Terminals: Siting, Safety, and Regulation," Congressional Research Service, 27 May 2004.

USS *Samuel B. Roberts* Deck Log, FFG 58, March 1988.

"USS *Samuel B. Roberts* FFG 58 Ammunition Expended 1987."

Visual message, *Simpson* to *Roberts* (FFG 58), 4 February 1988.

Visual message, *Stark* to *Roberts* (FFG 58), 1632Z 24 July 1986.

UNPUBLISHED MANUSCRIPTS

Haynes, FC1 Mark S. "Liberty Call," 1991.

Preston, John. "The Gulf Story," unpublished memoir, ca. 1989.

LETTERS

Boyd, Joseph, to DE-413 survivor Vince Goodrich, as reprinted in the 20 May 1988 Survivors' Association newsletter.

Breast, Capt. J. C., to Rinn, 16 May 1985.

Bulkeley, Rear Adm. John D., to Vice Adm. Joseph Metcalf III, 19 February 1986.

Cressman, Robert J., to Rinn, 1 February 1984.

Haggett, William, to Rinn, 11 April 1988.

Hass, YN1(SW) Paul D., to Pamela Rinn, 30 April 1988.

Joseph, Scot, to *Providence Journal,* 19 November 2000.

Luchino, Col. Gerald T., to Rinn, 8 January 1985.

McCauley, Vice Adm. W. F., to Rinn, 22 June 1987.

Murtha, Rep. John P., to William L. Ball III, 27 April 1988.

Rehder, Capt. W. A., to CNSG 4, 30 April 1987.

Rinn, Cdr. Paul X., to Capt. John P. Doolittle, 24 January 1985.

———. to crew, 30 April 1988.

——. to DE-413 Survivors' Association, 10 March 1988, reprinted in the organization's 20 April 1988 newsletter.

——. to Greg Rinn, 23 February 1988.

——. to Greg Rinn, ca. 13 March 1988.

——. to Whit [of the Survivors' Association], 2 May 1988.

Tatum, Randy, and Ted Johnson to *Wisner News Chronicle,* 14 April 1988.

Unhjem, Mark, to Rinn, 23 February 1988.

USS *Carl Vinson* Engineering Department to crew of USS *Samuel B. Roberts,* 16 April 1988, courtesy of Gordan Van Hook.

Valliere, Lt. (jg) Michael L., to crew's families, 18 April 1988.

BATH IRON WORKS DOCUMENTS

"A Legacy of Pride . . . A Future of Promise: The First Hundred Years of Bath Iron Works," BIW promotional booklet, 1984.

"List of Ships: The Hulls of Bath Iron Works," BIW promotional booklet, 2002.

"The Log," BIW employee newsletter, April 1986.

Platform List, FFG 58 Launch, 8 December 1984.

Press release, BIW, 24 October 1989.

OTHER

Briefing, Albert J. Tucker, Office of Naval Research, "Opportunities and Challenges in Ship Systems and Control and ONR." Presented at the IEEE Conference on Decision & Control, 4 December 2001.

Database, "Changes in Ships' Status, v. 3.4, 22 May 2005," compiled by Christopher P. Cavas.

Radio Address, Ronald Reagan, 21 May 1988.

Scrapbook, Gordan Van Hook.

Speech, CNO Adm. Carlisle Trost to USNI Annual Meeting, Newport, RI, 21 April 1988.

Transcript, *MacNeil/Lehrer NewsHour,* 18 April 1988.

Transcript, Pentagon press conference by NAVSEA chief Vice Adm. William Rowden and DCNO for plans, policy, and operations Vice Adm. Henry Mustin, 21 April 1988.

Transcript, U.S. House Armed Service Committee's Defense Policy Panel hearing into the USS *Vincennes'* attack on the Iranian airliner, 21 July 1992.

Videotapes, MSC Kevin Ford. Sent home as letters, January, February, April 1988.

Videotape, Navy Combat Camera B-roll, 15–16 April 1988.

Written recollections for NAVSEA investigators, GSE2 Randy A. Tatum, ca. 16 April 1988.

INTERVIEWS WITH AUTHOR

Former members of *Roberts* crew:

Baker, Joseph, 31 March 2004.

Burbine, David, 28 March 2004.
Chaffin, Lester, 9 February 2004.
Dumas, Charles R., 30 January 2002.
Eckelberry, John R., 26 October 2002.
Ford, Kevin, 30 March 2004.
Lambert, James, 7 February 2006.
Muehlberg, James, 23 January 2002.
Palmer, Glenn P., 4 January 2004.
Preston, John, 2 February 2002.
Raymond, Richard, 30 March 2004.
Rinn, Paul X., multiple occasions, 2001–05.
Sepelyak, Alan, 25 February 2004.
Sims, John, 22 February 2006.
Sobnosky, Robert B., 29 March 2004.
Sorensen, Eric, 29 November 2003.
Tilley, Mike, 5 August 2002.
Van Hook, Gordan E., 7 March 2004.
Walker, David J., 29 March 2004.

Others:
Blakelott, Bill, 6 August 2002.
Fitzgerald, Duane, 28 January 2002.
Haggett, William, 6 August 2002.
Hansen, Erik, 6 August 2002.
Less, Anthony, 29 October 2003.
Moll, Ed, 6 August 2002.
Rinn, Pamela, 30 July 2005.
Rowden, William, 16 December 2004.
Mustin, Henry, 11 December 2004.

CORRESPONDENCE

Substantive e-mail exchanges with these former members of *Roberts* crew: Joseph Baker, Robert C. Bent, David Burbine, Lester Chaffin, Larry Deem, Bill Dodson, John R. Eckelberry, Kevin Ford, Bradley G. Gutcher, Ted Johnson, Bill McCarty, Tom Mowry, James Muehlberg, Glenn P. Palmer, Christopher Pond, John Preston, Richard Raymond, Tom Reinert, Paul X. Rinn, Mike Roberts, David Robinson, Alan Sepelyak, Geary Shafer, Robert Sobnosky, Eric Sorensen, Randy Tatum, Doug Thomas, Mike Tilley, Gordan Van Hook, David J. Walker.

BRADLEY PENISTON is managing editor of *Defense News*. He has covered the U.S. military in more than a dozen countries and has spent time aboard more than fifty warships. His work has appeared in the *New York Times,* the *Washington Post, U.S. Naval Institute Proceedings,* and elsewhere. This is his second book.

THE NAVAL INSTITUTE PRESS is the book-publishing arm of the U.S. Naval Institute, a private, nonprofit, membership society for sea service professionals and others who share an interest in naval and maritime affairs. Established in 1873 at the U.S. Naval Academy in Annapolis, Maryland, where its offices remain today, the Naval Institute has members worldwide.

Members of the Naval Institute support the education programs of the society and receive the influential monthly magazine *Proceedings* and discounts on fine nautical prints and on ship and aircraft photos. They also have access to the transcripts of the Institute's Oral History Program and get discounted admission to any of the Institute-sponsored seminars offered around the country.

The Naval Institute also publishes *Naval History* magazine. This colorful bimonthly is filled with entertaining and thought-provoking articles, first-person reminiscences, and dramatic art and photography. Members receive a discount on *Naval History* subscriptions.

The Naval Institute's book-publishing program, begun in 1898 with basic guides to naval practices, has broadened its scope to include books of more general interest. Now the Naval Institute Press publishes about seventy titles each year, ranging from how-to books on boating and navigation to battle histories, biographies, ship and aircraft guides, and novels. Institute members receive significant discounts on the Press's more than eight hundred books in print.

Full-time students are eligible for special half-price membership rates. Life memberships are also available.

For a free catalog describing Naval Institute Press books currently available, and for further information about subscribing to *Naval History* magazine or about joining the U.S. Naval Institute, please write to:

Member Services
U.S. NAVAL INSTITUTE
291 Wood Road
Annapolis, MD 21402-5034
Telephone: (800) 233-8764
Fax: (410) 571-1703
Web address: www.navalinstitute.org